Trouble in Paradise

SLAVOJ ŽIŽEK

Trouble in Paradise

*From the End of History to the
End of Capitalism*

ALLEN LANE
an imprint of
PENGUIN BOOKS

To Jela – a messiah who arrived just in time.

ALLEN LANE

Published by the Penguin Group
Penguin Books Ltd, 80 Strand, London WC2R 0RL, England
Penguin Group (USA) Inc., 375 Hudson Street, New York, New York 10014, USA
Penguin Group (Canada), 90 Eglinton Avenue East, Suite 700, Toronto, Ontario, Canada M4P 2Y3
(a division of Pearson Penguin Canada Inc.)
Penguin Ireland, 25 St Stephen's Green, Dublin 2, Ireland (a division of Penguin Books Ltd)
Penguin Group (Australia), 707 Collins Street, Melbourne, Victoria 3008, Australia
(a division of Pearson Australia Group Pty Ltd)
Penguin Books India Pvt Ltd, 11 Community Centre, Panchsheel Park, New Delhi – 110 017, India
Penguin Group (NZ), 67 Apollo Drive, Rosedale, Auckland 0632, New Zealand
(a division of Pearson New Zealand Ltd)
Penguin Books (South Africa) (Pty) Ltd, Block D, Rosebank Office Park,
181 Jan Smuts Avenue, Parktown North, Gauteng 2193, South Africa

Penguin Books Ltd, Registered Offices: 80 Strand, London WC2R 0RL, England

www.penguin.com

First published 2014
001

Copyright © Slavoj Žižek, 2014

The moral right of the author has been asserted

Set in 9.75/13 pt Sabon LT Std
Typeset by Jouve (UK), Milton Keynes
Printed in Great Britain by Clays Ltd, St Ives plc

ISBN: 978-0-241-00496-8

www.greenpenguin.co.uk

MIX
Paper from
responsible sources
FSC
www.fsc.org   FSC™ C018179

Penguin Books is committed to a sustainable
future for our business, our readers and our planet.
This book is made from Forest Stewardship
Council™ certified paper.

Contents

INTRODUCTION *Divided we stand!*

Trouble in Paradise, Ernst Lubitsch's 1932 masterpiece, is the story of Gaston and Lily, a couple of happy burglars robbing the rich, whose life gets complicated when Gaston falls in love with Mariette, one of their wealthy victims. The lyrics of the song heard during the opening credits provide a definition of the 'trouble' alluded to, as does the image that accompanies the song: first we see the words 'trouble in', then beneath these words a large double bed appears, and then, over the surface of the bed, in large letters, 'paradise'. So 'paradise' is the paradise of a full sexual relationship: 'That's paradise / while arms entwine and lips are kissing / but if there's something missing / that signifies / trouble in paradise.' To put it in a brutally direct way, 'trouble in paradise' is Lubitsch's name for *il n'y a pas de rapport sexuel*.

So where is the trouble in paradise in *Trouble in Paradise*? There is a fundamental ambiguity about this key point. The first answer that imposes itself is this: although Gaston loves Lily as well as Mariette, the true 'paradisiacal' sexual relationship would have been the one with Mariette, which is why it is this relationship that has to remain impossible and unfulfilled. This lack of fulfilment confers on the film's end a touch of melancholy: all the laughter and boisterousness of the film's last minute, all the merry display of the partnership between Gaston and Lily, only fills in the void of this melancholy. Does Lubitsch not point in this direction with the repeated shot of the big empty double bed in Mariette's house, a shot which recalls the empty bed during the film's credits? There is, however, also the possibility of the exactly opposite reading:

Could it be that paradise is actually the scandalous love affair of Gaston and Lily, two chic thieves fending for themselves, and trouble is the sublimely statuesque Mariette? That, in a tantalizing irony, Mariette is the snake luring Gaston from his blissfully sinful Garden of Eden? ... Paradise, the good life, is the life of crime full of glamour and risks, and evil temptation comes in the form of Madame Colet, whose wealth holds the promise of an easy-going *dolce vita* without real criminal daring or subterfuge, only the humdrum hypocrisy of the respectable classes.[1]

The beauty of this reading is that paradisiacal innocence is located in the glamorous and dynamic life of crime, so that the Garden of Eden is equated with the underworld while the call of high-society respectability is equated with the snake's temptation. However, this paradoxical reversal is easily explained by Gaston's sincere and raw outburst, the first and only one in the film, enacted with no elegance or ironic distance, after Mariette refuses to call the police when he tells her that the chairman of the board of her company has for years been systematically stealing millions from her. Gaston's reproach is that, while Mariette is immediately ready to call the police when an ordinary burglar like him steals from her a comparatively small amount of money or wealth, she is ready to turn a blind eye when a member of her own respectable high class steals millions. Is Gaston here not paraphrasing Brecht's famous statement, 'What is the robbing of a bank compared to the founding of a bank'? What is a direct robbery like those of Gaston and Lily compared to the theft of millions in the guise of obscure financial operations?

There is, however, another aspect that has to be noted here: is Gaston's and Lily's life of crime really so 'full of glamour and risks'? Beneath the surface glamour of their thievery, aren't the two of them 'a quintessential bourgeois couple, conscientious professional types with expensive tastes – yuppies before their time. Gaston and Mariette, on the other hand, are the really romantic pair, the adventurous and risk-taking lovers. In returning to Lily and lawlessness, Gaston is doing the sensible thing – returning to his "station", as it were, opting for the mundane life he knows. And he does so with full regret, apparent in his lingering final exchange with Mariette, full of rue and stylish ardor on both sides.'[2]

G. K. Chesterton noted how the detective story

> keeps in some sense before the mind the fact that civilization itself is the most sensational of departures and the most romantic of rebellions . . . When the detective in a police romance stands alone, and somewhat fatuously fearless amid the knives and fists of a thieves' kitchen, it does certainly serve to make us remember that it is the agent of social justice who is the original and poetic figure, while the burglars and footpads are merely placid old cosmic conservatives, happy in the immemorial respectability of apes and wolves. The romance of the police . . . is based on the fact that morality is the most dark and daring of conspiracies.[3]

Is this not also the best definition of Gaston and Lily? Are these two burglars not living in their paradise before the fall into ethical passion? What is crucial here is the parallel between crime (theft) and sexual promiscuity: what if, in our postmodern world of ordained transgression, in which the marital commitment is perceived as ridiculously out of time, those who cling to it are the true subversives? What if, today, straight marriage is 'the most dark and daring of all transgressions'? This, exactly, is also the underlying premise of Lubitsch's *Design for Living*: a woman leads a satisfied, calm life with two men; as a dangerous experiment, she tries single marriage; however, the attempt miserably fails, and she returns to the safety of living with two men, so that the overall result can be paraphrased in the above-quoted Chesterton's words:

> marriage itself is the most sensational of departures and the most romantic of rebellions. When the couple of lovers proclaim their marriage vows, alone and somewhat fatuously fearless amid the multiple temptations to promiscuous pleasures, it does certainly serve to make us remember that it is marriage which is the original and poetic figure, while cheaters and participants in orgies are merely placid old cosmic conservatives, happy in the immemorial respectability of promiscuous apes and wolves. The marriage vow is based on the fact that marriage is the most dark and daring of sexual excesses.

A homologous ambiguity is at work in the basic political choice we are confronting today. Cynical conformism tells us that emancipatory ideals of more equality, democracy and solidarity are boring and even dangerous, leading to a grey, overregulated society, and that our true and only paradise is the existing 'corrupted' capitalist universe. Radical emancipatory engagement starts from the premise that it is the capitalist dynamics which are boring, offering more of the same in the guise of constant change, and that the struggle for emancipation is still the most daring of all ventures. Our goal is to argue for this second option.

There is a wonderful French anecdote about a British snob visiting Paris, who pretends to understand French. He goes to an expensive restaurant in *Quartier Latin* and, when asked by the waiter, '*Hors d'oeuvre?*', replies: 'No, I'm not out of work, I earn enough to be able to afford to eat here! Any suggestions for an appetizer?' The waiter proposes raw ham: '*Du jambon cru?*' The snob replies: 'No, I don't believe it was ham I had the last time here. But OK, let's have it again – and what about the main course?' '*Un faux-filet, peut-être?*' The snob explodes: 'Bring me the real one, I told you I have enough money! And quickly, please!' The waiter reassures him: '*J'ai hâte de vous servir!*', to which the snob snaps back: 'Why would you hate to serve me? I will give you a good tip!' Finally the snob gets the point that his knowledge of French is limited; to repair his reputation and prove that he is a man of culture, he decides, upon his departure late in the evening, to wish the waiter good night in Latin, since the restaurant is in *Quartier Latin*, and bids him '*Nota bene!*'

This book will proceed in five steps, mimicking the blunders of the unfortunate British snob. We will begin with the *diagnosis* of the basic coordinates of our global capitalist system; then we will move on to the *cardiognosis*, 'knowledge of the heart', of this system, i.e., to the ideology that makes us accept it. What will then follow is *prognosis*, the view of the future that awaits us if things continue as they are, as well as the putative openings, or ways out. We shall conclude with *epignosis* (a theological term that designates knowledge which is believed, engaging us in our acts, subjectively assumed), outlining the subjective and organizational forms appropriate for the new phase of our emancipatory struggle. The appendix will explore the impasses of today's emancipatory struggle apropos of the last Batman film.

The 'paradise' in the title of this book refers to the paradise of the End of History (as elaborated by Francis Fukuyama: liberal-democratic capitalism as the finally found best possible social order), and the 'trouble' is, of course, the ongoing crisis that compelled even Fukuyama himself to drop his idea of the End of History. My premise is that what Alain Badiou calls the 'Communist hypothesis' is the only appropriate frame with which to diagnose this crisis. The inspiration came from the series of talks I gave in Seoul in October 2013 as the Eminent Scholar at Kyunghee University. When I accepted the invitation, my first reaction was: is it not outright crazy to talk about the Idea of Communism in South Korea? Is the divided Korea not the clearest imaginable, almost clinical, case of where we stand today, after the end of the Cold War? On the one side, North Korea gives body to the dead end of the twentieth-century Communist project; on the other side, South Korea is in the midst of exploding capitalist development, reaching new levels of prosperity and technological modernization, with Samsung undermining even the primacy of Apple. Is South Korea in this sense not the supreme proof of how false is all the talk about global crisis?

The suffering of the Korean people in the twentieth century was immense. No wonder that – so I was told – even today, it is a taboo in Korea to speak of the atrocities the Japanese committed there during their Second World War occupation. They fear that talking about it would disturb the elders' peace of mind: destruction was so total that the Koreans do everything to forget that time and go on with their lives. Their attitude thus involves a profoundly Nietzschean inversion of the standard formula 'we will forgive but not forget'. With regard to Japanese atrocities, Koreans have a saying: *forget but never forgive*. And they are right: there is something very hypocritical in the formula 'forgive but do not forget' which is deeply manipulative, since it involves a superego blackmail: 'I forgive you, but by not forgetting your misdeed, I will make sure that you will for ever feel guilty about it.' So how did the Koreans survive this suffering? I would like to begin with the report by Franco Berardi, the Italian social theorist, on his recent journey to Seoul:

> By the end of the twentieth century – after decades of war, humiliation, starvation and horrific bombings – both the physical and the anthropological landscape of this country had been reduced to a sort of devastated abstraction. At that point, human life and the city gave themselves with docility to the transforming hand of the highest form of contemporary nihilism.
>
> Korea is the ground zero of the world, a blueprint for the future of the planet . . .
>
> After colonization and wars, after dictatorship and starvation, the South Korean mind, liberated by the burden of the natural body, smoothly entered the digital sphere with a lower degree of cultural resistance than virtually any other populations in the world. This, in my opinion, is the main source of the incredible economic performance that this country has staged in the years of the electronic revolution. In the emptied cultural space, the Korean experience is marked by an extreme degree of individualization, and simultaneously it is headed towards the ultimate cabling of the collective mind.
>
> These lonely monad walks in the urban space in tender continuous interaction with the pictures, tweets, games coming out of their small screens, perfectly insulated and perfectly wired into the smooth interface of the flow . . .
>
> South Korea has the highest suicide rate in the world . . . Suicide is the most common cause of death for those under 40 in South Korea . . . Interestingly, the toll of suicides in South Korea has doubled during the last decade . . . In the space of two generations their condition has certainly improved by the point of view of revenue, nutrition, freedom and possibility of travelling abroad. But the price of this improvement has been the desertification of daily life, the hyper-acceleration of rhythms, the extreme individualization of biographies, and work precariousness which also means unbridled competition . . .
>
> High-tech capitalism naturally implies ever-increasing productivity and ceaseless intensification of the rhythms of work, but it is also the condition that has made possible an impressive improvement in life standards, nourishment and consumption . . . But the present alienation

is a different sort of hell. The intensification of the rhythm of work, the desertification of the landscape and the virtualization of the emotional life are converging to create a level of loneliness and despair that is difficult to consciously refuse and oppose ... Isolation, competition, sense of meaninglessness, compulsion and failure: 28 persons out of 100,000 every year succeed in their attempt to escape and many more unsuccessfully try.

As suicide can be considered the ultimate mark of the anthropological mutation linked to the digital transformation and precarization, not surprisingly South Korea is number one in the world when it comes to the suicide rate.'[4]

Berardi's portrait of South Korea seems to follow the unsurpassed model of such portraits in the last decades, Baudrillard's famous portrait of Los Angeles (in his *America*) as a hyperreal Hell. It is all too easy to dismiss this genre of portraits as the pretentious pseudo-intellectual exercise of European postmodernists who use a foreign land or city as a screen onto which to project their morbid dystopias. In spite of all exaggerations, there is a grain of truth in them; or, more precisely, to paraphrase Adorno's well-known dictum about psychoanalysis, in Baudrillard's portrait of LA nothing is true except its exaggerations. And the same goes for Berardi's impressions of Seoul: what they provide is the image of a place deprived of its history, a *worldless* place. Badiou has reflected that we live in a social space which is progressively experienced as worldless. Even Nazi anti-Semitism, however ghastly it was, opened up a world: it described its critical situation by positing an enemy which was a 'Jewish conspiracy': it named a goal and the means of achieving it. Nazism disclosed reality in a way that allowed its subjects to acquire a global 'cognitive mapping', which included a space for their meaningful engagement. Perhaps it is here that one should locate one of the main dangers of capitalism: although it is global and encompasses the whole world, it sustains a *stricto sensu* worldless ideological constellation, depriving the large majority of people of any meaningful cognitive mapping. Capitalism is the first socio-economic order which *de-totalizes meaning*: it is not global at the level of meaning. There is, after all, no global 'capitalist world view', no 'capitalist civilization' proper: the fundamental lesson of globalization is precisely that capitalism can accommodate itself to all civilizations, from Christian to Hindu or Buddhist, from West to East. Capitalism's global dimension can only be formulated at the level of truth-without-meaning, as the Real of the global market mechanism.

Since, in Europe, modernization was spread over centuries, we had time to accommodate ourselves to it, to soften its shattering impact, through *Kulturarbeit*, through the formation of new social narratives and myths, while some other societies – exemplarily the Muslim ones – have been exposed to this impact directly, without a protective screen or temporal delay, so their symbolic universe has been perturbed much more brutally: they have lost their (symbolic) ground with no time left to establish a new (symbolic) balance. No wonder, then, that the only way for some of these societies to avoid total breakdown was to erect in panic the shield of 'fundamentalism', the psychotic-delirious-incestuous reassertion of religion as direct insight into the divine Real, with all the terrifying consequences that such a reassertion entails, up to the return with a vengeance of the obscene superego divinity demanding sacrifices. The rise of superego is another feature that postmodern permissiveness and the new fundamentalism share. What distinguishes them is the site of the enjoyment demanded: our own in permissiveness, God's own in fundamentalism.[5]

Perhaps the ultimate symbol of this devastated post-historical Korea is the pop-music event of summer 2012: 'Gangnam Style' performed by Psy. As a curiosity, it is worth noting that the 'Gangnam Style' video surpassed Justin Bieber's 'Beauty and a Beat' on Youtube, thus becoming the most watched Youtube video of all time. On 21 December 2012, it reached the magic number of one billion views – and since 21 December was the day when those who took seriously the predictions of the Mayan calendar were expecting the end of the world, one can say that the Ancient Mayas were right: the fact that a 'Gangnam Style' video gets a billion views effectively *is* the sign of the collapse of a civilization. The song is not only wildly popular, it also mobilizes people into a collective trance, with tens of thousands shouting and performing a dance that imitates horse riding, all in the same rhythm with an intensity unseen since the early days of the Beatles, venerating Psy as a new Messiah. The music is psydance at its worst, totally flat and mechanically simple, mostly computer-generated (recall that Psy – the singer's name – is a shortened version of 'psytrance'); what makes it interesting is the way it combines collective trance with self-irony. The words of the song (and the staging of the video) obviously poke fun at the meaninglessness and vacuity of Gangnam style, some claim even in a subtly subversive way – but we are nonetheless entranced, caught in the stupid marching rhythm, participating in it in pure mimesis; flash mobs pop up all around the world imitating moments of the song, etc. Gangnam style is not ideology in spite of ironic distance, it is ideology because of it. Irony plays the same role as the documentary style in von Trier's *Breaking the Waves*, in which the subdued pseudo-documentary form makes palpable the excessive content – in a strictly homologous way, the self-mocking irony of 'Gangnam Style' makes palpable the stupid *jouissance* of rave music. Many viewers find the song disgustingly attractive, i.e., they 'love to hate it', or, rather, they enjoy finding it disgusting, so they repeatedly play it to prolong their disgust – this compulsive nature of the obscene *jouissance* in all its stupidity is what true art should release us from. Should we not take a step further here and draw a parallel between the performance of 'Gangnam Style' in a large Seoul stadium and the performances staged not far away across the border, in Pyong Yang, to celebrate the glory of the North Korean beloved leaders? Do we not get in both cases a similar neo-sacred ritual of obscene *jouissance*?

It may seem that in Korea, as well as elsewhere, numerous forms of traditional wisdom survive to serve as a protecting cushion against the shock of modernization. However, it is easy to discern how these remnants of traditional ideology are already trans-functionalized, transformed into ideological tools destined to facilitate rapid modernization – like the so-called Oriental spirituality (Buddhism) with its more 'gentle', balanced, holistic, ecological approach (all the stories about how, say, when digging up earth for the foundations of a house, Tibetan Buddhists are careful not to kill any worms). It is not only that Western Buddhism, this pop-cultural phenomenon preaching inner distance and indifference in the face of the frantic pace of market competition, is arguably the most efficient way, for us, to fully participate in capitalist dynamics while retaining the appearance of mental sanity – in short, the paradigmatic ideology of late capitalism; one should add that it is no longer possible to oppose this Western Buddhism to its 'authentic' Oriental version, and here, the case of Japan delivers conclusive evidence. Not only does there exist today, among top Japanese managers, the widespread 'corporate Zen' phenomenon, but over the last 150 years Japan's rapid industrialization and militarization, with its ethics of discipline and sacrifice, were sustained by the large majority of Zen thinkers.

What we encounter here is the dialectical logic of historical trans-functionalization: in a changed historical constellation, a remnant of the pre-modern past can start to function as the symbol of what is traumatically unbearable in extreme modernity. The same goes for the role of vampires in our ideological imaginary. Stacey Abbott[6] has demonstrated how the medium of film has completely reinvented the vampire archetype: rather than representing the primitive and folkloric, the vampire has come to embody the very experience of modernity. No longer in a cape and coffin, today's vampire resides in major cities, listens to punk music, embraces technology and adapts to any situation.

This, of course, in no way implies that Buddhism can be reduced to a capitalist ideology. To clarify this point, let us take a surprising example. In 1991, Richard Taruskin published a book review in which he scathingly dismissed all of Sergei Prokofiev's music, save the juvenilia, as bad. The stuff Prokofiev wrote in the West is 'bruised or rotten, justifiably discarded and unrevivable' in its superficial modernity; it was meant to compete with Stravinsky but it failed to do so. Realizing this, Prokofiev slunk back to Russia and Stalin, where his works were ruined by 'careerism' and a 'perhaps culpable indifference ... camouflaged by his apolitical façade'. In the Soviet Union, Prokofiev was first a shill for Stalin and then his victim, but, underneath, there was always the 'perfect emptiness' of an 'absolute' musician 'who just wrote music, or rather, who wrote "just music"'.[7] Unfair as they are, these statements do point towards a kind of quasi-psychotic attitude on Prokofiev's part: in contrast to other Soviet composers dragged into the turmoil of Stalinist accusations (Shostakovich, Khachaturian, and others), there are in Prokofiev no inner doubts, hysteria, anxiety: he weathered the anti-formalist campaign of 1948 with an almost psychotic serenity, as if it didn't really concern him. (The very madness of his return to the USSR in 1936, the year of the harshest Stalinist purges, is a tell-tale sign of his state of mind.) The fate of his works under Stalinism is not without irony: most of his party-line-following works were criticized and rejected as insincere and weak (which they were), while he got Stalin prizes for his 'dissident' intimate chamber works (piano sonatas 7 and 8, first violin sonata, cello sonata). Of special interest is Prokofiev's (obviously sincere) ideological justification of his full compliance with the Stalinist demands: Stalinism was embraced in continuity with his adherence to Christian Science. In the Gnostic universe of Christian Science, material reality is just an appearance: one should rise above it and enter spiritual bliss through hard work and renunciation. Prokofiev transposed this same stance onto Stalinism, reading the key demands of the Stalinist aesthetics – simplicity, harmony, joy – through these Gnostic lenses. Using the term proposed by Jean-Claude Milner, one could say that, although Prokofiev's universe was not homogeneous with Stalinism, it was definitely *homogénéisable* ('homogenizable') – Prokofiev didn't simply accommodate himself opportunistically to the Stalinist reality. And this same question is to be raised today: although it would be stupid to claim that Buddhist spirituality is homogeneous with global capitalism, it is definitely homogenizable with it.

Back to Korea, this analysis seems confirmed by *Propaganda*, a documentary from 2012 (easily available online) about capitalism, imperialism and the mass manipulation of Western culture for the purpose of commodification, and how they permeate every aspect of the lives of the blissfully ignorant, borderline-zombie masses. It is a 'mockumentary' that pretends to be North Korean, although it was made by a group from New Zealand – but, as they say in Italy, *Se non è vero, è ben trovato*. The use of fear and religion to manipulate the masses, as well as the role of the media that provide colourful distractions to keep us from thinking about the bigger problems, are all touched upon. One of the best parts of the film is its annihilation of celebrity-worship culture: talking about Madonna and Brad and Angelina's 'shopping for children in third-world countries'; western obsession with the glamorous lives of celebrities and self-absorption while ignoring the plight of the homeless and the suffering; celebrities being tools of commodification to the point that they often don't even realize it, often driving them to the point of insanity – all this is so spot on it's scary. It is the world around us. All of it, particularly the part about Michael Jackson – a look at 'what America did to this man' – rings so true it's kind of hard to swallow. If, in *Propaganda*, one were to delete a brief passage here and there which mentions the wisdom of their great beloved leader etc., one would get a standard – not even traditional Marxist, but more specifically Western Marxist Frankfurt-School-style – critique of consumerism, commodification and *Kulturindustrie*. But what we should be attentive to is a warning at the film's beginning: the narrator's voice tells the viewers that, although the filth and perversity of what they will see will embarrass and shock them, the great beloved Leader has decided to trust them that they are mature enough to see horrible truth about the outside world – words that a benevolent protective maternal authority uses when it decides to inform children of an unpleasant fact.

To grasp the special ideological status of North Korea, one should not shirk from mentioning the mythical Shangri-la from James Hilton's *The Lost Horizon*, an isolated valley in Tibet where people leave happy modest lives totally isolated from the corrupted global civilization and under the benevolent rule of an educated elite. North Korea is the closest we get today to Shangri-la – in what sense? The idea, proposed by Pierre Legendre and some other Lacanians, is that the problem today is the decline of the Name-of-the-Father, of the paternal symbolic authority: in its absence, pathological Narcissism explodes, evoking the spectre of the primordial Real Father. Although this idea is to be rejected, it is fully justified in pointing out how the decline of the Master in no way automatically guarantees emancipation, but can well engender much more oppressive figures of domination. In North Korea, patriarchy is effectively undermined, but in an unexpected way. Is North Korea really the last bastion of Stalinism, mixing totalitarian control with Confucian authoritarianism? Here are the words of North Korea's most popular political song:

Ah, Korean Workers' Party, at whose breast only
My life begins and ends
Be I buried in the ground or strewn to the wind
I remain your son, and again return to your breast!
Entrusting my body to your affectionate gaze,
Your loving outstretched hand,
I cry out forever in the voice of a child,
Mother! I can't live without Mother!'

This is what the excessive mourning after Kim Il Sung's death signalled: 'I can't live without Mother!' As a further proof, here are the two entries 'mother' and 'father' from a North Korean *Dictionary of the Korean Language*, published in 1964:

mother: 1) The woman who has given birth to one: Father and mother; a mother's love. *A mother's benevolence is higher than a mountain, deeper than the ocean.* Also used in the sense of 'a woman who has a child': *What all mothers anxiously want is for their children to grow up healthy and become magnificent red builders.* 2) A respectful term for someone of an age similar to one's own mother: *Comrade Platoon Leader called Dŏngmani's mother 'mother' and always helped her in her work.* 3) A metaphor for being loving, looking after everything, and worrying about others: *Party officials must become mothers who ceaselessly love and teach the Party rank and file, and become standard-bearers at the forefront of activities.* In other words, someone in charge of lodgings has to become a mother to the boarders. This means looking carefully after everything: whether someone is cold or sick, how they are eating, and so on. 4) A metaphor for the source from which something originates: *The Party is the great mother of everything new. Necessity is the mother of invention.*

   father: the husband of one's birth mother.[8]

Maybe that's why, till the third Kim, the leader's wife was not mentioned in public: the Leader was hermaphroditic, with dominant feminine features. Is this in contradiction with North Korea's 'military first' policy, with its ruthless military disciplining and drilling? No, these are two sides of the same coin. The figure of the mother we are dealing with here is the so-called 'non-castrated' omnipotent devouring mother: apropos the real mother, Jacques-Alain Miller noted that 'not only is there an unsatisfied mother but also an all-powerful one. And the terrifying aspect of this figure of the Lacanian mother is that she is all-powerful and unsatisfied at the same time.'[9] Therein resides the paradox: the more 'omnipotent' a mother appears, the more unsatisfied (which means 'lacking') she is: 'The Lacanian mother corresponds to the formula *quaerens quem devoret*: she looks for someone to devour, and so Lacan presents her then as the crocodile, the subject with the open mouth.'[10] This devouring mother doesn't respond (to the child's demand for a sign of love), and it is as such that she appears omnipotent: 'Since the mother does not respond ... she is transformed into a real agent that yields raw power ... if the Other does not respond, he is transformed into a devouring power.'[11] This is why the feminized features clearly discernible in the official portraits of the two Kim's are not accidental. To quote B. R. Myers:

> Kim [Il Sung] was more a mother to his people than a stern Confucian patriarch: he is still shown as soft-cheeked and solicitous, holding weeping adults to his expansive bosom, bending down to tie a young soldier's bootlaces, or letting giddy children clamber over him. The tradition continues under Kim Jong Il, who has been called 'more of a mother than all the mothers in the world'. His military-first policy may come with the title of General, but reports of his endless tour of army bases focus squarely on his fussy concern for the troops' health and comfort. The international ridicule of his appearance is thus as unfair as it is tedious. Anyone who has seen a crowd of Korean mothers waiting outside an examination hall will have no difficulty recognizing Kim's drab parka and drooping shoulders, or the long-suffering face under the pillow-swept perm: this is a mother with no time to think of herself.[12]

Does North Korea then stand for something like the Indian Kali – the benevolent/murderous goddess – in power? One should distinguish levels here: in North Korea, the superficial level of manly-military discourse of the Leader as 'General', with the *Juche* idea of self-reliance, of humanity as a master of itself and its destiny, is sustained by a deeper level of the Leader as a maternal protector. Here is how Myers formulates the basic axiom of North Korean ideology: 'The Korean people are too pure blooded, and therefore too virtuous, to survive in this evil world without a great parental leader.'[13] Is this not a nice example of Lacan's formula of paternal metaphor, of the Name-of-the-Father as a metaphoric substitute for the desire of the mother? The Name-of-the-Father (Leader/General) and, beneath it, the mother's protective/destructive desire? [14]

One of the New Age commonplaces is that we in the West are too much dominated by the male/paternal principle of domination, discipline, struggle, and so on, and that, to re-establish balance, we should reassert the feminine principle of loving care and protection. However, cases of 'hard' feminine politicians from Indira Gandhi to Margaret Thatcher should make us think. Today the predominant figure of authority is no longer a patriarchal Master. Even 'totalitarianism' is not a discourse of the Master; however, the tragic experience of many revolutions in which the overthrowing of the old Master ended up in a much more murderous terror should in no way lead us to advocate a return to paternal symbolic authority as the only way out of the self-destructive deadlock of the late-capitalist narcissistic Protean Self. And this brings us back to Berardi. Although they are as different as one can imagine, North and South Korea share one basic feature: they are both post-patriarchal societies. The reason *Propaganda* often rings so true that it is hard to accept is thus not simply because of the fact, known from Montesquieu's *Persian Letters*, that a naïve foreign gaze can perceive in our culture things that we, immersed as we are in it, cannot note, but rather because the extreme opposition between North and South Korea is sustained by an underlying sameness indicated by the film's title: two extreme modes of timelessness, of suspending historicity proper. (This is why the very term 'propaganda' is indicative: the documentary uses as its title a word which best befits its own – North Korean – ideological universe.)

There is a well-known Jewish story about a child who, after being told a wonderful old legend by a rabbi, eagerly asks him: 'But did it really happen? Is it true?' The rabbi replies: 'It didn't really happen, but it is true.' This assertion of the 'deeper' symbolic truth in contrast to the factual should be supplemented by its opposite – our reaction to many a spectacular 'event' can only be: 'It did really happen, but it isn't true.' So we should be all the more grateful for any sign of hope, no matter how small it appears, like the existence of Café Photo in Sao Paolo. Publicized as 'entertainment with a special touch', it is – so I was told – a meeting place for high-class prostitutes with their prospective clients. Although this fact is very well known by the public, this information is not published on their website: officially, 'it is a place to meet the best company for your evening'. Things really do proceed there with a special touch: prostitutes themselves – mostly students of humanities – choose their customers. Men (prospective clients) enter, take a seat at a table, buy a drink and wait, being observed by women. If a woman finds one of them acceptable, she sits at his table, lets him buy her a drink and starts a conversation on some intellectual topic, usually a theme of cultural life, sometimes even art theory. If she finds the man bright and attractive enough, she asks him if he would like to go to bed with her and tells him her price. This is prostitution with a feminist twist, if ever there was one – even if, as is often the case, the feminist twist is paid for by a class limitation: both prostitutes and clients come from the upper or at least upper-middle classes. So I humbly dedicate this book to the prostitutes of the Café Photo in Sao Paolo.

I

DIAGNOSIS *Hors d'oeuvre?*

CRISIS, WHAT CRISIS?

The situation of South Korea today cannot but evoke the famous opening lines of Charles Dickens's *Tale of Two Cities*: '... it was the spring of hope, it was the winter of despair, we had everything before us, we had nothing before us, we were all going direct to Heaven, we were all going direct the other way.' So, in South Korea, we find top economic performance, but with the frantic intensity of the work rhythm; unbridled consumerist heaven, but permeated with the hell of solitude and despair; abundant material wealth, but with the desertification of the landscape; imitation of ancient traditions, but with the highest suicide rate in the world. This radical ambiguity disturbs the image of South Korea as today's ultimate success story – success, yes, but what kind of success?

The Christmas 2012 issue of the *Spectator* magazine opened with the editorial 'Why 2012 was the best year ever', which argues against the perception that we live in 'a dangerous, cruel world where things are bad and getting worse':

> It may not feel like it, but 2012 has been the greatest year in the history of the world. That sounds like an extravagant claim, but it is borne out by evidence. Never has there been less hunger, less disease or more prosperity. The West remains in the economic doldrums, but most developing countries are charging ahead, and people are being lifted out of poverty at the fastest rate ever recorded. The death toll inflicted by war and natural disasters is also mercifully low. We are living in a golden age.[1]

The same idea was developed in detail by Matt Ridley – here is the blurb for his *Rational Optimist*:

> A counterblast to the prevailing pessimism of our age, [the book] proves, however much we like to think to the contrary, that things are getting better. Over 10,000 years ago there were fewer than 10 million people on the planet. Today there are more than 6 billion, 99 per cent of whom are better fed, better sheltered, better entertained and better protected against disease than their Stone Age ancestors. The availability of almost everything a person could want or need has been going erratically upwards for 10,000 years and has rapidly accelerated over the last 200 years: calories; vitamins; clean water; machines; privacy; the means to travel faster than we can run, and the ability to communicate over longer distances than we can shout. Yet, bizarrely, however much things improve from the way they were before, people still cling to the belief that the future will be nothing but disastrous.[2]

And Steven Pinker's *The Better Angels of Our Nature* gives us more of the same. Here is its blurb:

> Believe it or not, today we may be living in the most peaceful moment in our species' existence. In his gripping and controversial new work, *New York Times* bestselling author Steven Pinker shows that despite the ceaseless news about war, crime, and terrorism, violence has actually been in decline over long stretches of history. Exploding myths about humankind's inherent violence and the curse of modernity, this ambitious book continues Pinker's exploration of the essence of human nature, mixing psychology and history to provide a remarkable picture of an increasingly enlightened world.[3]

One often hears in mass media, especially those of non-European countries, a more modest version of this optimism, focusing on economy: crisis, what crisis? Look at the BRIC countries, or Poland, South Korea, Singapore, Peru, many sub-Saharan African states: they are all progressing. The losers are only Western Europe and, up to a point, the US, so we are not dealing with a global crisis, but just with the shift of the dynamics of progress away from the West. Is a potent symbol of this shift not the fact that recently many people from Portugal, a country in deep crisis, are returning to Mozambique and Angola, ex-colonies of Portugal – but this time as economic immigrants, not as colonizers? Our much-decried crisis is hardly worthy of the name if it is merely a local crisis in a picture of overall progress. Even with regard to human rights: is the situation in China and Russia now not better than fifty years ago? Decrying the ongoing crisis as a global phenomenon is typically a Eurocentric view – and, what's more, a view coming from Leftists who usually pride themselves on their anti-Eurocentrism.

With many provisos, one can roughly accept the data to which these 'rationalists' refer. Yes, today we definitely live better than our ancestors did 10,000 years ago in the Stone Age, and even an average prisoner in Dachau (the Nazi *working* camp, not Auschwitz, the *killing* camp) was living at least marginally better, probably, than a slave prisoner of the Mongols. And so on and so forth. But there is something that this story misses.

First – we should restrain our anti-colonialist joy here – the question to be raised is: if Europe is in gradual decay, *what is replacing its hegemony?* The answer is: 'capitalism with Asian values' (which, of course, has nothing to do with Asian people and everything to do with the clear and present tendency of contemporary capitalism as such to suspend democracy). From Marx on, the truly radical Left was never simply 'progressist'. It was always obsessed by the question: what is the price of progress? Marx was fascinated by capitalism, by the unheard-of productivity it unleashed; it was just that he insisted that this very success engenders antagonisms. And we should do the same with the progress of global capitalism today: keep in view its dark underside, which is fomenting revolts.

What all this implies is that today's conservatives are not really conservative. While fully endorsing capitalism's continuous self-revolutionizing, they just want to make it more efficient by supplementing it with some traditional institutions (religion, for instance) to constrain its destructive consequences for social life and to maintain social cohesion. Today, a true conservative is the one who fully admits the antagonisms and deadlocks of global capitalisms, the one who rejects simple progressivism, and who is attentive to the dark obverse of progress. In this sense, only a radical Leftist can be today a true conservative.

People do not rebel when 'things are really bad' but when their expectations are disappointed. The French Revolution occurred after the king and the nobles had for decades been gradually losing their grip on power; the 1956 anti-Communist revolt in Hungary exploded after Nagy Imre had already been prime minister for two years, after (relatively) free debates among intellectuals; people rebelled in Egypt in 2011 because there had been some economic progress under Mubarak, which had given rise to a whole class of educated young people who participated in the universal digital culture. And this is why the Chinese Communists are right to be in a panic: precisely because, on average, Chinese are now living considerably better than forty years ago, but the social antagonisms (between the newly rich and the rest) have exploded, plus people's expectations are now generally much higher. That's the problem with development and progress: they are always uneven, they give birth to new instabilities and antagonisms, they generate new expectations which cannot be met. In Tunisia or Egypt just prior to the Arab Spring, the majority probably lived a little bit better than decades ago, but the standards by which they measured their (dis)satisfaction were much higher.

So yes, the *Spectator*, Ridley, Pinker and their fellow travellers are in principle right, but the very facts that they emphasize are creating conditions for revolt and rebellion. The mistake to be avoided is the one best exemplified by the story (apocryphal, maybe) about the Left-Keynesian economist John Galbraith. Before a trip to USSR in the late 1950s, he wrote to his anti-Communist friend Sidney Hook: 'Don't worry, I will not be seduced by the Soviets and return home claiming they have socialism!' Hook answered him promptly: 'But that's what worries me – that you will return claiming USSR is NOT socialist!' What worried Hook was the naive defence of the purity of the concept: if things go wrong with building a socialist society, this does not invalidate the idea itself, it just means we didn't implement it properly. Do we not detect the same naivety in today's market fundamentalists? When, during a recent TV debate in France, Guy Sorman claimed that democracy and capitalism necessarily go together, I couldn't resist asking him the obvious question: 'But what about China today?' He snapped back: 'In China there is no capitalism!' For the fanatically pro-capitalist Sorman, if a country is non-democratic, it simply means it is not truly capitalist but practises capitalism's disfigured version, in exactly the same way that, for a democratic Communist, Stalinism was simply not an authentic form of Communism. The underlying mistake is not difficult to identify. It is the same as in the well-known joke: 'My fiancée is never late for an appointment, because the moment she is late she is no longer my fiancée!' This is how today's free-market apologist explains the crisis of 2008: it was not the failure of the free market that caused the crisis but excessive state regulation, i.e. the fact that our market economy was not a true one, that it was still in the clutches of the welfare state. When we stick to such a purity of market capitalism, dismissing its failures as accidental mishaps, we end up in a naive progressivism that ignores the mad dance of the opposites.

One of the most striking cases of this mad dance is, in the economic sphere, the weird coexistence of intense employment with the threat of unemployment: the more intensely those who are employed work, the more generalized is the threat of unemployment. Today's situation therefore compels us to shift the accent of our reading of Marx's *Capital* from the general topic of capitalist reproduction to, as Frederick Jameson puts it, 'the fundamental structural centrality of unemployment in the text of *Capital* itself': 'unemployment is structurally inseparable from the dynamic of accumulation and expansion which constitutes the very nature of capitalism as such.'[4] In what is arguably the extreme point of the 'unity of the opposites' in the economic sphere, it is the very success of capitalism (raised productivity, etc.) that produces unemployment (renders more and more workers useless): what should be a blessing (less hard labour needed) becomes a curse. In this way the world market is, with regard to its immanent dynamic, 'a space in which everyone has once been a productive labourer, and in which labour has everywhere begun to price itself out of the system'.[5] That is to say, in the ongoing process of capitalist globalization, the category of the unemployed has acquired a new quality beyond the classic notion of the 'reserve army of labour'. One should consider, in terms of the category of unemployment, 'those massive populations around the world who have, as it were, "dropped out of history", who have been deliberately excluded from the modernizing projects of First World capitalism and written off as hopeless or terminal cases':[6] so-called 'failed states' (Congo, Somalia), victims of famine or ecological disasters, caught in pseudo-archaic 'ethnic hatreds', objects of philanthropy and NGOs or (often the same people) of the 'war on terror'. The category of the unemployed should thus be expanded to encompass the wide span of population from the temporarily unemployed, through the no-longer-employable and permanently unemployed, up to people living in slums and other types of ghettos (all those often dismissed by Marx himself as 'lumpenproletarians') and, finally, entire areas, populations or states excluded from the global capitalist process, like the blank spaces in ancient maps. Does this extension of the circle of the 'unemployed' not take us back from Marx to Hegel: the 'rabble' returns, emerging in the very core of emancipatory struggles? That is to say, such a re-categorization changes the entire 'cognitive mapping' of the situation: the inert background of History becomes a potential agent of emancipatory struggle.

We should nonetheless add three qualifications to Jameson's deployment of this idea. First, one should correct the semiotic square proposed by Jameson, whose terms are (1) workers, (2) the reserve army of the (temporarily) unemployed, (3) the (permanently) unemployable and (4) the 'formerly employed'[7] but now unemployable. Would not a more appropriate fourth term be the *illegally employed*, from those working in black markets and slums up to different forms of slavery? Second, Jameson fails to emphasize how those 'excluded' are often nonetheless *included* in the world market. Take the case of today's Congo: behind the façade of the 'primitive ethnic passions' exploding yet again in the African 'heart of darkness', it is easy to discern the contours of global capitalism. After the fall of Mobutu, Congo no longer exists as a united operating state; its eastern part in particular is a multiplicity of territories ruled by local warlords controlling their patch of land with armies that as a rule include drugged children. Each warlord has business links to a foreign company or corporation exploiting the wealth – mostly mineral – in the region. This arrangement fits both partners: the corporation gets mining rights without paying taxes and so forth, while the warlord gets paid. The irony is that many of these minerals are used in high-tech products like laptops and mobile phones. So, in short, forget about blaming conflict on the 'savage customs' of the local population: just take away from the equation the foreign high-tech companies and the whole edifice of 'ethnic warfare fuelled by old passions' will fall apart.[8] And third, the category of 'formerly employed' should be supplemented by its opposite: the educated unemployed. Today, a whole generation of students has almost no chance of finding appropriate employment, something which leads to massive protest. The worst way to resolve this gap is to directly subordinate education to the demands of the market – if for no other reason than that the market dynamic itself renders the education provided by universities 'obsolete'. These unemployable students are destined to play a key organizing role in the forthcoming emancipatory movements (as they already have done in Egypt and in European protests from Greece to the UK). Radical change is never triggered by the poor alone. The addition of a generation of unemployable educated youth (combined with widely available modern digital technology) offers the prospect of a properly revolutionary situation.

Jameson adds here another (paradoxical, but deeply justified) key step: he characterizes this new structural unemployment as a form of *exploitation*. The exploited are not only workers producing surplus-value appropriated by capital; also exploited are those who are structurally prevented from getting caught in the capitalist vortex of exploited wage labour, including whole zones and nations. How, then, are we to rethink the concept of exploitation? A radical change is needed here: in a properly dialectical twist, exploitation includes its own negation – the exploited are not only those who produce or 'create', but also (and even more) those who are condemned *not* to create. Here, are we not back at the structure of the well-known joke from the last decade of the Soviet Union about Rabinovitch, a Jew who wants to emigrate? The bureaucrat at the emigration office asks him why, and Rabinovitch answers: 'There are two reasons why. The first is that I'm afraid that in the Soviet Union the Communists will lose power, and the new power will put all the blame for the Communist crimes on us Jews – there will again be anti-Jewish pogroms . . .' 'But,' interrupts the bureaucrat, 'this is pure nonsense; nothing can change in the Soviet Union, the power of the Communists will last forever!'

'Well,' responds Rabinovitch calmly, 'that's my second reason.' We can easily imagine a state bureaucrat asking a worker: 'Why do you think you are exploited?' and the worker replying, 'For two reasons. First, when I work, the capitalist appropriates my surplus-value.' 'But you are now unemployed; no one is appropriating your surplus-value because you create none!' 'This is the second reason …' Everything hinges on the fact that the totality of capitalist production not only needs workers, but also generates the 'reserve army' of those who cannot find work: the latter are not simply outside the circulation of capital, they are actively produced as not-working by this circulation.

There is a wonderfully dialectical joke in Lubitsch's *Ninotchka*. The hero visits a cafeteria and orders coffee without cream, to which the waiter replies: 'Sorry, but we have run out of cream. Can I bring you coffee without milk?' In both cases, the customer gets coffee alone, but this One-coffee is each time accompanied by a different negation, first coffee-with-no-cream, then coffee-with-no-milk. What we encounter here is the logic of differentiality, in which the lack itself functions as a positive feature – the paradox rendered nicely by an old Yugoslav joke about a Montenegrin (people from Montenegro were stigmatized as lazy in ex-Yugoslavia): why does a Montenegrin guy, when going to sleep, put at the side of his bed two glasses, one full and one empty? Because he is too lazy to think in advance if he will be thirsty during the night. The point of this joke is that the absence itself has to be positively registered: it is not enough to have one full glass of water, since, if the Montenegrin will not be thirsty, he will simply ignore it – this negative fact itself has to be taken-note-of by the empty glass, i.e., no-need-for-water has to be materialized in the void of the empty glass.

Why waste time with such dialectical jokes? Because they allow us to grasp how ideology at its purest functions in our allegedly post-ideological times. To detect so-called ideological distortions, one should note not only what is said, but the complex interplay between what is said and what is not said, the un-said implied in what is said: do we get coffee without cream or coffee without milk? There is a political equivalent of these lines: in a well-known joke from socialist Poland, a customer enters a store and asks: 'You probably don't have butter, or do you?' The answer: 'Sorry, but we are the store which doesn't have toilet paper; the one across the street is the one that doesn't have butter!' And what about a scene in today's Brazil where, in a carnival, people from all backgrounds dance together on the street, momentarily obliterating their race and class differences. But when a jobless worker delivers himself up to the free dance, forgetting his worries about how to take care of his family, it is obviously not the same as when a rich banker lets himself go and feels good about being at one with the people, in the process forgetting that he refused a loan to the poor worker. They are both the same on the street, but the worker is dancing without milk, while the banker is dancing without cream. The labelling of food provides another striking example of absence as a determining factor: recall how often we read on food products 'without added sugar' or 'without preservatives or additives' – not to mention 'without calories', 'without fat', etc. – the catch being that for each 'without' you have to accept (knowingly or not) the presence of another 'with' (Coke without calories and sugar? OK, but with the artificial sweeteners which bring their own health risks).

This paradox reaches its climax when what we are offered is a thing without itself – coffee without coffee. Recall the ongoing debate about universal healthcare in the US: the Republicans who claim that universal healthcare deprives individuals of their freedom of choice are effectively promoting a freedom of choice *without actual freedom of choice*. That is to say, what the Republican opponents of universal healthcare are unable to see is how state-imposed universal health-care effectively functions as a safety network which enables the majority to enjoy a much wider space of free endeavours. They are not simply not-working – their not-working is their positive feature, in the same way that 'coffee without milk' is its positive feature.

BREAKING EGGS WITHOUT GETTING AN OMELETTE

The crisis whose indication is the new role of unemployment reveals 'the structural limits that capital meets in the attempt to subjugate the immaterial economy and the internet to the logic of commercialization, where the principle of gratuitousness continues to predominate despite the attempts to establish economic barriers to the access and the reinforcement of intellectual property rights.'[9] In other words, the crisis is not just the result of inadequate financial regulations, it expresses 'the intrinsic difficulty to make immaterial capital function like capital and cognitive capitalism to function like capitalism'.[10] As such, this crisis signals the end of the 1990s project of the New Economy, the idea that capitalism can be revitalized in its digital form, with programmers and other intellectual workers turning into 'creative' capitalists (the dream embodied in the journal *Wired*). That's why stronger and stronger state intervention is needed to keep the system viable. We should not miss the double irony here: there is some truth in the claim that state-socialism disintegrated in 1990 because it was not able to adapt itself to the digitalization of economic and social life; however, the same traditional Marxist notion of the contradiction between productive forces and relations of production is now undermining capitalism itself. (Basic income should thus be re-conceptualized not as an extended support of the unemployed, i.e., as a redistributive measure of social security, but as a financial recognition of the fact that, in a knowledge-based-economy, collective productivity of the 'general intellect' is the key source of wealth.[11])

Communism remains the horizon, the *only* horizon, from which one can not only judge but even adequately analyse what goes on today – a kind of immanent measure of what went wrong. That's why one should abandon the 'neo-Ricardian compromise between wage labour and productive capital against the power of finance',[12] which tries to resuscitate the Social-Democratic welfare-state model: every demonization of financial capital is a manoeuvre to obfuscate the basic antagonism of capitalist production by transposing it onto 'parasitic' financial capital. And one should no less reject attempts at what one cannot but ironically call 'Left Friedmanism', the idea advocated by Wang Hui (among others), according to which what we are witnessing today is not the consequence of the market economy but its distortion: 'resistance against monopolization and domineering market tyranny cannot be simply equalled with the struggle "against" the market, because such social resistance itself includes the efforts striving for fair competition in the market and for economic democracy.'[13] Recall Habermas's notion of distorted communication (distorted because of extra-linguistic power relations of oppression and domination): Wang Hui seems to imply the notion of distorted market competition and exchange – distorted due to the external pressures of political, cultural and social conditions:

> the movement of economy is always embedded in politics, culture and other social conditions, so to strive for the conditions of fair market competition does not equal getting rid of the state political system, social customs, and any regulating mechanism. On the contrary, the perfecting of market conditions aims to reform, limit, and expand these systems in order to create social conditions for fair interaction. In this sense, the struggle for social justice and fair market competition cannot be equalled with the opposition to state intervention. It rather requires socialist democracy, namely, to prevent the state from becoming the protector of domestic monopoly and multinational monopoly through the society's democratic control of the state.[14]

Here, one should remain shamelessly orthodox Marxist: Wang Hui underestimates the immanent logic of market relations, which tends towards exploitation and destabilizing excesses. Are we substantializing economy too much here? It would be easy to perform the standard deconstructionist operation on 'economy' and claim that there is no Economy as a substantial unified field, that what we designate as 'economy' is an inconsistent space traversed by a multitude of practices and discourses: material production from primitive hand labour to automated production, money operations, publicity machines, interventions of state apparatuses, legal regulations and obligations, ideological dreams, religious myths, tales of domination, suffering and humiliation, private obsessions with wealth and pleasures, and so on. While this is undoubtedly true, there is nonetheless not a deeper 'essence' of Economy, but rather something like a 'mathem' of capital, a formal matrix of the self-reproduction of capital, like that which Marx was trying to elaborate in his *Capital*. This mathem, this trans-historical and trans-cultural formal matrix, is the 'real' of capital: the thing that stays the same through the entire process of global capitalism, the madness of which becomes palpable in moments of crisis. Marx describes the contours of this madness when he talks about the traditional miser as 'a capitalist gone mad', hoarding his treasure in a secret hide-out, in contrast to the 'normal' capitalist, who augments his treasure by throwing it into circulation:

> The restless never-ending process of profit-making alone is what he aims at. This boundless greed after riches, this passionate chase after exchange-value, is common to the capitalist and the miser; but while the miser is merely a capitalist gone mad, the capitalist is a rational miser. The never-ending augmentation of exchange-value, which the miser strives after, by seeking to save his money from circulation, is attained by the more acute capitalist, by constantly throwing it afresh into circulation.[15]

This madness of the miser is nonetheless not something which simply disappears with the rise of 'normal' capitalism or its pathological deviation. It is, rather, *inherent* in it: the miser has his moment of triumph in the economic *crisis*. In a crisis, it is not – as one would expect – money which loses its value, and we have to resort to the 'real' value of commodities; commodities themselves (the embodiment of 'real [use] value') become useless, because there is no one to buy them. In a crisis,

> money suddenly and immediately changes from its merely nominal shape, money of account, into hard cash. Profane commodities can no longer replace it. The use-value of commodities becomes value-less, and their value vanishes in the face of their own form of value. The bourgeois, drunk with prosperity and arrogantly certain of himself, has just declared that money is a purely imaginary creation. 'Commodities alone are money,' he said. But now the opposite cry resounds over the markets of the world: only money is a commodity . . . In a crisis, the antithesis between commodities and their value-form, money, is raised to the level of an absolute contradiction.[16]

Does this not mean that at this moment, far from disintegrating, fetishism is fully asserted in its direct madness? In crisis, the underlying belief, disavowed and just practised, is thus directly asserted. And the same holds for today's ongoing crisis, one of the spontaneous reactions to which is to turn to some commonsense guideline: 'Debts have to be paid!', 'You cannot spend more than you produce!', or something similar – and this, of course, is the worst thing one can do, since in this way, one gets caught in a downward spiral.

First, such elementary wisdom is simply wrong – the United States was doing quite well for decades by spending much more than it produced. At a more fundamental level, we should clearly perceive the paradox of debt. The problem with the slogan 'You cannot spend more than you produce!' is that, taken universally, it is a tautological platitude, a fact and not a norm (of course humanity cannot consume more than it produces, like you cannot eat more food than you have on the plate), but the moment one moves to a particular level, things get problematic and ambiguous. At the direct material level of social totality, debts are in a way irrelevant, inexistent even, since humanity as a whole consumes what it produces – by definition one cannot consume more. One can reasonably speak of debt only with regard to natural resources (destroying the material conditions for the survival of future generations), where we are indebted to future generations which, precisely, do not yet exist and which, not without irony, will come to exist only through – and thus be indebted for their existence to – ourselves. So here, also, the term 'debt' has no literal sense, it cannot be 'financialized', quantified into an amount of money. The debt we can talk about occurs when, within a global society, some group (nation or whatever) consumes more than it produces, which means that another group has to consume less than it produces – but here, relations are by no means as simple and clear as they may appear. Relations would be clear if, in a situation of debt, money was a neutral instrument measuring how much more one group consumed with regard to what it produced, and at whose expense – but the actual situation is far from this. According to public data, around 90 per cent of money circulating is 'virtual' credit money, so if 'real' producers find themselves indebted to financial institutions, one has good reasons to doubt the status of their debt: how much of this debt is the result of speculations which happened in a sphere without any link to the reality of a local unit of production?

So when a country finds itself under the pressure of international financial institutions, be it the IMF or private banks, one should always bear in mind that their pressure (translated into concrete demands: reduce public spending by dismantling parts of the welfare state, privatize, open up your market, deregulate your banks ...) is not the expression of some neutral objective logic or knowledge, but of a doubly partial ('interested') knowledge. At the formal level, it is a knowledge which embodies a series of neoliberal presuppositions, while at the level of content, it privileges the interests of certain states or institutions (banks etc.).

When the Romanian Communist writer Panait Istrati visited the Soviet Union in the late 1920s, the time of the first purges and show trials, a Soviet apologist trying to convince him about the need for violence against the enemies of the Soviet Union invoked the proverb, 'You can't make an omelette without breaking eggs,' to which Istrati tersely replied: 'All right. I can see the broken eggs. Where's this omelette of yours?' We should say the same about the austerity measures imposed by the IMF, about which the Greeks would be fully justified in saying: 'OK, we are breaking our eggs for all of Europe, but where's the omelet you are promising us?'

If the ideal of financial speculation is to get an omelette without breaking any eggs, in a financial meltdown we end up with just broken eggs, as was the case in Cyprus. Recall the classic cartoon scene of a cat which simply continues to walk over the edge of the precipice, ignoring the fact that she no longer has ground under her feet – she falls only when she looks down and notices she is hanging over the abyss. Is this not how ordinary people in Cyprus must feel these days? They are aware that Cyprus will never be the same, that ahead lies a catastrophic fall in living standards, but the full impact of this fall is not yet properly felt, so for a short period they can afford to go on with their normal daily lives, like the cat who calmly walks in the empty air. And we should not condemn them. Such delaying of the full impact of the crash is also a survival strategy: the real impact will come silently, when the panic is over. This is why it is now, when the Cyprus crisis has largely disappeared from the media, that one should think and write about it.

Back to the joke about Rabinovitch, it is easy to imagine a similar conversation between a European Union financial administrator and a Cypriot Rabinovitch today. Rabinovitch complains: 'There are two reasons we are in a panic here. First, we are afraid that the EU will simply abandon Cyprus and let our economy collapse ...' The EU administrator interrupts him: 'But you can trust us, we will not abandon you, we will tightly control you and advise you what to do!' 'Well,' responds Rabinovitch calmly, 'that's my second reason.' Such a deadlock is at the core of Cyprus's sad predicament: it cannot survive in prosperity without Europe, but nor can it do so *with* Europe. Both options are worse, as Stalin would have put it. Recall the cruel joke from Lubitsch's *To Be Or Not to Be*: when asked about the German concentration camps in the occupied Poland, the responsible Nazi officer, 'concentration-camp Erhardt', replies: 'We do the concentrating, and the Poles do the camping.' Does the same not hold true for the ongoing financial crisis in Europe? The strong Northern Europe, centred on Germany, does the concentrating, while the weakened and vulnerable South does the camping. Visible on the horizon are thus the contours of a divided Europe: its Southern part will be more and more reduced to a zone with a cheap labour force, outside the safety network of the welfare state, a domain appropriate for outsourcing and tourism. In short, the gap between the developed world and those lagging behind is now opening within Europe itself.

This gap is reflected in the two main stories about Cyprus, which resemble the two similar stories about Greece. There is what can be called the German story: free spending, debts and money laundering cannot go on indefinitely. And there is the Cyprus story: the brutal EU measures amount to a new German occupation which is depriving Cyprus of its sovereignty. Both stories are wrong, and the demands they imply are nonsensical: Cyprus by definition cannot repay its debt, while Germany and the EU cannot simply go on throwing money into the bottomless Cypriot financial hole. Both stories obfuscate the key fact: that there is something wrong with a system in which uncontrollable banking speculation can cause a whole country to go bankrupt. The Cyprus crisis is not a storm in the cup of a small marginal country, it is a symptom of what is wrong with the entire EU system. This is why the solution is not just more regulation to prevent money laundering and so on, but (at least) a *radical change in the entire banking system* – to say the unsayable, some kind of *socialization of banks*. The lesson of crashes that accumulated worldwide from 2008 onwards (Wall Street, Iceland, and so on) is clear: the whole network of financial funds and transactions, from individual deposits and retirement funds up to the functioning of all kinds of derivatives, will have to be somehow brought under social control, streamlined and regulated. This may sound utopian, but the true utopia is the notion that we can somehow survive with small cosmetic changes.

But there is a fatal trap to be avoided here: the socialization of banks that is needed is not a compromise between wage labour and productive capital against the power of finance. Financial meltdowns and crises are obvious reminders that the circulation of Capital is not a closed loop which can fully sustain itself – i.e. that this circulation points towards the reality of producing and selling actual goods that satisfy actual people's needs. However, the more subtle lesson of crises and meltdowns is that *there is no return to this reality* – all the rhetoric of 'let us move from the virtual space of financial speculation back to real people who produce and consume' is deeply misleading; it is ideology at its purest. The paradox of capitalism is that you cannot throw out the dirty water of financial speculations and keep the healthy baby of real economy: *the dirty water effectively is the 'bloodline' of the healthy baby.*

NOW WE KNOW WHO JOHN GALT IS!

This paradox was rendered palpable in the autumn 2013 shutdown of the US state apparatus. What was this shutdown really about? In the middle of April 2009, I was taking a rest in a hotel room in Syracuse, NY, jumping between two channels: a PBS documentary on Pete Seeger, the great American country singer of the Left, and a Fox News report on the anti-tax 'Tea Party' in Austin, Texas, in which another country singer performed an anti-Obama populist song full of complaints about how Washington is taxing hard-working ordinary people to finance rich Wall Street financiers. There was a weird similarity between the two singers: both formulated an anti-establishment populist complaint against the exploitative rich and the state, calling for radical measures including civil disobedience. All of which is another painful reminder that, at least with regard to the form of organization, today's radical-populist Right strangely reminds us of the old radical-populist Left. Are today's Christian survivalist-fundamentalist groups, with their half-legal status and seeing the main threat to their freedom in the oppressive state apparatus, not organized like the Black Panthers back in the 1960s? In both cases, we have a militarized group getting ready for the final battle. How long will this masterful ideological manipulation continue to work? How long will the base of the Tea Party stick to the fundamental irrationality of its agenda to protect the interest of the hard-working ordinary people by privileging the 'exploitative rich' and thereby literally countering their own interests?

Some of us remember the old infamous Communist tirades against the bourgeois 'formal' freedom – ridiculous as they are, there is an element of truth in this distinction between 'formal' and 'actual' freedom. A manager in a company in crisis has the 'freedom' to fire worker A or B, but not the freedom to change the situation which imposes on him this choice. The moment we approach the US healthcare debate in this way, the 'freedom to choose' appears in a different way. True, a large part of the population will be effectively delivered of the dubious 'freedom' to worry about who will cover their illness, to find a way through the intricate network of financial and other decisions. Being able to take basic healthcare for granted, to count on it like one counts on a water supply without worrying about having to choose the water company, people will simply gain more time and energy to dedicate to other things. The lesson to be learned is that freedom of choice is something which actually functions only if a complex network of legal, educational, ethical, economic and other conditions exists as the invisible thick background of the exercise of our freedom. This is why, as an antidote to the ideology of choice, countries like Norway should be held as a model: although all main agents respect a basic social agreement and large social projects are enacted in solidarity, social productivity and dynamics are at an extraordinary level, flatly denying the common wisdom that such a society should be stagnating.

Not many people know – and even fewer appreciate the irony of the fact – that 'My Way', Frank Sinatra's iconic song that supposedly expresses American individualism, is an Americanized version of the French song 'Comme d'habitude', which means 'as usual', or 'as is customary'. It is all too easy to see this couple – the French original and its American version – as yet another example of the opposition between sterile French manners and American inventiveness (the French follow established customs, while Americans look for new solutions) – but what if we drop the false appearance of opposition and discern in the habit of 'comme d'habitude' the hidden sad truth of the much-praised search for new ways? In order to be able to do it 'my way', each of us has to rely on quite a lot of things going on comme d'habitude. Quite a lot of things, in other words, have to be regulated if we are to enjoy our non-regulated freedom.[17]

One of the weird consequences of the 2008 financial meltdown and the measures taken to counteract it (enormous sums of money to help banks) was the revival in the work of Ayn Rand, the fullest ideological expression of radical 'greed is good' capitalism: the sales of her magnum opus Atlas Shrugged exploded. According to some, there are already signs that the scenario described in Atlas Shrugged – the 'creative capitalists' themselves going on strike – is now being enacted. Yet this reaction almost totally misreads the situation: most of the gigantic sums of bail-out money went precisely to those deregulated Randian 'titans' who failed in their 'creative' schemes and in doing so brought about the meltdown. It is not the great creative geniuses who are now helping lazy ordinary people; rather, it is the ordinary taxpayers who are helping the failed 'creative geniuses'. One should simply recall that the ideologico-political father of the long economic process which ended up in the 2008 meltdown was Alan Greenspan, a card-carrying Randian 'objectivist'. So now we finally know who John Galt is – the idiot responsible for the 2008 financial meltdown and, consequentially, for the threat of the shutdown of state apparatuses.

In order truly to awaken from the Randian capitalist 'dogmatic dream' (as Kant would have put it), we should apply to our situation Brecht's old quip from his Beggars' Opera: 'What is the robbing of a bank compared to the founding of a bank?' What is the stealing of a couple of thousand dollars, for which one goes to prison, compared to financial speculations which deprive tens of millions of their homes and savings, and are then rewarded by state help of sublime grandeur? Maybe Jose Saramago was right when he proposed treating the big bank managers and others responsible for the meltdown as perpetrators of crimes against humanity, whose place is in the Hague Tribunal; maybe one should not treat this proposal just as a poetic exaggeration in the style of Jonathan Swift, but take it seriously. This, however, will never happen since, after the doctrine of the bank *too big to fail* (the logic being that its bankruptcy would have catastrophic consequences for the entire economy), we now have the doctrine of the bank *too big to indict*[18] (since, one can argue, its indictment would have catastrophic consequences for the financial and moral status of the ruling elites).

These elites, the main culprits for the 2008 financial meltdown, now impose themselves as experts, the only ones who can lead us on the painful path of financial recovery, and whose advice should therefore trump parliamentary politics, or, as Mario Monti put it: 'Those who govern must not allow themselves to be completely bound by parliamentarians.'[19] What, then, is this higher force whose authority can suspend the decisions of the democratically elected representatives of the people? The answer was provided back in 1998 by Hans Tietmeyer, then governor of the Deutsches Bundesbank, who praised national governments for preferring 'the permanent plebiscite of global markets' to the 'plebiscite of the ballot box'.[20] Note the democratic rhetoric of this obscene statement: global markets are more democratic than parliamentary elections since the process of voting goes on in them permanently (and is permanently reflected in market fluctuations) and at a global level – not only every four years, and within the confines of a nation-state. The underlying idea is that, freed from this higher control of markets (and experts), parliamentary-democratic decisions are 'irresponsible'.

The consequences of such thinking have been – and are being – felt all around Europe. In one of his last interviews before his fall, Nicolae Ceauşescu was asked by a Western journalist how he justified the fact that Romanian citizens could not travel freely abroad even though freedom of movement was guaranteed by the Romanian constitution. Ceauşescu's answer followed the best of Stalinist sophistry: true, the constitution guaranteed the freedom of movement, but it also guaranteed the right of the people to a safe and prosperous home. So we have here a potential conflict of rights: if Romanian citizens were to be allowed to leave the country freely, the prosperity of the homeland would be threatened and they would have put in danger their right to the homeland. In this conflict of right, one has to make a choice, and the right to a prosperous and safe homeland enjoys a clear priority.

It seems that this same spirit of Stalinist sophistry is alive and well in today's Slovenia where, on 19 December 2012, the Constitutional Court found that a proposed referendum on the legislation to set up a 'bad bank' and a sovereign holding would be unconstitutional – thus in effect banning a popular vote on the matter. The referendum had been mooted by trade unions, against the government's neo-liberal economic politics, and the proposal attracted enough signatures to make it constitutionally obligatory. The government's idea was to transfer all bad credits from the main banks onto a new 'bad bank', which would then be salvaged by state money (i.e., at the taxpayers' expense), preventing any serious inquiry into who was responsible for the financial fiasco. This measure, a matter of financial and economic policy, was debated for months and was far from being generally accepted even by financial specialists. So why prohibit the referendum? In 2011, when Papandreou's government in Greece proposed a referendum on austerity measures, there was panic in Brussels, but even there no one dared directly to prohibit it.

According to the Slovene Constitutional Court, the referendum 'would have caused unconstitutional consequences' – but how? The Constitutional Court conceded that the referendum was a constitutional right, but claimed that its execution would endanger other constitutional values which should be given priority in a situation of economic crisis: the efficient functioning of the state apparatus, especially in creating conditions for economic growth; the realization of human rights, especially the rights to social security and to free economic initiative. In short, in its assessment of the consequences of the referendum, the Constitutional Court simply accepted as an undisputed fact the reasoning of international financial authorities which are exerting pressure on Slovenia to enact more austerity measures: failing to obey the dictates of international financial institutions (or to meet their expectations) can lead to political and economic crisis and is thus unconstitutional. To put it bluntly: since meeting these financial dictates/expectations is the condition of maintaining the constitutional order, they have priority over the constitution (and *eo ipso* state sovereignty).

No wonder, then, that the Court's decision shocked many legal specialists. Dr France Bučar, an old dissident and one of the fathers of Slovene independence, pointed out that, following the logic the Constitutional Court used in this case, the Court can prohibit any referendum, since every such act has social consequences: 'With this decision, the constitutional judges issued to themselves a blank cheque allowing them to prohibit anything anyone can concoct. From when does the Constitutional Court have the right to assess the state of economy or bank institutions? It can assess only if a certain legal regulation is in accord with the constitution or not. That's it!'

There can of course be a conflict between different constitutional rights: if a group of people, say, were to propose an openly racist referendum, asking the people to endorse a law endorsing police torture, it should undoubtedly be prohibited. However, the reason for prohibition in this case is that the principle promoted by the referendum (the acceptability of torture) directly conflicts with other articles of the constitution, while in the Slovene case, the reason for prohibition does not concern principles, but the (possible) pragmatic consequences of an economic measure.

Slovenia may be a small marginal country, but the decision of its Constitutional Court was the symptom of a global tendency towards the limitation of democracy. The idea is that, in a complex economic situation like today's, the majority of the people are not qualified to decide – they just want to keep their privileges intact, unaware of the catastrophic consequences which would ensue if their demands were to be met. This line of argument is not new. In a TV interview a decade ago, the theorist Ralf Dahrendorf linked the growing distrust in democracy to the fact that, after every revolutionary change, the road to new prosperity leads through a 'valley of tears'. After the breakdown of socialism, one cannot directly pass to the abundance of a successful market economy – the limited, but real, socialist welfare and security had to be dismantled, and these first steps are necessarily painful. The same goes for Western Europe, where the passage from the post-Second World War welfare state to new global economy involves painful renunciations, less security, less guaranteed social care.

A rumour circulated in 1990s Germany (*se non è vero, è ben trovato*) that, on a visit to Berlin after he lost power, Gorbachev paid a surprise call on the ex-Chancellor Willy Brandt. However, when he (with his guards) approached Brandt's house and rang the doorbell, Brandt refused to see him. Later, he explained to a friend why: he had never forgiven Gorbachev for allowing the dissolution of the Communist bloc – not because Brandt was a secret believer in Soviet Communism, but because he was well aware that the disappearance of the Communist bloc would also entail the disappearance of the West European Social Democratic welfare state. That is to say, Brandt knew that the capitalist system is ready to make considerable concessions to the workers and the poor only if there is a serious threat of an alternative, of a different mode of production which promises workers their rights. To retain its legitimacy, capitalism has to demonstrate how it works better even for the workers and the poor – and the moment this alternative vanishes, one can proceed to dismantle the welfare state.

For Dahrendorf, however, the problem is best encapsulated by the simple fact that this painful passage through the 'valley of tears' lasts longer than the average period between (democratic) elections, so that there is a great temptation to postpone difficult changes for short-term electoral gains. In Dahrendorf's view, the paradigmatic constellation here is the disappointment of the large strata of post-Communist nations with the economic results of the new democratic order. In the glorious days of 1989, they equated democracy with the abundance of the Western consumerist societies; now, ten years later, when the abundance is still missing, they blame democracy itself. Unfortunately, Dahrendorf focuses much less on the opposite temptation: if the majority resists the necessary structural changes in the economy, would (one of) the logical conclusion(s) not be that, for a decade or so, an enlightened elite should take power, even by non-democratic means, to enforce the necessary measures and thus to lay the foundations for the truly stable democracy? Along these lines, Fareed Zakaria has pointed out how democracy can only 'catch on' in economically developed countries: if developing countries are 'prematurely democratized', the result is a populism which ends in economic catastrophe and political despotism. No wonder that today's economically most successful Third World countries (Taiwan, South Korea, Chile) embraced full democracy only after a period of authoritarian rule. And, furthermore, does this line of thinking not provide the best argument for the authoritarian regime in China?

It is hardly surprising that there is today, among some Russian nationalists, a nostalgia for Yuri Andropov, the KGB head who became CPSU General Secretary in 1982 but died after only sixteen months of power. This longing is for a kind of alternative history: if Andropov were to have lived longer, the USSR would have survived in a Chinese way. Andropov wanted to introduce radical economic reforms, and his programme, on which he was working from 1965, was like that of Pinochet in Chile: authoritarian and centralized state power introduces by non-democratic means and without public discussion a complex of unpopular modernizing transformations directed at the Westernization of the country. Andropov was well aware that, for several years, a harsh, almost Stalinist dictatorship would be needed because of the opposition these liberal reforms would generate. He also wanted to abolish the ethno-territorial divisions of the USSR, since in his view dispensing with the non-Russian republics would have been to destroy much of the party *nomenklatura*. Consequently, he considered banning the activity of all parties in the country (which meant the banning of the CPSU). In place of the republics, Andropov wanted to create ten competing economic zones, the best of which would guide the country as a whole and overcome the degradation of the system more generally, much as the Chinese have done. To run these zones, Andropov knew he had to find new professionals, and for that he looked to certain officers in the KGB and others who were prepared to work with the KGB in this direction. Andropov's decision to pursue ultra-liberal policies by authoritarian means reflected the Reagan–Thatcher spirit of the 1980s – for Russia, the alternative of Swedish socialism was considered inappropriate.[21]

What is new today is that, with the continuing crisis which began in 2008, this same distrust of democracy – once confined to the Third World or post-Communist developing countries – is gaining ground in developed Western countries themselves: what was a decade or two ago patronizing advice to others now concerns ourselves. But what if this distrust is justified? What if only experts can save us, with full or less-than-full democracy? The least one can say is that the current crisis offers many proofs of how it is not the people but the experts themselves who, in large part, don't know what they are doing. In Western Europe, we are effectively witnessing a growing incapability of the ruling elite – they know less and less how to rule. Look at how Europe is dealing with the Greek crisis: putting pressure on Greece to repay debts, but at the same time ruining its economy through imposed austerity measures and thereby ensuring the Greek debt will never be repaid. At the end of December 2012, the IMF itself released research showing that the economic damage from aggressive austerity measures may be as much as three times larger than previously assumed, thereby cancelling its own advice on austerity in the Eurozone crisis. Now, the IMF admits that forcing Greece and other debt-burdened countries to reduce their deficits too quickly would be counterproductive – now, after hundreds of thousands of jobs have been lost because of such 'miscalculations'. And herein resides the true message of the 'irrational' popular protests all around Europe. The protesters know very well what they don't know: they don't pretend to have fast and easy answers, but what their instinct is telling them is nonetheless true – that those in power also don't know it. In Europe today, the blind are leading the blind. Austerity politics is not really science, not even in a minimal sense. It is much closer to a contemporary form of superstition – a kind of gut reaction to an impenetrably complex situation, a common sense reaction of 'things went wrong, we are somehow guilty, we have to pay the price and suffer, so let's do something that hurts and spend less.' Austerity is not 'too radical', as some Leftist critics claim, but, on the contrary, too superficial: an act of avoiding the true roots of the crisis.

Another example of such magic thinking (and a true model of what Hegel called abstract thinking) is the so-called 'Laffer curve', evoked by free-market advocates as a reason against excessive taxation. The Laffer curve is a representation of the relationship between possible rates of taxation and the resulting levels of government revenue, illustrating how taxable income will change in response to changes in the rate of taxation. It postulates that no tax revenue will be raised at the extreme tax rates of 0 per cent and 100 per cent, and that there must be at least one rate where tax revenue would be a non-zero maximum: even from the standpoint of the government which taxes business, the highest revenue is not gained by the highest taxes. There is a point at which higher taxes start to work as a disincentive, causing capital flight and consequently lower tax revenues. The implicit premise of this reasoning is that today the tax rate is already too high, and that lowering the tax rate would therefore not only help business but also raise tax revenues. The problem with this reasoning is that, while in some abstract sense it is true, things get more complex the moment we locate taxation into the totality of economic reproduction. A great part of the money collected by taxation is again spent on the products of private business, thereby giving incentive to it. More important even, the proceeds of taxation are also spent on creating the appropriate conditions for business. Let us take two comparable cities, one with lower and the other with a higher business tax rate. In the first city public education and healthcare are in a bad condition, crime is exploding, and so on; the second city, meanwhile, spends higher revenues on better education, better energy supply, better transport, etc. Is it not reasonable to suppose that many businesses would find the second city more attractive for investment? So, paradoxically, if the first city decides to follow the second in its tax policy, raising taxes may give more incentive to private business. (And, incidentally, many half-developed ex-Communist countries to which developed countries are outsourcing their industries are exploited, in the sense that Western business gains access to a cheaper skilled workforce that has benefited from public education: thus, the socialist state provides free education for the workforces of Western companies.)[22]

BEING-TOWARDS-DEBT
AS A WAY OF LIFE

A spectre is haunting capitalism today – the spectre of debt. All the powers of capitalism have entered into a holy alliance to exorcise this spectre, but do they really want to get rid of it? Maurizio Lazzarato[23] provides a detailed analysis of how, in today's global capitalism, debt works across a whole range of social practices and levels, from nation states down to individuals. The hegemonic neoliberal ideology endeavours to extend the logic of market competition to all areas of social life so that, for example, health and education – or even political decisions (voting) themselves – are perceived as investments made by the individual in his or her individual capital. In this way, the worker is no longer conceived merely as labour power, but as personal capital making good or bad 'investment' decisions as s/he moves from job to job and increases or decreases his/ her capital value. This reconceptualization of the individual as an 'entrepreneur-of-the-self' means a significant change in the nature of governance: a move away from the relative passivity and enclosure of disciplinary regimes (the school, the factory, the prison), as well as from the biopolitical treatment of the population (by the welfare state). How can one govern individuals who are conceived of as autonomous agents of free market choices, i.e., as 'entrepreneurs-of-the-self'? Governance is now exercised at the level of the environment in which people make their apparently autonomous decisions: risks are outsourced from companies and states to individuals. Through this individualization of social policy and privatization of social protection through its alignment with market norms, protection becomes conditional (no longer a right), and is tied to individuals whose behaviours are thus opened up for evaluation. For the majority of people, being an 'entrepreneur-of-the-self' refers to the individual's ability to deal with outsourced risks without having the necessary resources or power to do so adequately:

> contemporary neoliberal policies produce a human capital or 'entrepreneur-of-the-self' more or less indebted and more or less poor but always precarious. For the majority of the population, becoming an entrepreneur-of-the-self is limited to managing one's employability, one's debts, the drop in one's salary and income and the reduction in social services according to business and competitive norms.[24]

As individuals become poorer through the shrinkage of their salaries and the removal of social provision, neoliberalism offers them compensation through debt and by the promotion of shareholding. In this way, wages or deferred salaries (pensions) don't rise, but people have access to consumer credit and are encouraged to provide for retirement through personal share portfolios; people no longer have a right to housing but have access to housing/mortgage credit; people no longer have a right to higher education, but can take out student loans; mutual and collective protection against risks are dismantled, but people are encouraged to take out private insurance. In this way, without replacing all existing social relationships, the creditor–debt nexus comes to overlay them: workers become indebted workers (having to pay back their company shareholders for employing them); consumers become indebted consumers; citizens become indebted citizens, having to take responsibility for their share of their country's debt.

Lazzarato relies here on Nietzsche's idea, developed in his *A Genealogy of Morals,* that what distinguished human societies, as they moved away from their primitive origins, was their capacity to produce a human able to promise to pay others back and to recognize their debt towards the group. This promise grounds a particular type of memory oriented to the future ('I remember I owe you, so I will behave in ways that will allow me to pay you back'), and so becomes a way of governing future conducts. In more primitive social groups, debts to others were limited and could be discharged, while with the coming of empires and monotheisms, one's social or divine debt become effectively unpayable. Christianity perfected this mechanism: its all-powerful God meant a debt that was infinite; at the same time, one's guilt for non-payment was internalized. The only way one could possibly repay in any way was through obedience: to the will of God, to the church. Debt, with its grip on past and future behaviours and with its moral reach, was a formidable governmental tool. All that remained was for it to be secularized.

This constellation gives rise to a type of subjectivity characterized by moralization and specific temporalization. The indebted subject practises two kinds of work: salaried labour, and the work upon the self that is needed to produce a subject who is able to promise, to repay debts, and who is ready to assume guilt for being an indebted subject. A particular set of temporalities are associated with indebtedness: to be able to repay (to remember one's promise), one has to make one's behaviour predictable, regular and calculating. This not only militates against any future revolt, with its inevitable disruption of the capacity to repay; it also implies an erasure of the memory of past rebellions and acts of collective resistance which disrupted the normal flow of time and led to unpredictable behaviours. This indebted subject is constantly opened up to the evaluating inspection of others: individualized appraisals and targets at work, credit ratings, individual interviews for those in receipt of benefits or public credits. The subject is thus compelled not only to show that he or she will be able to repay debt (and to repay society through the right behaviours), but also to show the right attitudes and assume individual guilt for any failings. This is where the asymmetry between creditor and debtor becomes palpable: the indebted 'entrepreneur-of-the-self' is more active than the subject of the previous, more disciplinary modes of governance; however, deprived as he or she is of the ability to govern his or her time, or to evaluate his or her own behaviours, his or her capacity for autonomous action is strictly curtailed.

In case it might seem that debt is simply a governmental tool suited to modulating the behaviour of individuals, it should be noted that similar techniques can (and do) apply to the governance of institutions and countries. Anyone following the unfolding, slow-motion car crash that is the current crisis cannot but be aware of how countries and institutions are under constant evaluation (by credit rating agencies for example), have to accept moral fault for their previous errors and self-indulgence, and have to commit to future good behaviour that will ensure that, no matter what cuts have to be made in the body of their social provision, or their workers' rights, they will be able to repay the lending agent's pound of flesh.[25]

In this way, the ultimate triumph of capitalism comes about when each worker becomes his or her own capitalist, the 'entrepreneur-of-the-self' who decides how much to invest in his or her own future (education, health and so forth), paying for these investments by becoming indebted. What were formally rights (to education, healthcare, housing) thus become free decisions to invest, which are formally at the same level as the banker's or capitalist's decision to invest in this or that company, so that – at this formal level – everyone is a capitalist getting indebted in order to invest. We are here a step further from the formal equality between the capitalist and the worker in the eyes of the law. Now they are both capitalist investors; however, the same difference in the 'physiognomy of our *dramatis personae*' which, according to Marx, appears after the exchange between labour and capital is concluded, reappears here between the capitalist investor proper and the worker who is compelled to act as the 'entrepreneur-of-the-self': 'The one smirks self-importantly and is intent on business; the other is timid and holds back, like someone who has brought his own hide to market and has nothing else to expect but — a tanning.'[26] And he is right to remain timid: the freedom of choice imposed on him is a false one; it is the very form of his servitude.[27]

How does today's rise of the indebted man, specific to the conditions of global capitalism, compare to the relationship of debtor/creditor as a universal anthropological constant articulated by Nietzsche? It is the paradox of direct realization which turns into its opposite. Today's global capitalism brings the relationship of debtor/creditor to its extreme and simultaneously undermines it: debt becomes an openly ridiculous excess. We thus enter the domain of obscenity: when a credit is accorded, the debtor is not even expected to return it – debt is directly treated as a means of control and domination.

It is as if the providers and caretakers of debt accuse the indebted countries of not feeling enough guilt: they are accused of feeling innocent. Recall the ongoing EU pressure on Greece to implement austerity measures, a pressure that fits perfectly what psychoanalysis calls 'superego'. Superego is not an ethical agency proper, but a sadistic agent which bombards the subject with impossible demands, obscenely enjoying the subject's failure to comply with them. The paradox of the superego is that, as Freud saw it clearly, the more we obey its demands, the more we feel guilty. Imagine a vicious teacher who gives to his pupils impossible tasks, and then sadistically jeers when he sees their anxiety and panic. This is what is so terribly wrong with the EU demands/commands: they don't even give Greece a chance. The Greek failure is part of the game. Here, the goal of politico-economic analysis is to deploy strategies of how to step out of this infernal circle of debt and guilt.

A similar paradox was operative from the very beginning, of course, since a promise/obligation which cannot ever be fully met is at the very base of the banking system. When one puts money into a bank, the bank is obliged to return the money on demand – but we all know that, while the bank can do this to some of the people who deposited money, it by definition cannot do it for all of them. However, this paradox, which originally held for the relationship between individual depositors and their bank, now also holds for the relationship between the bank and (legal or physical) persons who borrowed money from it. What this implies is that the true aim of lending money to the debtor is not to get the debt reimbursed with a profit, but the indefinite continuation of the debt which keeps the debtor in permanent dependency and subordination. A decade or so ago, Argentina decided to repay its debt to the IMF ahead of time (with financial help from Venezuela). The IMF's reaction was on the face of it surprising: instead of being glad that it was getting its money back, the IMF (or, rather, its top representatives) expressed their concern that Argentina would use this new freedom and financial independence from international institutions to abandon tight financial politics and engage in careless spending. This uneasiness made palpable the true stakes of the debtor/creditor relationship: debt is an instrument with which to control and regulate the debtor, and, as such, it strives for its own expanded reproduction.

Another surprise here is that theology and poetry knew this long ago – confirmation once more of the validity of Berardi's topic 'poetry and finance'. Let us jump back to early modernity. Why was the story of Orpheus *the* opera subject in the first century of its history, with almost one hundred known versions of it? The figure of Orpheus asking the Gods to bring him back his Eurydice stands for an intersubjective constellation which provides as it were the elementary matrix of the opera or, more precisely, of the operatic aria: the relationship of the subject (in both senses of the term: autonomous agent as well as the subject of legal power) to his Master (Divinity, King, or Lady of the courtly love) is revealed through the hero's song (the counterpoint to the collectivity embodied in the chorus), which is basically a supplication addressed to the Master, a call for him to show mercy, to make an exception, or otherwise to forgive the hero his trespass. The first, rudimentary, form of subjectivity is this voice of the subject beseeching the Master to suspend, for a brief moment, his own Law. A dramatic tension in subjectivity arises from the ambiguity between power and impotence that pertains to the gesture of grace by means of which the Master answers the subject's entreaty. As to the official ideology, grace expresses the Master's supreme power, the power to rise above one's own law: only a really powerful Master can afford to distribute mercy. What we have here is a kind of symbolic exchange between the human subject and his divine Master: when the subject, the human mortal, through his offer of self-sacrifice, surmounts his finitude and attains the divine heights, the Master responds with the sublime gesture of Grace, the ultimate proof of *his* humanity. Yet this act of grace is at the same time branded by the irreducible mark of a forced empty gesture: the Master ultimately makes a virtue out of necessity, in that he promotes as a free act what he is in any case compelled to do. If he refuses clemency, he runs the risk of the subject's respectful entreaty turning into open rebellion. Of special interest is here Mozart's late opera *Clemenza di Tito*, in which we witness a sublime/ridiculous explosion of mercies. Just before the final pardon, Tito himself fulminates at the proliferation of treasons that obliges him to proliferate acts of clemency:

> The very moment that I absolve one criminal, I discover another ... I believe the stars conspire to oblige me, in spite of myself, to become cruel. No: they shall not have this satisfaction. My virtue has already pledged itself to continue the contest. Let us see which is more constant, the treachery of others or my mercy ... Let it be known to Rome that I am the same and that I know all, absolve everyone, and forget everything.

One can almost hear Tito complaining, like Rossini's Figaro, *'Uno per volta, per carita!'* – 'Please, not so fast, one after the other, in the line for mercy!' Living up to his task, Tito forgets everyone, but those whom he pardons are condemned to remember it forever:

SEXTUS: It is true, you pardon me, Emperor; but my heart will not absolve me; it will lament the error until it no longer has memory.

TITUS: The true repentance of which you are capable is worth more than constant fidelity.

These lines from the finale blurt out the obscene secret of *Clemenza*: the pardon does not really abolish the debt. Rather, it makes the debt infinite – we are forever indebted to the person who pardoned us. No wonder Tito prefers repentance to fidelity: in fidelity to the Master, I follow him out of respect, while in repentance, what attached me to the Master is the infinite indelible guilt. In this, Tito is a thoroughly Christian master. The ridiculous proliferation of mercy in *Clemenza* means that power no longer functions in a normal way, so that it has to be sustained by mercy all the time: if the Master has to show mercy, it means that the law has failed, that the legal state machinery is not able to run on its own and needs incessant intervention from the outside.[28] And the same holds true for today's capitalism. Peter Buffett (Warren's son) recently published a *New York Times* op-ed in which he explained 'Philanthropic Colonialism':

> Inside any important philanthropy meeting, you witness heads of state meeting with investment managers and corporate leaders. All are searching for answers with their right hand to problems that others in the room have created with their left . . . Philanthropy has become the 'it' vehicle to level the playing field and has generated a growing number of gatherings, workshops and affinity groups.
>
> As more lives and communities are destroyed by the system that creates vast amounts of wealth for the few, the more heroic it sounds to 'give back'. It's what I would call 'conscience laundering' – feeling better about accumulating more than any one person could possibly need to live on by sprinkling a little around as an act of charity. But this just keeps the existing structure of inequality in place. The rich sleep better at night, while others get just enough to keep the pot from boiling over.
>
> And with more business-minded folks getting into the act, business principles are trumpeted as an important element to add to the philanthropic sector . . . Micro-lending and financial literacy (now I'm going to upset people who are wonderful folks and a few dear friends) – what

is this really about? People will certainly learn how to integrate into our system of debt and repayment with interest. People will rise above making $2 a day to enter our world of goods and services so they can buy more. But doesn't all this just feed the beast?[29]

Although Buffet's critique remains ideologically constrained by simple concerns for more decent human life, avoiding questions about basic system changes ('I'm really not calling for an end to capitalism; I'm calling for humanism'), he provides an adequate description of how the ideology (and practice) of charity plays a key role in global capitalism. Peter Sloterdijk, referring to George Bataille's notion of the 'general economy' of sovereign expenditure, which he opposes to the 'restrained economy' of capitalism's endless profiteering, provides (in *Zorn und Zeit*) the outlines of capitalism's split from itself, its immanent self-overcoming. Capitalism culminates when it 'creates out of itself its own most radical – and the only fruitful – opposite, totally different from what the classic Left, caught in its miserablism, was able to dream about.'[30] Sloterdijk's positive mention of Andrew Carnegie shows the way: the sovereign self-negating gesture of the endless accumulation of wealth is to spend this wealth for things beyond price, and outside market circulation: public good, arts and sciences, health, and so on. This concluding 'sovereign' gesture enables the capitalist to break out of the vicious cycle of endless expanded reproduction, of gaining money in order to earn more money. When he donates his accumulated wealth to public good, the capitalist self-negates himself as the mere personification of capital and its reproductive circulation: his life acquires meaning. It is no longer just expanded reproduction as self-goal. Furthermore, the capitalist thus accomplishes the shift from *eros* to *thymos*, from the perverted 'erotic' logic of accumulation to public recognition and reputation.

What Sloterdijk's idea amounts to is nothing less than the elevation of figures like George Soros or Bill Gates into personifications of the inherent self-negation of the capitalist process itself: their work of charity, their immense donations to public welfare, is not just a personal idiosyncrasy, whether sincere or hypocritical, it is the logical concluding point of capitalist circulation, necessary from the strictly economic standpoint since it allows the capitalist system to postpone its crisis. It re-establishes balance – a kind of redistribution of wealth to the truly needy – without falling into a fateful trap: the destructive logic of resentment and enforced statist redistribution of wealth which can only end in generalized misery. (It also avoids, one might add, the other mode of re-establishing a kind of balance and asserting *thymos* through sovereign expenditure, namely wars.) Or, to quote the old Latin saying, *velle bonum alicui*: charity (doing good deeds) is the pastime (amusement, distraction) of those who are indifferent (who don't really care).

When we are buying products like toothpaste or soft drinks, the top of the container or bottle is often in a different colour, with big letters telling us, '20 per cent free!': you buy the product, and you get a surplus gratis. Maybe, we could say that the entire capitalist system addresses us in a similar way: 'Buy global capitalism, participate in it, and you will get 20 per cent of it back for free in the form of charity and philanthropic donations!' However, in the case of capitalism, the Godfather is making us an offer we can and should refuse.

2

CARDIOGNOSIS *Du jambon cru?*

FREEDOM IN THE CLOUDS

Visiting Julian Assange at the Ecuadorian embassy in London in December 2013 was a rather depressing experience, in spite of the kindness of the embassy staff. The embassy is a six-roomed apartment with no garden, so that Assange cannot even take a daily walk; nor can he step out of the apartment into the main corridor – policemen are waiting for him there. There are always a dozen of them around the house and in some of the surrounding buildings. There's even one beneath a tiny toilet window, in case Assange tries to escape through that hole in the wall. The apartment is bugged from above and below and the internet connection is suspiciously slow.

So how come the British state employs almost fifty people full time to guard Assange under the legal pretence that he refuses to go to Sweden and be questioned about a minor sexual misconduct (there are no charges against him!)? One is tempted to become a Thatcherite and ask: how does this fit in with austerity politics? If a nobody like myself were wanted by the Swedish police for a similar interrogation, would the UK also employ fifty people to guard me? The serious question is this: where does such a ridiculously excessive desire for revenge stem from? What did Assange, his colleagues and whistle-blowing sources do to deserve this? In a way, one can understand the authorities. Assange and his colleagues are often accused of being traitors, but they are something much worse (in the eyes of the authorities):

Even if Snowden were to sell his information discreetly to another intelligence service, this act would still count as part of the 'patriotic games', and if needed he would have been liquidated as a 'traitor'. However, in Snowden's case, we are dealing with something entirely different. We are dealing with a gesture which questions the very logic, the very status quo, which for quite some time serves as the only foundation of all 'Western' (non)politics. With a gesture which, as it were, risks everything, with no consideration of profit and without its own stakes: it takes the risk because it is based on the conclusion that what is going on is simply wrong. Snowden didn't propose any alternative. Snowden – or, rather, the logic of his gesture, like, say, before him, the gesture of Chelsea Manning – *is* the alternative.[1]

WikiLeaks' achievement is nicely encapsulated by Assange's ironic self-designation as a 'spy for the people'. 'Spying for the people' is not a direct negation of spying (which would be acting as a double agent, selling our secrets to the enemy) but its self-negation, i.e., it undermines the very principle of spying, the principle of secrecy, since its goal is to make secrets public. It thus functions in a way similar to how the Marxist 'dictatorship of the proletariat' was supposed to function (but rarely ever did, of course): as an immanent self-negation of the very principle of dictatorship. To those who see Communism as a scarecrow we should say that what WikiLeaks is doing is the practice of Communism. WikiLeaks simply enacts the commons of information.

In the struggle of ideas, the rise of bourgeois modernity was exemplified by the French *Encyclopédie* (1751–72), a gigantic venture that systematically presented all available knowledge to a broad audience. The addressee of this knowledge was not the state but the public as such. It may seem that Wikipedia is today's *Encyclopédie*, but something is missing from it: the knowledge which is ignored by and repressed from the public space, repressed because it concerns precisely the way state mechanisms and agencies control and regulate us all. The goal of WikiLeaks should be to make this knowledge available to all of us with a simple click. Assange is today's d'Alembert, the editor of this new *Encyclopédie*, the true people's encyclopedia for the twenty-first century. Why?

Our informational commons recently emerged as one of the key domains of class struggle in two of its aspects: economic in the narrow sense and socio-political. On the one hand, new digital media confront us with the impasse of 'intellectual property'. The very nature of the World Wide Web seems to be Communist, tending towards the free flow of data – CDs and DVDs are gradually disappearing, millions of people simply downloading music and videos, mostly for free. This is why the business establishment is engaged in a desperate struggle to impose the form of private property on this flow by enforcing intellectual property laws. This free circulation, of course, brings about its own dangers, as was pointed out by Jaron Lanier,[2] who sees a threat in the very feature of the digital space that is usually celebrated as its greatest social achievement, the free circulation of data and ideas: this very openness gave birth to non-creative providers (Google, Facebook) who exert an almost monopoly power to regulate the flow of data, while individuals who create the content are lost in the anonymity of the network. Lanier's solution is a massive return to private property: everything that circulates on the web including personal data (which sites I am visiting, say, or which books I check on Amazon) should be treated as a valuable commodity and remunerated, plus everything should be clearly attributed to an individual human source. While Lanier is right that the anonymous anarchic free circulation engenders its own power networks, one should nonetheless question his proposed solution: is global privatization/commodification really the only way to do it? Are there no other forms of global regulation?

On the other hand, digital media (especially with the almost universal access to the internet and mobile phones) opened up new ways for millions of ordinary people to establish a network and coordinate their collective activities, while also offering state agencies and private companies undreamt-of possibilities of tracking our public and private acts. It is into this struggle that WikiLeaks intervened in such an explosive way. For Jacques Lacan, the axiom of the ethics of psychoanalysis was: 'Do not compromise your desire.' Is this axiom also not an accurate designation of the whistle-blowers' acts? This uncompromising stance is a constant reminder that, in our daily lives, we more and more resemble baboons. That is to say, why do baboons have big, protruding, hairless red butts? The main reason seems to be that the buttocks of a female in heat will swell so the male knows that she is ready to mate. It also functions as a sign of submission, where one animal turns and presents its rump to the other, implicitly saying, 'I know you're stronger than me, so let's not fight any more!' The baboons with the redder, more hairless butts attract more mates and have more offspring, and, in their turn, the offspring are favoured because, on average, they have redder, more hairless butts than the rest. Is this not how the struggle for ideological hegemony also looks? Individuals display their hairless protruding butts, offering themselves to be penetrated by ideological messages. There is no need for violent imposition; the victim voluntarily offers itself – as was made clear when we recently found out about the massive digital control of our lives.

This is why it is not enough to see WikiLeaks as an anti-American phenomenon. That is to say, how do President Obama's acts fit into the constellation formed through WikiLeaks' disclosures? While the Republicans are denouncing Obama as a dangerous Leftist dividing American people and posing a threat to the American way of life, some Leftists denounce him as 'worse than Bush' in his pursuit of imperialist foreign policy. When, back in 2009, Obama got the Nobel peace prize, we all knew this was not a prize for his achievements, but a gesture of hope, a desperate attempt to put additional pressure on Obama so that he would keep his electoral promises and work as the anti-Bush president. The idea of giving the Nobel peace prize to Chelsea Manning should be embraced as a justified reaction to the fact that Obama failed to meet these expectations. To account for this disappointment, one should bear in mind the way Obama won re-election in 2012. Jean-Claude Milner recently proposed the notion of a 'stabilizing class': not the old ruling class, but the broad class of all those who are fully committed to the stability and continuity of the existing social, economic and political order, the class of those who, even when they call for a change, do so only to enforce changes that will make the system more efficient and ensure that nothing will really change.[3] This is the key to the interpretation of electoral results in today's developed Western states: who succeeded in winning over this class? Far from truly being perceived as a radical transformer, Obama won *them* over, and that's why he was re-elected. The majority that voted for him were put off by the radical changes advocated by the Republican market and religious fundamentalists.

We all remember Obama's smiling face, full of hope and trust, when he repeatedly delivered the motto of his first campaign: 'Yes, we can!': we can get rid of the cynicism of Bush's era and bring justice and welfare to the American people, we can make America the land of hope and dreams again. Now that the US continues with covert operations, using drones and expanding its control and intelligence network, spying even on its allies, some protesters have been displaying signs with a slightly changed motto: 'Yes, we scan!' Perhaps a more pertinent variation would have been to imagine Obama looking at us with a mockingly evil smile and replying 'Yes, we can!' to the protesters shouting at him: 'You can't use drones for killing!' 'You can't surely want to spy even on our allies!'

However, such simple personalization misses the point: the threat to our freedom disclosed by whistle-blowers has much deeper systemic roots. Edward Snowden should be defended not only because his acts annoyed and embarrassed the US secret services – what he revealed is something that not only the US but also all other great (and not so great) powers (from China to Russia, from Germany to Israel) are doing (to the extent that they are technologically able to do it). His acts thus provide a factual foundation to our premonitions of how much we are all monitored and controlled – their lesson is global, reaching far beyond standard US-bashing. We didn't really learn from Snowden (or from Manning) anything we didn't already presume to be true – but it is one thing to know it in general, and another to get concrete data. It is a little bit like knowing that one's sexual partner is playing around. One can accept the abstract knowledge of it, but pain arises when one learns the steamy details, when one gets pictures of what they were doing . . .

Sometimes, we learn such steamy details from smaller, marginal countries instigating security measures in a much more open and direct way. For example, in the summer of 2012, the Hungarian parliament passed a new national security law that

> enables the inner circle of the government to spy on people who hold important public offices. Under this law, many government officials must 'consent' to being observed in the most intrusive way (phones tapped, homes bugged, emails read) for up to two full months each year, except that they won't know which 60 days they are under

surveillance. Perhaps they will imagine they are under surveillance all of the time. Perhaps that is the point. More than twenty years after Hungary left the world captured in George Orwell's novel *1984*, the surveillance state is back.

Now, if the Fidesz government of Prime Minister Viktor Orbán finds something it doesn't like – and there's no legal limit to what it may find objectionable – those under surveillance can be fired. The people at the very top of the government are largely exempt from surveillance – but this law hits their deputies, staffers and the whole of the security services, some judges, prosecutors, diplomats, and military officers, as well as a number of 'independent' offices that Orbán's administration is not supposed to control.[4]

And here is how the Hungarian government justifies such measures:

Officials of the Hungarian government will say that what they are doing is nothing novel. Other countries, they will point out, have ways to determine whether high-level officials have played fast and loose with state secrets or whether people holding the public trust are corrupt. The US government has now been shown to be gathering up everyone's phone calls and emails, so how can anyone be critical of what the Hungarian government is doing?[5]

When confronted with such facts, should every decent American citizen not feel like a baboon suddenly overwhelmed by the shame of his or her protruding red butt? Back in 1843, the young Karl Marx claimed that the German *ancien régime* 'only imagines that it believes in itself and demands that the world should imagine the same thing'.[6] In such a situation, shaming those in power becomes a weapon – or, as Marx explains, 'The actual pressure must be made more pressing by adding to it consciousness of pressure, the shame must be made more shameful by publicizing it.'[7] And this is exactly our situation today: we are facing the shameless cynicism of the existing global order whose agents only imagine that they believe in their ideas of democracy, human rights and so on, and, thanks to WikiLeaks, the shame (our shame for tolerating such power over us) is made more shameful by publicizing it. What we should be ashamed of is the worldwide process of the gradual narrowing of the public use of reason. When Paul says that, from a Christian standpoint, 'there are no men and women, no Jews and Greeks,' he claims that ethnic roots, national identity and gender are *not categories of truth*; or, to put it in precise Kantian terms, when we reflect upon our ethnic roots, we engage in a *private use of reason*, constrained by contingent dogmatic presuppositions, i.e., we act as 'immature' individuals, not as free human beings who believe in the universality of reason. The public space of the 'world civil society' designates the paradox of universal singularity, of a singular subject who, in a kind of short-circuit, bypasses the mediation of the particular and directly participates in the Universal. This is what Kant, in the famous passage of his 'What is Enlightenment?', means by 'public' as opposed to 'private': 'private' does not mean one's individual as opposed to communal ties, but the very communal-institutional order of one's particular identification; while 'public' is the trans-national universality of the exercise of one's Reason. We see where Kant parts with our liberal common sense: the domain of state itself is in its own way 'private', private in the precise Kantian sense of the 'private use of Reason' in state administrative and ideological apparatuses, while individuals reflecting on general issues use reason in a 'public' way.

This Kantian distinction is especially pertinent in the case of the internet and other new media torn between their free 'public use' and their growing 'private' control. Our struggle should thus focus on the threats to the trans-national public sphere, like the recent trend for organizing cyberspace into 'clouds': in this way, details are abstracted from consumers, who no longer have need for expertise in, or control over, the technology infrastructure 'in the cloud' that supports their activity. Two words are revealing here: *abstracted* and *control* – in order to manage a cloud, there needs to be a monitoring system which controls its functioning, and this system is by definition hidden from users. The paradox is that, the more the small item (smartphone or iPod) I hold in my hand is personalized, easy to use, 'transparent' in its functioning, the more the entire set-up has to rely on the work being done elsewhere, in a vast circuit of machines which coordinate the user's experience. The more our experience is non-alienated, spontaneous, transparent, the more it is regulated and controlled by the invisible network of state agencies and large private companies that follow their secret agendas.

What makes the all-encompassing control of our lives so dangerous is not that we lose our privacy, that all our secrets are exposed to the view of the Big Brother. There is no state agency which is able to exert such control – not because they don't know enough, but because they know too much. The sheer size of data sets is too large, and in spite of all the intricate programs for detecting suspicious messages, computers that register so many details are too stupid to interpret and evaluate them properly, leading to ridiculous mistakes in which innocent bystanders are listed as potential terrorists. This is what makes state control of our communications so dangerous. Without knowing why, without doing anything illegal, we can all of a sudden find ourselves on a list of potential terrorists. Recall the legendary answer of a Hearst newspaper editor to Hearst's inquiry as to why he doesn't want to take a well-deserved holiday: 'I am afraid that if I go, there will be chaos, everything will fall apart – but I am even more afraid to discover that, if I go, things will just go on as normal without me, a proof that I am not really needed!' Something similar can be said about state control of our communications: we should fear that we no longer have any secrets, that secret state agencies know everything, but what we should fear even more is that they might fail to do so.

Whistle-blowers play a crucial role in keeping the 'public reason' alive. Assange, Manning, Snowden: these are our new heroes, exemplary cases of the new ethics that befits our digital era. They are no longer just whistle-blowers who denounce the illegal practices of private companies (banks, tobacco and oil companies and so forth) or public authorities; they denounce these public authorities themselves when they engage in the 'private use of reason'. We need more Mannings and Snowdens also in China, in Russia, everywhere. States like China and Russia are of course much more oppressive than the US – just imagine what would have happened to someone like Manning in a Russian or Chinese court (there would probably have been no public trial; a Chinese Manning would have just disappeared). However, one should not exaggerate the softness of the US: true, the US doesn't treat prisoners as brutally as China or Russia – because of their technological priority, they simply do not need the openly brutal approach (which they are more than ready to apply when it is needed). In this sense, the US is even more dangerous than China insofar as their measures of control are not perceived as such, while Chinese brutality is openly displayed. That is to say, while, in a country like China, the limitations of freedom are clear to everyone – there are no illusions about it, the state is an openly oppressive mechanism – in the US formal freedoms are officially guaranteed, so that most individuals experience their lives as free and are not even aware of the extent to which they are controlled by state mechanisms. Just imagine how much one can learn about each of us by checking our bank accounts, which books we buy on Amazon, our emails, and so on. Whistle-blowers do something much more important than stating the obvious by way of denouncing the openly oppressive regimes: they render public the unfreedom that underlies the very situation in which we experience ourselves as free.

This feature is not limited to digital space. It thoroughly pervades the form of subjectivity that characterizes 'permissive' liberal society. Since free choice is elevated into a supreme value, social control and domination can no longer appear as infringing the subject's freedom; it has to appear as (and be sustained by) the very self-experience of individuals as free. This unfreedom often appears in the guise of its opposite: when we are deprived of universal healthcare, we are told that we are given a new freedom of choice (to choose our healthcare provider); when we can no longer rely on long-term employment and are compelled to search for a new precarious job every couple of years or maybe even every couple of weeks, we are told that we are given the opportunity to re-invent ourselves and discover our unexpected creative potential; when we have to pay for the education of our children, we are told that we become 'entrepreneurs-of-the-self', acting like a capitalist who has to choose freely how he will invest the resources he possesses (or has borrowed) – in education, health, travel. Constantly bombarded by such imposed 'free choices', forced to make decisions for which we are not even properly qualified (or do not possess enough information about), we increasingly experience our freedom as a burden that causes unbearable anxiety. Unable to break out of this vicious cycle alone, as isolated individuals, since the more we act freely, the more we get enslaved by the system, we need to be awakened from this dogmatic slumber of fake freedom by the push of a Master figure.

Back in May 2002, it was reported that scientists at New York University had attached a computer chip transmitting elementary signals directly to a rat's brain, which allowed them to control the rat's movements by means of a steering mechanism (as in a remote-controlled toy car). For the first time, the 'will' of a living animal agent, its 'spontaneous' decisions about the movements it makes, were taken over by an external machine. Of course, the great philosophical question here is how the unfortunate rat 'experienced' these movements decided from outside: did it continue to 'experience' them as spontaneous (in other words, was it totally unaware that its movements were being steered?), or was it aware that something was wrong? And, maybe, therein resides the difference between Chinese citizens and us, free citizens of Western liberal countries: the Chinese human rats are at least aware they are controlled, while we are the stupid rats strolling around unaware of how our movements are monitored.

It is crucial that the new encyclopedia emerging around WikiLeaks acquires an independent international base, so that the humiliating game of playing one big state against another (like Snowden having to look for protection in Russia) will be kept to a minimum. Our axiom should be that Snowden and Pussy Riot are part of the same struggle – we need a new International, an international network to organize the protection of whistle-blowers and the dissemination of their message. The list is already growing: Manning, Assange, Snowden ... and Utku Kali, a Turkish gendarmerie private who leaked the intelligence report revealing that the massacre in Reyhanli, Syria (a blast that killed more than 170 people on 11 May 2013; the official number is 53), was organized by the radical Islamist group El-Nusra. Right after the blast, the Turkish government blamed Assad's regime in Syria, but the leak showed that the Turkish government knew in advance about it and did not prevent it – or maybe even 'guided' this false-flag operation. Utku Kali was immediately arrested and is now in prison, accused of leaking military secrets.[8] Such leaks provide an insight into what is really going on behind the scenes in Syria today.

Whistle-blowers are our heroes because they prove that if they – those in power – can do it, we can also do it. We often hear today that democracy can only be renewed from the grass-roots level of local communities, since state mechanisms are too ossified and insensitive to people's pressing concerns; however, the problems we are confronting today also call for global organizations and forms of activity – the good old nation-state is simultaneously too large and too small. The ideal counterforce to the state would be a direct short-circuit between the two levels: local civil-society organizations forming trans-national networks. The problem, of course, is that protesters who form these networks are a clear minority. The reaction of the large majority, after Snowden's revelations were widely reported in the media, might best be summed up by the memorable lines of the last song from Altman's *Nashville*, performed by Barbara Harris: 'You may say I ain't free, but it don't worry me.'

VAMPIRES VERSUS ZOMBIES

This fight to control cyberspace is at bottom a class issue, which demonstrates that class struggle is alive and well. When President Obama was accused of irresponsibly introducing 'class warfare' into politics, Warren Buffett gloated: 'There's class warfare, all right, but it's my class, the rich class, that's making war, and we're winning.'[9] If class warfare is still anathema in American public discourse, this repressed topic is returning with a vengeance in Hollywood. One doesn't have to look far for class struggle there – like it or not, we encounter it quickly and unexpectedly. Just think about post-apocalyptic blockbusters (and even video games) such as Neil Blomkamp's *Elysium* (2013), set in 2154, when the rich live on a gigantic man-made space station while the rest of the population resides on a ruined Earth that looks like an expanded Latin American favela.[10] This film is the latest in a series which begins with John Boorman's *Zardoz* (1974), depicting a post-apocalyptic Earth in 2293 inhabited mostly by 'Brutals', ordinary humans living in miserable, violent conditions. They are ruled by 'Eternals', who use a privileged group of Brutals called 'Exterminators' as their warrior class to keep in check ordinary

Brutals. Exterminators worship the god Zardoz, a huge, flying, hollow stone head whose message is: 'The gun is good, the penis is evil. The penis shoots seeds and makes new life to poison the Earth with a plague of men, as once it was, but the gun shoots death and purifies the Earth of the filth of Brutals. Go forth ... and kill!' The Zardoz godhead supplies the Exterminators with weapons, while the Exterminators supply it with grain to feed the Eternals who live in Vortex, a secluded community of civilized beings protected by an invisible forcefield. The immortal Eternals lead a pleasant but ultimately stifling existence, and, predictably, the film ends with the shield being broken down so that the Eternals rediscover sex and mortality.[11]

These films take place in a society which is radically divided along class lines, but in a very specific way – a way described by Peter Sloterdijk in his *In the World Interior of Capital*, a shameless assertion of the grand narrative of our global-capitalist modernity.[12] Sloterdijk explains that, in the end phase of globalization, the world system completed its development and, as a capitalist system, came to determine all conditions of life. The first sign of this development was the Crystal Palace in London, the site of the first world exhibition in 1851: it captured the inevitable exclusivity of globalization as the construction and expansion of a world interior whose boundaries are invisible yet virtually insurmountable from without, and which is inhabited by one and a half billion winners of globalization. Three times this number are left standing outside the door. Consequently, 'the world interior of capital is not an agora or a trade fair beneath the open sky, but rather a hothouse that has drawn inwards everything that was once on the outside.'[13] This interior, built on capitalist excesses, determines everything: 'The primary fact of the Modern Age was not that the earth goes around the sun, but that money goes around the earth.'[14] After the process that transformed the world into the globe, 'social life could only take place in an expanded interior, a domestically organized and artificially climatized inner space.'[15] As cultural capitalism rules, all world-forming upheavals are contained: 'No more historic events could take place under such conditions – at most, domestic accidents.'[16]

On 1 December 2013, at least seven people died when a Chinese-owned clothing factory in an industrial zone in the Italian town of Prato, 10 kilometres from the centre of Florence, burned down, killing workers trapped in an improvised cardboard dormitory built onsite.[17] The accident occurred in the Macrolotto industrial district of the town, known for its large number of garment factories. Riberto Pistonina, a local trade union functionary, commented: 'No one can say they are surprised at this because everyone has known for years that, in the area between Florence and Prato, hundreds if not thousands of people are living and working in conditions of near-slavery.'[18] Prato alone has at least 15,000 immigrants legally registered (out of a total population of around 200,000), as well as more than 4,000 Chinese-owned businesses. Thousands more Chinese immigrants are believed to be living in the city illegally, working up to 16 hours per day for a network of wholesalers and workshops turning out cheap clothing. We thus do not have to look for the miserable life outside the global Dome far away in the suburbs of Shanghai (or at least in Dubai and Qatar) and hypocritically criticize China. Foxconn is right here, in our house – we just don't see it (or, rather, we pretend not to see it).

What Sloterdijk correctly points out is that capitalist globalization not only stands for openness, conquest, but also for a self-enclosed globe separating the Inside from the Outside. The two aspects are inseparable: capitalism's global reach is grounded in the way it introduces a radical class division across the entire globe, separating those protected by the sphere from those outside its cover.

A more surprising example of class struggle in Hollywood is provided by the two films on Abraham Lincoln released in 2012: Spielberg's big feel-good liberal 'high quality' *Lincoln* and its obviously ridiculous poor cousin *Abraham Lincoln: Vampire Hunter*. As a reviewer has noted, Spielberg 'whitewashes Lincoln much as Martin Luther King Jr has been whitewashed by our political culture, which emphasizes healing and unity at the expense of truth and justice.'[19] Just prior to victory in the civil war, Lincoln succeeds in imposing the amendment banning slavery through 'clever lawyering, petty patronage and personal will. The action centres on the governing elites, depicting Lincoln as the ultimate insider.'[20] In clear contrast to it, *Abraham Lincoln: Vampire Hunter* shows how 'revolutionary change gets accomplished through the militancy and mobilization of outsiders and the oppressed'.[21] Lincoln, whose mother is killed by vampires, discovers that vampires are also behind the Confederate secessionists. The vampire leader makes a deal with Jefferson Davis: vampires will help the confederate army if the South regularly delivers to the vampires black slaves as the source of the blood they need for food. When Lincoln finds out, he uses the silver reserves of the US to quickly manufacture silver bullets for the army and thus secures the Northern victory at Gettysburg. Ridiculous? Yes, definitely. But this ridiculousness is itself a symptom of ideological repression or, even stronger, psychotic foreclosure: what is excluded from the Symbolic returns in the Real of a hallucination, and what is excluded is class struggle in all its brutality. One could venture the hypothesis that horror movies register the class difference in the guise of the difference between vampires and zombies. Vampires are well mannered, exquisite and aristocratic, and they live among normal people, while zombies are clumsy, inert and dirty, and attack from the outside, like a primitive revolt of the excluded. The equation between zombies and the working class was made explicit in *White Zombie* (1932, directed by Victor Halperin and Edward Halperin), the first full-length zombie film made before the Hays Code, which prohibited direct references to brutal capitalists and the workers' struggle, began to regulate Hollywood movies. There are no vampires in this film – but, significantly, the main villain controlling the zombies is played by Bela Lugosi, who had become famous a year earlier as Dracula. *White Zombie* takes place on a plantation in Haiti, the site of the most famous slave revolt. Lugosi receives another plantation owner and shows him his sugar factory where workers are zombies who, as Lugosi is quick to explain, don't complain about long working hours, demand no trade unions, never strike, but just go on and on working. Such a film was possible only before the imposition of the Hays Code.

It is only against this background of class struggle that we can discern the underlying logic of conflicting political positions. Alain Badiou[22] has distinguished four main socio-political orientations today, and it is easy to see how they form yet another Greimasian semiotic square: (1) pure liberal global capitalism; (2) its softer welfare state version (we accept capitalism, but with a proviso that it should be regulated to ensure healthcare, education, solidarity with the poor and so on); (3) direct reactionary fundamentalist anti-capitalism; (4) radical emancipatory movements. These four positions can be arranged along three axes: pro-capitalism (1-2) versus anti-capitalism (3-4); political Right (1-3) versus political Left (2-4); pure (1-4) versus impure (2-3), where 'purity' designates a consistent position which draws all the consequences from its basic (capitalist or anti-capitalist) premise, while 'impure' designates a compromise (say, welfare-state Social Democracy stands for capitalism that is regulated, controlled, mixed with motifs of universal solidarity and justice). And, perhaps, there are two more positions: (5) authoritarian capitalism (like the 'Asian values' capitalism in Singapore and China); (6) whatever remains of the old 'totalitarian' Communist Left (Cuba, Khmer Rouge in Cambodia, North Korea, Maoist rebels in India and Nepal). (5) is Rightist, pro-capitalist, and impure; (6) is Leftist, anti-capitalist, and pure. There are positions which clearly mirror each other – for instance, (5) and (2) are clearly the mirror-image of each other: opposed along the axis of Right versus Left, they both try to regulate the excess of pure liberal capitalism, the first with traditional values and an authoritarian state, the second with welfare-state instruments. Similarly, (3) and (6) mirror each other along the Left–Right axis: they both endeavour to step out of the capitalist universe by means of reorganizing social life according to the 'totalitarian' project of a 'closed' society. And, finally, (1) and (4) also mirror each other along the same axis in the sense that they both clearly embody the two poles of the basic socio-political antagonism: global capitalism versus its emancipatory overcoming. The key point, of course, is to distinguish (6) from (4), as well as (5) from (3). In the case of (5) authoritarian capitalism and (3) direct reactionary anti-capitalism, the difference seems clear, but *de facto* it tends to disappear. All 'fundamentalist' religious regimes, no matter how anti-capitalist their rhetoric, tend to find a way not only to get used to global capitalism but even to perfectly integrate themselves into it (think of Saudi Arabia). In the case of (4) versus (6), we have the opposite: both the Khmer Rouge regime and an authentic radical-emancipatory movement are pure, Leftist and anti-capitalist, but there is a difference more radical than any other that separates them.

To discern this difference, it is crucial to recognize differences between statements that may sound similar or even identical. For example, one of the common threads in the ongoing popular revolts in Europe, especially in Spain, is the rejection of the entire 'political elite', Left or Right. They are all dismissed as corrupt, out of touch with the actual needs of ordinary people and so forth. However, such a statement can cover two radically opposed positions: on the one hand, the populist-moralistic rejection of the entire political class ('they are all the same, politics is a whore'), which, as a rule, conceals the call for a new Master who will clear this nest of corruption and introduce honesty; on the other hand, something *entirely different*, truly stepping out of the binary opposition which defines the contours of the hegemonic political space (Republicans versus Democrats, Conservatives versus Labour). In this second case, the underlying logic is not 'they are all the same' but, 'Of course our principal enemy is the capitalist Right, but we also reject the blackmail of the established Left which enjoins us to support them as the only way to stop the Right.' This second position is the position of 'neither nor': we don't want X, but we also don't want its inherent negation, the opposition to it that remains within the same field. This doesn't mean 'they're all the same', but, precisely, that they are not 'all' (in the Lacanian sense of the paradoxes of non-All, of the All grounded in an exception). 'They are all the same' means that we want the exception, a direct/honest politics exempted from the corrupted politics as usual, neither Right nor Left. However, in the case of 'neither nor', the negation of the Right gives us the (established) Left, but the negation of the Left does not give us the Right again, but rather a non-Left which is of the Left more than the (established) Left itself.

THE CYNIC'S NAIVETY

To find our way in this mess, we have to break out of our ideological constraints – but how? Is this still a viable option today, when the cynicism of those in power is often so direct and open that there seems to be no need for the critique of ideology? Why should we lose time and engage in arduous 'symptomatic reading', discerning gaps and repressions in the public discourse of those in power, when this discourse more or less openly and shamelessly admits its particular interests? There are nonetheless multiple problems with this thesis. Such a notion of a cynical society in which those in power brutally admit what they are doing is not sufficient at all. It is precisely when they openly and 'realistically' admit that it is ultimately all about power, money or influence that they err to the extreme; their realism without illusions is the very form of their blindness. What they fatefully underestimate is the efficiency of illusions that structure and sustain their ruthless power games or financial speculations. At the beginning of Hitler's rule, it was the big capitalist cynics who told themselves, 'Let's allow Hitler to take over and get us rid of the Left, and then we'll get rid of him.' The financial crisis of 2008 was brought about by the cynical bankers who acted upon the 'greed is good' principle, not by blind idealists. Therein resides the limit of Sloterdijk's old formula of cynical reason: 'They know what they are doing, and they are nonetheless doing it.'[23] They are blind to the illusions inherent in the brutal 'realist' stance. Recall Marx's brilliant analysis of how, in the French revolution of 1848, the conservative-republican Party of Order functioned as the coalition of the two branches of royalism (Orléanists and legitimists) in the 'anonymous kingdom of the Republic'.[24] The parliamentary deputies of the Party of Order perceived their republicanism as a mockery: in parliamentary debates, they constantly ridiculed the Republic to let it be known that their true aim was to restore the monarchy. What they were not aware of was that they themselves were duped as to the true social impact of their rule. What they were in fact doing was establishing the conditions of the bourgeois republican order that they despised so much (for instance, by guaranteeing the safety of private property). So it is not that they were royalists who were just wearing a republican mask: although they saw themselves as such, it was their very 'inner' royalist conviction which was the deceptive front masking their true social role. In short, far from being the hidden truth of their public republicanism, their sincere royalism was the fantasmatic support of their actual republicanism. As Marx put it, the royalists

> deceived themselves concerning the fact of their united rule. They did not comprehend that if each of their factions, regarded separately, by

itself, was royalist, the product of their chemical combination had necessarily to be *republican* ... Thus we find these royalists in the beginning believing in an immediate restoration, later preserving the republican form with foaming rage and deadly invective against it on their lips, and finally confessing that they can endure each other only in the republic and *postponing the restoration indefinitely* [*die Restauration aufs Unbestimmte vertagen*]. The *enjoyment* of the united rule [*der Genuß der vereinigten Herrschaft*] itself strengthened each of the two factions, and made each of them still more unable and unwilling to subordinate itself to the other, that is, to restore the monarchy.[25]

Marx describes here a precise case of perverted libidinal economy: there is a Goal (restoration of the monarchy) that members of the group experience as their true goal, but which, for tactical reasons, has to be publicly disavowed; however, what brings enjoyment is not the multiple ways of obscenely making fun of the ideology they have to follow publicly (rage and invectives again republicanism), but the very indefinite postponement of the realization of their official Goal (which allows them to rule united). Imagine the following scenario: in the private sphere, I am unhappily married, I mock my wife all the time, declaring my intention to abandon her for my mistress whom I really love, and while I get small pleasures from invectives against my wife, the enjoyment that sustains me is generated by the indefinite postponement of really leaving my wife for my mistress. And, back to politics, weren't American Republicans during Ronald Reagan's administration a lot like the Party of Order? Their Orléanists were new-tech liberal capitalists, and their legitimists were the anti-establishment populists (which later morphed into the Tea Party movement) – they hated each other, but they knew they could only rule together, so each of them endlessly postponed the measures they really cared about (such as a ban on abortion). This is the formula of today's cynical politics: its true dupes are the cynics themselves, who are not aware that their truth is in what they are mocking, not in their hidden beliefs. As such, cynicism is a perverted attitude: it transposes onto its other (non-cynical) dupes its own division. This is why, as Freud pointed out, perverse activity is not an open display of the unconscious, but its greatest obfuscation.

There is one thing about Henry Kissinger, the ultimate cynical *Realpolitiker*, which truly stands out: how utterly wrong all his predictions were. When news reached the West about the anti-Gorbachev military coup in 1991, he immediately accepted the new regime (which ignominiously collapsed three days later) as a fact. In short, when socialist regimes were already the living dead, he was counting on a long-term pact with them. What this example perfectly demonstrates is the limitation of cynicism: cynics are Lacan's *les non-dupes qui errent*; what they fail to recognize is the symbolic efficiency of illusions, the way those illusions regulate the activity that generates social reality. The position of cynicism is that of wisdom – the paradigmatic cynic tells you privately, in a confidential low-key voice: 'But don't you get it that it is all really about money/power/sex, that all high principles and values are just empty phrases which count for nothing?' In this sense, philosophers effectively believe in the power of ideas, they believe that ideas rule the world, and cynics are fully justified in accusing them of this sin – however, what the cynics don't see is their own naivety, the naivety of their cynical wisdom. It is the philosophers who are the true realists: they are well aware that the cynical position is impossible and inconsistent, that cynics effectively follow the principle they publicly mock. Stalin was a cynic if there ever was one – but that's precisely why he sincerely believed in Communism.

The general theoretical point that underlies this blindness of cynicism is that a critique of ideology has to include a theory of constructed ignorance. Much like knowledge, ignorance is also socially constructed, in all its fifty shades, from simple direct ignorance, where we don't even know we don't know, to politely ignoring what we know very well, and covering all intermediate levels, especially the institutional Unconscious.[26] Recall the liberal appropriation of Martin Luther King, in itself an exemplary case of un-learning. Henry Louis Taylor recently remarked:

> Everyone knows, even the smallest kid knows about Martin Luther King, can say his most famous moment was that 'I have a dream' speech. No one can go further than one sentence. All we know is that this guy had a dream. We don't know what that dream was.[27]

King had come a long way from the crowds who cheered him at the 1963 March on Washington, when he was introduced as 'the moral leader of our nation': by taking on issues outside segregation, he had lost much of his public support and was beginning to be seen as a pariah. As Harvard Sitkoff put it, he took on issues of poverty and militarism because he considered them vital 'to mak[ing] equality something real and not just racial brotherhood but equality in fact'.[28] To put it in Badiou's terms, King followed the 'axiom of equality' well beyond the topic of racial segregation: he was working on anti-poverty and anti-war issues at the time of his death. He had spoken out against the Vietnam War and was in Memphis in support of striking sanitation workers when he was killed in April 1968. 'Following King meant following the unpopular road, not the popular one.'[29] In short, elevating King into a moral icon involved a lot of systematic erasure of what was known about him.

Another case of systematic unlearning concerns psychoanalysis: as Gerard Wajcman has rightfully observed, in our era, which sees itself as permissive, as violating all sexual taboos and repressions, thereby making psychoanalysis obsolete, Freud's fundamental insight into child sexuality is strangely ignored:

> The sole remaining prohibition, the one sacred value in our society that seems to remain, is to do with children. It is forbidden to touch a hair on their little blond heads, as if children had rediscovered that angelic purity on which Freud managed to cast some doubt. And it is undoubtedly the diabolical figure of Freud that we condemn today, seeing him as the one who, by uncovering the relationship of childhood to sexuality, quite simply depraved our virginal childhoods. In an age when sexuality is exhibited on every street corner, the image of the innocent child has, strangely, returned with a vengeance.[30]

One can go on endlessly enumerating similar cases – suffice it to recall the systematic unlearning of the facts about a colonized people imposed by the colonizers. This unlearning concerns not only facts, but even more the ideological space which provides the coordinates for our understanding of the 'primitives'. (For example, when early ethnologists encountered a tribe whose totem was a bird, they automatically attributed to the tribe members the ridiculous belief that they had developed from this bird.) But the most basic ignorance is immanent to the Law: it concerns its own obscene underside.

On 3 December 2013, the Israeli *Haaretz* newspaper reported that ultra-Orthodox unofficial 'modesty patrols' were selling glasses with special blur-inducing stickers on their lenses: the glasses provided clear vision for up to a few metres so as not to impede movement, but anything beyond that got blurry – including women.[31] Along similar lines, one can well imagine aggressive Zionists selling glasses which somehow blur Palestinians and their buildings, so that one can see the Holy Land the way it should have been.

THE OBSCENE UNDERSIDE OF THE LAW

Legend has it that Alfred Hitchcock (a Catholic) was once driving through a small Swiss town. All of a sudden, he pointed his finger at something through the car window and said: 'This is the most terrifying scene I've ever seen!' A friend sitting at his side looked in the direction pointed by Hitchcock and was surprised: he saw nothing unusual, just a priest who, while talking to a young boy, had placed his hand on the boy's arm. Hitchcock stopped the car, rolled down the window and shouted: 'Run, boy, save your life!' While this anecdote could be taken as a display of Hitchcock's eccentric showmanship, it does bring us to the 'heart of darkness' of the Catholic Church. How?

Let's clarify this point through a series of examples from different areas. In an episode from Monty Python's *The Meaning of Life*, a teacher asks his pupils how to arouse the vagina. Caught in their ignorance, the embarrassed pupils avoid his gaze and stammer half-articulate answers, while the teacher reprimands them severely for not practising the subject at home. With his wife's assistance, he thereupon demonstrates the penetration of the penis into the vagina. Bored, one of the schoolboys casts a furtive glance through the window, and the teacher asks him sarcastically: 'Would you be kind enough to tell us what is so attractive out there in the courtyard?' This scene is so uncanny because it exhibits, in broad daylight, the way sexual enjoyment is sustained by a superego-imperative: it doesn't come spontaneously, it is a duty.

The very beginning of this episode makes the point even more clearly. The pupils are waiting for the teacher to arrive; they are bored, sitting at their benches, yawning and staring into the air. When the boy standing close to the door shouts 'The teacher is coming!', the pupils explode into the wild activity of shouting, throwing papers around, shaking their tables and so on – all the stuff pupils are supposed to do when the teacher is absent, so that, when the teacher enters, he can be annoyed and shout at them: 'Stop this circus! Quiet!' What this scene makes clear is that the 'transgressive' commotion that annoys the teacher is in fact directed at him – it is not spontaneous amusement, but something performed for the teacher. Does the same not hold for our most intense forms of enjoyment, that they are not spontaneous outbursts but something learned by imitation, an acquired taste? Recall the first experience of smoking or drinking hard liquor: as a rule, it is a slightly older peer who tells me in half secret that adults are doing this, and then offers a taste of a cigarette or a drink, and my first reaction is, as expected, disgust – I start coughing, spitting it out, and exclaim: 'Is this supposed to be *pleasurable*?' Then, gradually, I learn to enjoy it and maybe even get addicted. (There is something of this even in Coke: when one tastes it for the first time, one sees immediately why Coke, with its bitter taste, was first introduced as a medicine.) When one wants just direct pleasure, one doesn't mess with the likes of tobacco or alcohol – a good fruit juice or chocolate drink does it better. And doesn't the same ultimately hold even for sex? A directly pleasurable thing is probably rhythmic squeezing of oneself, masturbation maybe, and definitely not the complex effort of a full act of copulation which, again, has to be learned.

A similar lesson can be learned from swearing. It may appear that when, in the middle of a polite conversation, one gets really mad and cannot hold back any more, one explodes into wild swearing . . . but is it so? I have a ritual with (some of) my good friends: for the first five minutes after we meet, we engage in a formulaic session of rough and tasteless swearing (all the 'screw your mother up her ass' and 'may you suffocate in your own shit' one can imagine); then, after we get tired, we acknowledge with a brief nod that this rather boring but unavoidable introductory ritual is over and, relieved that we did our duty, we relax and start to talk in a normal, polite way, as the kind and considerate people we really are. So, again, the lesson is that, while pleasures can be spontaneous, there is nothing spontaneous in excessive outbursts of enjoyment – they have to be learned the hard way.

We should apply this lesson also to forms of collective violence like gang rapes and killings. One of the terrifying effects of the non-contemporaneity of different levels of social life is the rise of violence against women – not just random violence, but systemic violence, violence which is specific to a certain social context, follows a pattern, and transmits a clear message. While we were right to be terrified by the gang rapes in India, the world-wide echo of these cases is nonetheless suspicious. As Arundhati Roy pointed out, the cause of this unanimous outburst of moral judgment was that the rapists were poor. So, perhaps, it would be commendable to widen our perception and include other similar phenomena. The serial killings of women in Ciudad Juarez at the Mexican border with Texas are not just private pathologies, but a ritualized activity, part of the subculture of local gangs (first gang rape, then torture till death, which includes cutting off breast nipples with scissors), and directed at single young women working in new assembling factories – a clear case of macho reaction to the new class of independent working women.[32] Even more unexpected are serial rapes and murders of aboriginal women in Western Canada, close to reservations around Vancouver, belying Canada's claim to be a model tolerant welfare state: a group of white men abduct, rape and kill a woman, and then deposit the mutilated body just within the reservation territory, which puts it legally under the jurisdiction of the tribal police, totally unprepared to deal with such cases. When Canadian authorities are contacted, they tend to limit their investigation to the native community in order to present the crime as a case of local family violence due to drugs and alcohol.[33] In all these cases, the social dislocation due to fast industrialization and modernization provokes a brutal reaction from men who experience this development as a threat. And the crucial feature in all these cases is that the violent act is not a spontaneous outburst of raw, brutal energy, breaking the chains of civilized customs, but something learned, externally imposed, ritualized, part of the symbolic substance of a community. What is repressed for the 'innocent' public gaze is not the cruel brutality of the act, but precisely its 'cultural', ritualistic character of symbolic custom.

The same perverted social-ritual logic is at work in the cases of paedophilia that constantly shake the Catholic Church: when Church representatives insist that these cases, deplorable as they are, are an internal problem, and display great reluctance to collaborate with police in their investigations, they are, in a way, right. The paedophilia of Catholic priests is not something that concerns merely those who happened to choose to be priests because of contingent reasons of private history with no relation to the Church as an institution; it is a phenomenon that concerns the Catholic Church as such, that is inscribed into its very functioning as a socio-symbolic institution. It does not concern the 'private' unconscious of individuals, but the 'unconscious' of the institution itself. It is not something that happens because the institution has to accommodate itself to the pathological realities of libidinal life in order to survive, but something that the institution itself needs in order to reproduce itself. One can well imagine a non-paedophile priest who, after years of service, gets involved in paedophilia because the very logic of the institution seduces him into it. Such an *institutional Unconscious* designates the obscene disavowed underside that, precisely because it is disavowed, sustains the public institution. (In the army, this underside consists of the obscene sexualized rituals which sustain group solidarity.) In other words, it is not simply that, for conformist reasons, the Church tries to hush up the embarrassing paedophile scandals; in defending itself, the Church defends its innermost obscene secret. What this means is that identifying with this secret side is a key constituent of the very identity of a Christian priest: if a priest seriously (not just rhetorically) denounces these scandals, he thereby excludes himself from the ecclesiastic community. He is no longer 'one of us' (in exactly the same way that a citizen who denounced the Ku Klux Klan to the police in the American South in the 1920s excluded himself from his community, i.e., betrayed its fundamental solidarity).[34]

Structurally similar cases can be found everywhere in the way authority works. During the long rule of Kemal Ataturk, the 'father' of modern Turkey, from the end of the First World War until his death in the 1930s, there was a persistent rumour among the Turks that, in contrast to his official image as an ascetic leader working night and day for his country, he was a great playboy who slept with the wives of all of his collaborators. However, those in the know claim that, at least from the mid 1920s onwards, the real Ataturk was an impotent drunkard who was only able occasionally to play with very young boys – the rumour about his serial seductions was a carefully propagated official myth. What is interesting here is that, although this rumour was officially denied (one was even in danger of being severely punished for talking too much about Ataturk's sexual promiscuity), it was discreetly propagated by the very authorities who ruthlessly punished those who besmirched Ataturk's official image by spreading stories about his erotic adventures, and it played a crucial role in sustaining his aura. One can easily imagine an embarrassing situation in Turkey in 1930: at a public meeting, an official Kemalist speaker attacks those who spread filthy rumours about the leader's promiscuity; an unknown man from the public stands up and fully supports the speaker, emphasizing how everyone knows that rumours about Ataturk's sexual prowess are utterly false. Although he only confirms what the official speaker claims, he thereby denies the obscene obverse of the official ideology. That is to say, when the official speaker was attacking rumours about Ataturk, everyone knew that he did that just *pro forma*, effectively confirming their truth as something that one should not talk about in public.[35]

Back to the Catholic Church. In the summer of 2012 there occurred in Slovenia an almost clinically pure display of the Catholic Church's obscenity. It involved two actors, the conservative Cardinal Franc Rode, a Slovene with the highest place in the Church *nomenklatura*, and Alojz Uran, the archbishop who was first deposed by the Vatican and then even ordered immediately to leave Slovenia until certain accusations against him were clarified. Since Uran was very popular among ordinary Catholic believers, rumours started to circulate about what could possibly have warranted this extraordinarily harsh punishment. After a week or so of embarrassed silence, the Church authorities grudgingly said that Uran was suspected of fathering an illegitimate child – an explanation which, for a series of reasons, was met with widespread disbelief. First, rumours about Uran's paternity had been circulating for decades, so why did the Church not take measures earlier, when Uran was nominated to be the archbishop of Slovenia? Second, Uran himself publicly proclaimed that he was ready to undergo DNA or any other tests to prove that he has no children. Last but not least, it is well known that, in the Slovene Church, a struggle was going on for many years between conservatives (among them Rode) and moderates (among them Uran). But whatever the truth, the public was shocked by the double standards displayed by the Catholic *nomenklatura*: while Uran was ordered to leave Slovenia due to a mere *suspicion* that he had fathered a child, the reaction of the Church was infinitely more soft in the numerous cases of paedophilia among priests – these cases were never reported to the police, the responsible priest was never punished but just moved to another part of Slovenia, there was pressure on the parents of the abused children to keep things quiet, and so on.[36]

What made things even worse was the open, cynical 'realism' displayed by Cardinal Rode: in one of his radio interviews, he said that 'statistically, this is an *irrelevant* problem – one or at the utmost two out of a hundred priests had a kind of adventure.'[37] What drew the attention of the public right away was the term 'a kind of adventure' used as a euphemism for paedophilia: the brutal crime of raping children was presented as a normal display of adventurous 'vivacity' (another term used by Rode), and, as Rode quipped in another interview: 'In forty years time you would expect some small sins to occur, wouldn't you?'[38] This is Catholic obscenity at its purest: no solidarity with the victims (children), and what we find beneath the morally upright posture is just the barely concealed solidarity with the perpetrators on behalf of cynical realism (that's life, priests can also be adventurous and vivacious . . .), so that, in the end, the only true victims would seem to be the Church and the perpetrators themselves who had been exposed to an unfair media campaign. The lines are thus clearly drawn: paedophilia is ours, our own dirty secret, and as such normalized, the secret foundation of our normality, while fathering a child is a true violation to be ruthlessly rejected – or, as G. K. Chesterton put it a century ago in his *Orthodoxy* (unaware of the full consequences of his words, of course):

The outer ring of Christianity is a rigid guard of ethical abnegations and professional priests; but inside that inhuman guard you will find the old human life dancing like children, and drinking wine like men; for Christianity is the only frame for pagan freedom.[39]

The perverse conclusion is unavoidable here: do you want to enjoy the pagan dream of pleasurable life without paying the price of melancholic sadness for it? Choose Christianity! We can discern traces of this paradox in the figure of the Catholic priest (or nun) as the ultimate bearer of sexual wisdom. Recall what is arguably the most powerful scene from *The Sound of Music*: after Maria escapes from the von Trapp family back to the monastery, unable to deal with her sexual attraction towards Baron von Trapp, she cannot find peace there since she is still longing for the Baron. The Mother Superior summons her and advises her to return to the von Trapp family and try to sort out her relationship with the Baron. She delivers this message in a weird song titled 'Climb Every Mountain!', whose surprising motif is: Do it! Take the risk and try everything your heart wants! Do not allow petty considerations to stand in your way! The uncanny power of this scene resides in its unexpected display of the spectacle of desire, which makes the scene truly *embarrassing*: the very person whom one would expect to preach abstinence and renunciation turns out to be the agent of fidelity to one's desire. Today, with cases of paedophilia popping up everywhere in the Catholic Church, one can easily imagine a new version of the scene from *The Sound of Music*: a young priest approaches the abbot, complaining that he is still tortured by desires for young boys, and demanding further punishment.

This is the immanent contradiction at the very core of the Church's identity, making it the main anti-Christian force today. The legend says that when, in 1804, the Pope was approaching Napoleon to put the Emperor's crown on his head, Napoleon took the crown from his hands and put it on his head himself. The Pope quipped back: 'I know your aim is to destroy Christianity. But believe me, Sire, you will fail – the Church has been trying to do this for 2,000 years and still hasn't succeeded . . .' With people like Cardinal Rode from Slovenia, we can see how the Church continues to do so, and there is no reason to rejoice at this sad fact – the Christian legacy is all too precious and, today, more pertinent than ever. In his *Notes Towards a Definition of Culture*, T. S. Eliot remarked that there are moments when the only choice is the one between heresy and non-belief, when the only way to keep a religion alive is to perform a sectarian split from its main corpus. This is what has to be done today.

SUPEREGO, OR, THE PROHIBITED PROHIBITION

This inherent inconsistency of the ideologico-legal order is not limited to church institutions – one of the most conspicuous cases today is that of China. How do official Communist theorists react when confronted with the all too obvious contradiction: a Communist Party which still legitimizes itself in Marxist terms, but renounces Marxism's basic premise, that of workers self-organization as a revolutionary force in order to overthrow capitalism? It is difficult to avoid the impression that all the resources of legendary Chinese politeness are mobilized here; it is considered impolite to directly raise (or insist on) these questions. This resort to politeness is necessary because it is the only way to combine what cannot be combined: to enforce Marxism as official ideology while openly prohibiting its central axioms would cause the collapse of the entire ideological edifice, thereby rendering it meaningless. As a result, while certain things are clearly prohibited, this prohibition cannot be publicly stated, but is itself prohibited. It is not merely prohibited to raise the question of workers' self-organization against capitalist exploitation as the central tenet of Marxism; it is also prohibited to publicly claim that it is prohibited to raise this question.[40] In this way, we violate what Kant called the 'transcendental formula of public law': 'All actions relating to the right of other men are unjust if their maxim is not consistent with being rendered public.' A secret law, a law unknown to its subjects, would legitimize the arbitrary despotism of those who exercise it – compare with this formula the title of a recent report on China: 'Even what's secret is a secret in China.'[41] Troublesome intellectuals who report on political oppression, ecological catastrophes and rural poverty get years of prison for betraying a state secret. The catch is that many of the laws and regulations that make up the state-secret regime are themselves classified, making it difficult for individuals to know how and when they're in violation – and what Snowden's revelations made palpable is the extent to which the agencies that monitor terrorists' secret plans function in the Chinese way.

Such a self-referential redoubling of the prohibiting Law which itself becomes prohibited transforms it into a traumatic Real, and this brings us back to the superego – the Freudian name for a Law which functions as real-impossible. In the courtroom scene in *The Merchant of Venice*, Portia, disguised as Balthazar, orders Shylock not to leave the court after he loses his bid for the pound of flesh: 'Tarry a little / . . . / Tarry, Jew, / The law hath yet another hold on you.'[42] Which Law? The obscene superego one, the obverse of mercy (legally nonsense) – you wanted it (a pound of flesh), you *have* to get it! We get here an ironic reference to Paul's claim that Christians do not need external circumcision but the circumcision of the heart – and it is as if *The Merchant of Venice* realizes this literally, forcing Shylock to get his pound of flesh as a circumcision of the heart.[43] The pressure of the superego is exercised here with an additional twist: you wanted it, now you have to have it, you cannot renounce it.

But let us turn to a contemporary example of this obscene ambiguity of legal power: the deadlock of the anti-smoking campaigns. In August 2012, it was reported that, from that December, tobacco companies in Australia would no longer be allowed to display their distinctive colours, brand designs and logos on cigarette packs. To make smoking as unglamorous as possible, the packs would come in a uniformly drab shade of olive and feature graphic health warnings and images of cancer-riddled mouths, blinded eyeballs and sickly children.[44] What we are witnessing here is a kind of *Selbst-Aufhebung* of the commodity-form: no logo, no 'commodity-aesthetics' which could seduce us into buying the product. On the contrary, the package openly and graphically draws attention to the fact that the product is harmful, providing reasons against buying it. The anti-commodity presentation of a commodity is in itself not a novelty – it also accounts for the allure of 'cultural' products like painting or music which are 'not strictly a commodity; it is . . . worth buying only when the pretence that it is not a commodity can be successfully maintained.'[45] Here, the antagonism between commodity and non-commodity functions as the complete opposite of logo-less cigarettes: the superego injunction is, 'You should be ready to pay an exorbitant price for this commodity precisely because it is much more than a mere commodity!' In the case of logo-less cigarettes, we get the raw use value deprived of its logo form (in a similar way, we can buy logo-less sugar, coffee and sweets from discount stores); in the case of a painting, the logo itself 'sublates' use value, i.e., as Marx has noted, the price seems to determine the value.

But does this direct 'pragmatic contradiction' really take us out of commodity-fetishism? Does it not rather provide yet another example of the fetishist split signalled by the well-known phrase *je sais très bien, mais quand même . . . ?* A decade or so ago there was a German publicity poster for Marlboro cigarettes: their standard cowboy figure was this time directly pointing with his finger down towards the obligatory statement 'Smoking is dangerous for your health!', with the words '*Jetzt erst rechts!*' added, which can be vaguely translated as 'Now things are getting serious!' The implied meaning is clear: now that you know how dangerous it is to smoke, you have a chance to prove that you have the courage to go on smoking! In other words, the expected response is: 'I know very well the dangers of smoking, but I am not a coward, I am a true man and, as such, ready to take the risk and remain faithful to my smoking commitment!' It is only in this way that smoking effectively becomes a form of consumerism: 'I am ready to consume cigarettes "beyond the pleasure-principle", beyond the petty utilitarian considerations about health.' And is not this dimension of lethal excessive enjoyment at work in every publicity or commodity appeal? Are all utilitarian considerations (this food is healthy, it was organically grown, it was produced under fair-trade conditions and so on) not just a deceptive surface containing a deeper superego injunction: 'Enjoy! Enjoy to the end, irrespective of consequences!'? The Australian 'negative' packaging will thus bring out the superego injunction which was here all the time – that is to say, will a smoker, when he buys the 'negatively' packed cigarettes, not hear beneath the negative message the silent, but all the more present and pressing, voice of the superego? This voice will answer his question: 'If all these dangers of smoking are true – and I accept they are true – why am I then still buying the package?'

This same superego injunction works in an inverted way in another climactic moment of the anti-smoking campaign that clearly displays its moralistic edge: the ongoing wave of prohibitive measures targeting e-cigarettes. Two years ago, Michael Bloomberg, then Mayor of New York City, signed into law a ban on using electronic cigarettes anywhere conventional cigarette use is prohibited; then, the big US airlines followed; restaurant owners also tend towards prohibiting electronic cigarettes; and so on. But why, when all that e-cigarettes emit is an odourless water vapour? The basic argument is that when one smokes an e-cigarette in a public place, one demonstrates craven addiction, as well as a weakness of willpower (one is not strong enough to resist the temptation of smoking), and this may exert a bad influence on others or at least annoy them. In short, one is not punished for health reasons, for the effects of what one is doing, but simply for displaying a stance or disposition, without posing a threat to anyone – it is like prohibiting the public consumption of sugarless cakes because in eating them one displays an addiction to eating cakes. The superego twist resides here in the fact that I am guilty even if I am innocent because I am innocent in a wrong way (admitting my desire to smoke in the guise of my very effort not to smoke).

So, again, what is the superego? *Ne čakaj na maj* (*Don't Wait for May*) – a popular Slovene film from 1957, one of the first post-Second World War Slovene films which asserted the right of the young generation to enjoy life and have fun – is a surprisingly refined romantic comedy almost as good as the Ernst Lubitsch masterpieces. It tells the story of a couple of students passionately in love with each other: she, Vesna, is the daughter of a severe high-school mathematics professor, a widower who lives with his unmarried sister, an old maid who has never had sex; he, Samo, is an amateur pilot of sport planes. Here is the much simplified plot: when the two go on a short skiing vacation together with a group of friends, Vesna's father, worried about the dangers of a holiday away from her family, asks his sister to accompany them and keep an eye on Vesna. Supposed to be the gatekeeper, the old lady, of course, ends up as the one who brings the lovers together. After some misunderstandings that cause jealousy, the couple find themselves alone, but they merely exchange a few kisses – Vesna doesn't want to engage in full sex, since she wants a lifelong connection, not just a brief affair. After they return home and Vesna tells her father that she wants to marry, the father sternly prohibits marriage until they finish their studies. Vesna then concocts a plan: she leaves false traces indicating that she is already pregnant (she 'forgets' a book on pregnancy on her bed and she pretends to have morning sickness), and then escapes with Samo. When her father and their noisy neighbours learn the news, rumours explode about how promiscuous the young generation is and how they have no moral compass. Gradually, nonetheless, the father and his sister relent and joyfully prepare for Vesna and Samo's wedding and baby, buying a small bed and ordering children's clothes. Then, when they are all gathered in front of their house, Vesna and Samo unexpectedly return home, telling them that there is no pregnancy since they didn't use the opportunity for illicit sexual pleasures. The same gossipy neighbours react critically again, with the main moralist uttering, with a dismissive sneer: 'You see, the boy didn't even use his opportunity! I knew all along that he was of no real use!' Even Vesna's father is disappointed and attacks Samo's mother: 'What kind of son did you raise that he didn't even know how to get my daughter pregnant! He isn't worthy of her!' The lovers run away; when they are alone on the plane, high above the city, Vesna whispers something we cannot understand into Samo's ear, the two lovers laugh and embrace, and here the film ends . . . One can guess what she whispers into his ear – something like 'Now you can fuck me!'

Vesna's strategy in faking her pregnancy is complex: its goal is not just to make her family accept her marriage by confronting them with a (fake) *fait accompli*, it concerns also (and even primarily) the inner psychic economy of the couple's relationship, how to bring themselves to perform the full act. That is to say, it is evident that Vesna doesn't want to follow the path of the simple transgression of violating the norm imposed by the father; she is not ready to assume full responsibility for the (sexual) act in defiance of the big Other (in this case, paternal authority). What she wants is not only to have sex legitimately, but, even more perversely, to be forced into doing it by the very authority whose function is to prohibit it, and this is why she does the opposite of what young lovers usually do: instead of keeping the appearance of chastity and engaging in sex discreetly, out of the Other's view, she engenders the (false) appearance of illicit sex while in reality persisting in chastity. The premise is that we are not hypocrites who pretend to be pure and chaste but secretly engage in illicit pleasures; on the contrary, we are hypocrites who pretend to enjoy illicit pleasures while secretly preferring chastity. The false appearance of illicit pleasures generates obscene expectations which are disappointed when this appearance is proven false – and at this point she can finally engage in sex under the aegis of the big Other of paternal authority, obeying its obscene injunction. This strategy lays bare the ambiguity of paternal authority. It forces the authority to openly display its obscene underside. At the same time, it demonstrates how a successful sexual act is not just a matter of intimate passions, but has to be mediated through the big Other of some symbolic authority.

The changed reaction of the gossipy neighbours provides a perfect example of how superego works: it exerts pressure to impose sexual constraints, to impede sexual contact; however, beneath this surface appearance, its true injunction is: 'Do it, enjoy! I want you to do precisely what I am prohibiting you from doing!' In other words, you are guilty if you violate the prohibition, but you are even guiltier if you obey it (which explains the superego paradox: the more you obey its command, the more you are guilty). Freud brings this fundamental ambiguity constitutive of the *superego* agency – when you violate the moral standard, you are guilty, when you don't use the opportunity to violate it, you are even guiltier – to the extreme: 'It seems that the superego is saying: in any case you are guilty.'[46]

This constitutive guilt accounts for another reversal of common sense, which concerns *Strafbeduerfnis*, the need to be punished, the weird satisfaction provided by a painful punishment: it is not the crime that causes the guilt feeling and punishment; it is the need to be punished that generates guilt and gives birth to criminal intentions (and occasionally acts). Where, then, does this original need-to-be-punished come from? Instead of grounding it directly in some kind of primordial masochism, striving for pleasure-in-pain, Freud proposes a more complex scenario which concerns the very basic matrix of socialization, of entering a legal order. It is not only that, in a pseudo-Hegelian way, the legal order needs occasional transgressions (crimes) in order to assert its authority through punishing the perpetrators – all of us, also those who have never perpetrated any crime, are constituted as legal subjects through being considered as potential criminals. Freud elaborated this scenario in his well-known analysis of Dostoyevsky's *The Brothers Karamazov*, in which a group of brothers is suspected of killing their father, an obscene *père-jouisseur*:

> It is a matter of indifference who actually committed the crime; psychology is only concerned to know who desired it emotionally and who welcomed it when it was done. And for that reason all of the brothers, except the contrasted figure of Alyosha, are equally guilty – the impulsive sensualist, the sceptical cynic and the epileptic criminal. In *The Brothers Karamazov* there is one particularly revealing scene. In the course of his talk with Dmitri, Father Zossima recognizes that Dmitri is prepared to commit suicide, and he bows down at his feet. It is impossible that this can be meant as an expression of admiration; it must mean that the holy man is rejecting the temptation to despise or detest the murderer and for that reason humbles himself before him. Dostoyevsky's sympathy for the criminal is, in fact, boundless; it goes far beyond the pity which the unhappy wretch has a right to, and reminds us of the 'holy awe' with which epileptics and lunatics were regarded in the past. A criminal is to him almost a Redeemer, who has taken on himself the guilt which must else have been borne by others. There is no longer any need for one to murder, since *he* has already murdered; and one must be grateful to him, for, except for him one would have been obliged oneself to murder.[47]

Insofar as the primordial crime (the murder of the obscene *Ur-Vater*) is constitutive of the social body kept together by a Law, the definition of an *innocent* subject of the Law is: *someone who no longer needs to kill since another one – the 'sacred murderer' – already did it for him*, realizing the innocent's desire. We are thus incorporated into a legal order through crime and guilt: a subject of Law is by definition a potential criminal. This shared guilt that constitutes the universality of legal citizens brings us back to the reflexive redoubling of the (legal) prohibition. The Law not only prohibits, it is itself prohibited:

The law is prohibition: this does not mean that it prohibits, but that it is itself prohibited, a prohibited place ... one cannot reach the law, and in order to have a rapport of respect with it, one must not have a rapport with the law, one must interrupt the relation. One must enter into relation only with the law's representatives, its examples, its guardians. These are interrupters as much as messengers. One must not know who or what or where the law is.'[48]

Why not? Because if one were to get to know it, the Law would lose its legitimacy: its foundation in an act of illegal violence would become apparent. (This is why Kant prohibited questioning the origins of legal order.) What has to remain prohibited is the criminal underside of the Law, the 'mythic violence' (Benjamin) of its instauration, the violence that continuously sustains the rule of Law. This prohibition (repression) works by way of transposing pressure onto the subject: the subject has to be perceived as *a priori* (formally) guilty, so that the guilt (obscene violence) of the big Other, of the Law itself, remains invisible. However, in order to function, this transposition has to assume two forms: first, that of the guilty subject who effectively committed the crime, and, then, that of the innocent bystanders who profited from it since the criminal's act delivered them from the need to murder: 'I take the crime upon myself so that the big Other [the Law] remains pure, unblemished.'

The notion of sacrifice usually associated with Lacanian psychoanalysis is that of a gesture that enacts the disavowal of the impotence of the big Other. At its most elementary, the subject does not offer his sacrifice to profit from it himself, but to fill in the lack in the Other, to sustain the appearance of the Other's omnipotence or, at least, consistency. In the film *Beau Geste* (1939), Gary Cooper, who plays the oldest of the three brothers living with their benevolent aunt, steals an enormously expensive diamond necklace, which is the pride of the aunt's family, in what seems to be a gesture of excessive, ungrateful cruelty. He disappears with it, knowing that his reputation is ruined, that he will be for ever known as the ungracious embezzler of his benefactress. So, why did he do it? At the end of the film, we learn that he did it in order to prevent the embarrassing disclosure that the necklace was a fake: unbeknownst to everyone else, some time ago the aunt had had to sell the necklace to a rich maharaja in order to save the family from bankruptcy, replacing it with a worthless imitation. Just prior to his 'theft', he learned that a distant uncle who co-owned the necklace wanted it sold for financial gain; if the necklace were to be sold, the fact that it was a fake would undoubtedly have been discovered. Consequently, the only way to retain the aunt's (and, thus, the family's) honour was to stage its theft. This is the proper deception of the crime of stealing: to occlude the fact that, ultimately, *there is nothing to steal* – in this way, the constitutive lack of the Other is concealed (i.e., the illusion is maintained that the Other possessed what was stolen from it). If, in love, one gives what one doesn't possess, in a crime of love, one steals from the beloved Other what the Other doesn't possess. This is what the *beau geste* of the film's title alludes to. And, therein also resides the meaning of sacrifice: one sacrifices oneself (one's honour and future) to maintain the appearance of the Other's honour, to save the beloved Other from shame.

Then, there is the virtual guilt of the innocent bystanders, of the collective who profit from a (necessary) crime. The Freudian paradox 'The more you are innocent, the more you are guilty,' holds for them: the more they are innocent of the actual crime, the more they are guilty for enjoying its fruits without paying the price for them. Superego-pressure enters here, capitalizing on this guilt in a very specific way: the superego-pressure does not squash the subject's individuality, its effect is not to immerse the subject into a crowd where his or her individuality is dissolved; on the contrary, the superego-pressure *individualizes* the subject, or, to quote Balibar's wonderful reversal of Althusser's classic formula, *the superego interpellates subjects into individuals*. The superego addresses me as a unique individual, confronting me with my guilt and responsibility: 'Don't escape into generalities, don't resort to objective circumstances, look deep into your heart and ask yourself where you failed with regard to your duties!' This is why superego-pressure gives rise to anxiety: in the eyes of the superego, I am alone, there is no big Other behind which I can hide, and I am 'guilty as charged' because the very position of being charged makes me formally guilty – if I plead my innocence, it only signals my additional guilt for denying guilt.

A series of situations that characterize today's society perfectly exemplify this type of superego-individualization: ecology, political correctness and poverty. The predominant ecological discourse which addresses us as *a priori* guilty, indebted to mother nature, under the constant pressure of the ecological superego-agency, addresses us as individuals: What did you do today to repay your debt to nature? Did you put all newspapers into the proper recycling bin? And all the bottles of beer or cans of Coke? Did you use your car when you could have used a bike or public transport? Did you use air conditioning instead of just opening the windows?[49] The ideological stakes of such individualization are easily discernible: I get lost in my own self-examination instead of raising much more pertinent global questions about our entire industrial civilization.

The same goes for the endless politically correct self-examination: was my look at the female flight attendant too intrusive and sexually offensive? Did I use any words with a possible sexist undertone while addressing her? The pleasure, thrill even, provided by such self-probing is evident – recall how self-critical regret is mixed with joy when you discover that your innocent joke was not so innocent after all, that it had a racist undertone. As for charity, recall how we are all the time bombarded by messages destined to make us feel guilty for our comfortable way of life while children are starving in Somalia or dying unnecessarily from easily curable diseases – messages which simultaneously offer an easy way out ('You *can* make a difference! Give $10 monthly and you will make a black orphan happy!'). Again, the ideological underpinning is easily discernible here. Lazzarato's notion of 'the indebted man' provides the general structure of such subjectivity for which the superego-pressure of being indebted is constitutive – to paraphrase Descartes, I am in debt, therefore I exist as a subject integrated into the social order.

And does the same not hold even for the pathological fear of some Western liberal Leftists that they may be guilty of Islamophobia? Any critique of Islam is denounced as an expression of Western Islamophobia, Salman Rushdie is denounced for unnecessarily provoking Muslims and being (partially, at least) responsible for the *fatwa* condemning him to death, and so on. The result of such stances is what one should expect in such cases: the more the Western liberal Leftists

probe into their guilt, the more they are accused by Muslim fundamentalists of being hypocrites who try to conceal their hatred of
Islam. Again, this constellation perfectly reproduces the paradox of
the superego: the more you obey what the Other demands of you, the
guiltier you are. It is as if the more you tolerate Islam, the stronger its
pressure on you will be. What this implies is that terrorist fundamentalists, be they Christian or Muslim, are not really fundamentalists in
the authentic sense of the term – what they lack is a feature that is
easy to discern in all authentic fundamentalists, from Tibetan Buddhists to the Amish in the US: the absence of resentment and envy, the
deep indifference towards the non-believers' way of life. If today's
so-called fundamentalists really believe they have found their way to
Truth, why should they feel threatened by non-believers, why should
they envy them? When a Buddhist encounters a Western hedonist, he
hardly condemns. He just benevolently notes that the hedonist's search
for happiness is self-defeating. In contrast to true fundamentalists, the
terrorist pseudo-fundamentalists are deeply bothered, intrigued and
fascinated by the sinful life of the non-believers. One can feel that, in
fighting the sinful other, they are fighting their own temptation. The
passionate intensity of a fundamentalist mob bears witness to the lack
of true conviction; deep in themselves, terrorist fundamentalists also
lack true conviction – their violent outbursts are proof of it. How fragile the belief of a Muslim would be if he felt threatened by, say, a
stupid caricature in a low-circulation Danish newspaper? Fundamentalist Islamic terror is *not* grounded in the terrorists' conviction of
their superiority and in their desire to safeguard their cultural-religious
identity from the onslaught of global consumerist civilization. The
problem with fundamentalists is not that we consider them inferior to
us, but, rather, that *they themselves* secretly consider themselves inferior. This is why our condescending politically correct assurances that
we feel no superiority towards them only makes them more furious
and feeds their resentment. The problem is not cultural difference
(their effort to preserve their identity), but the opposite: the fact that
the fundamentalists are already like us, that, secretly, they have
already internalized our standards and measure themselves by them.
Paradoxically, what the fundamentalists really lack is precisely a dose
of that true 'racist' conviction of one's own superiority.

The mechanism of crowd-formation described in detail by Freud should be conceived precisely as a reaction to this individualizing superego-pressure: the activity of the crowd is a kind of 'return of the repressed', of the mythic violence, and the dissolving of the participants' individuality also dissolves the anxiety and guilt that affected them as isolated individuals. In this sense, one can say that crowd activity turns around the Freudian superego paradox: when we engage in crowd violence (such as pogroms), *the more we are guilty, the more we are innocent* – the more brutal our violence, the more we escape the vicious cycle of the superego.

And, we may add, the more we are caught in Christian-capitalist obscene spirituality, the more we act like egotist animals. Vladimir Solovyov, the Russian Orthodox critic of Communism, expressed the tension of atheist socialism, caught between Darwinist materialism and its high-compassion ethics, with the following *non sequitur*: 'Man has evolved out of a monkey – therefore it is our duty to love one another.'[50] But is there really a gap between the two propositions? Is a ruthless survivalist ethics which condemns the weak to death really the immanent outcome of Darwinist materialism? What if the atheist socialist's apparent *non sequitur* just turns around the ideological *non sequitur* of our Christian-capitalist societies? The Christian-capitalist ideology is effectively telling us: 'Man is a creature of God with an immortal soul – therefore we should immerse ourselves in the human-animal utilitarian pursuit of pleasure.'

3

PROGNOSIS *Un faux-filet, peut-être?*

Nietzsche wrote, apropos of *Hamlet*: 'What must a person have suffered if he needs to be a clown that badly! – Is *Hamlet* understood? It is not doubt but *certainty* that drives you mad.'[1] There are two distinct propositions combined in this passage: first, Nietzsche's version of the old wisdom about the despair that lurks behind the mask of a clown – Hamlet must suffer tremendously if he feels compelled to play a crazy clown; and second, what makes him suffer, what drives him mad, is not his doubt but his certainty about who murdered his father; and his doubt, his search for the ultimate proof of Claudius' guilt, is an escape from his certainty. Another mode of escape from unbearable certainty can be to indulge in what may appear as tasteless jokes. A Bosnian cultural analyst was surprised to discover that dozens of jokes about the Serb massacre circulate among people whose relatives died in Srebrenica. Here is one example (which refers to buying beef in old Yugoslavia: the butcher usually asked, 'With or without bones?', as bones were often used for beef soup): 'I want to buy some land for a house close to Srebrenica – do you know what the prices are?' 'Prices vary, they depend on what kind of land you want – with or without bones.' Far from expressing tasteless disrespect, such jokes are the only way to deal with an unbearably traumatic reality; they render quite adequately our helpless perplexity, belying all pathetic compassion with the victims as a truly tasteless blasphemy.

Recall Paul Robeson's rewriting of his legendary 'Ol' Man River', a model of simple and efficient critico-ideological intervention. In the original version from the Hollywood musical *Show Boat* (1936), the river (the Mississippi) is presented as the embodiment of the enigmatic and indifferent Fate, an old wise man who 'must know somethin', but don't say nothin',' and just keeps rolling, retaining its silent wisdom. In the new version,[2] the river is no longer the bearer of an anonymous, unfathomable collective wisdom, but, rather, the bearer of collective *stupidity*, of passive tolerance of meaningless suffering, and the victim's response to it should be sovereign laughter. Here are the final lines of the original song:

> . . . you gets a little drunk, an' you land in jail.
> But I gets weary, and sick of tryin',
> I'm tired of livin', and scared of dyin'.
> But ol' man river, he just keeps rollin' along.

And here is the changed version:

> . . . you show a little grit, an' you lands in jail.
> But I keeps laughin', instead of cryin',
> I must keep fightin', until I'm dyin'.
> And ol' man river, he'll just keep rollin' along.

A more radical strategy for escaping from unbearable reality is that of 'de-realization'. In his analysis of the big trench battles of the First World War, such as Ypres and the Somme, where hundreds of thousands died to gain a few yards of land, Paul Fussell pointed out how the hellish nature of what went on made the participants experience their situation as theatrical: it was impossible for them to believe that they were taking part in such a murderous endeavour in person, as 'themselves'. The whole affair was all too farcical, perverse, cruel and absurd to be perceived as being part of their 'real lives'. In other words, the experience of the war as a theatrical performance enabled the participants to escape from the reality of what went on. It allowed them to follow their orders and perform their military duties without making it part of their 'true self' and, in this way, without having to abandon their innermost conviction that the real world was still a rational place and not a madhouse.[3]

It is a commonplace that the Great War functioned as an immense shock, an encounter of the Real which signalled the end of an entire civilization. Although everyone was expecting it, people were no less surprised when the war actually exploded, and (an even more enigmatic fact) this very surprise was quickly re-normalized, as War became a new way of life. How was this re-normalization achieved? Unsurprisingly, it was through the massive use of ancient ideological myths and narratives, which made the War appear as part of the normal flow of things: the no-man's-land between the trenches full of unexploded mines, holes and desolation became a new version of the Waste Land from the Grail myth.[4] This mobilization of ancient myths and legends is the ultimate proof of the traumatic novelty of the Great War: precisely because something unheard of had taken place, all ancient myths had to be put to work to account for this novelty. Of course, such myths tend to be paranoiac fantasy tales rather than proper symbolic narratives. To paraphrase Lacan, what is too traumatic to be integrated into the Symbolic returns in the Real as a paranoiac construct or hallucination. No wonder the Great War triggered an explosion of interpretive paranoia – its problem was the same as that of Stalinism: how to account for the embarrassing failures of what was supposed to be the best system? The Stalinist answer was to see counter-revolutionary plots and traitors everywhere, much like the answer given by Reginald Grant's *S.O.S.*, published in the course of the First World War, an unsurpassed collection of lies, legends and myths, all taken extremely seriously. Grant's problem was a simple one: he could not believe that the Germans were astute enough to locate targets for their artillery across the enemy line by analysing the sound and light of enemy fire, so he thought the Belgian countryside behind the British lines must have been full of treacherous farmers signalling the positions of British guns to the Germans. He believed that they were doing this in several ways: (1) windmills all of a sudden starting to turn in the opposite direction to the wind;[5] (2) the hour hands on local church towers showing the wrong time; (3) housewives hanging laundry to dry in front of their houses, the colours of the laundry (two white shirts, then one black . . .) sending a coded signal.

The problem is how to distinguish this false (ideological) paranoia from the basic paranoiac stance which is an irreducible ingredient of every critique of ideology. On a beach in a Mediterranean country, I was shown a lone fisherman repairing a net; while my hosts wanted to demonstrate traditional labour based on artisanal ancient experience and wisdom, my immediate reaction to this display was paranoia: what if the spectacle I saw in front of me was a staged authenticity, something meant to impress tourists, like preparing fresh food in department stores or other such instances of false transparency in the production process? What if I got too close to the net, saw a small sign saying 'made in China' and noticed that the 'authentic' fisherman was just mimicking productive gestures? Or, even better, what if we re-imagine the scene as a detail from some Hitchcock film: the fisherman is a foreign agent and he is weaving the net in a specially coded way so that another agent will decode in it a secret (terrorist) message?

The most brilliant hallucinatory legend of the Great War was the persistent rumour that gangs of half-crazy deserters lived somewhere in the no-man's-land between the trenches on the front lines, in a desolate wasteland of barren, scorched earth full of rotting corpses, bomb craters, abandoned trenches, caves and tunnels. These gangs were supposedly made up of members of all participating armies and nations – Germans, French, British, Australians, Poles, Croats, Belgians, Italians – and they all lived in friendship and peace, avoiding detection and helping each other. Living in rags, with long beards, they never allowed themselves to be seen – from time to time, one just heard their crazy shouts and songs. They came out of their netherworld only during the night, after a battle, in order to scavenge the corpses and collect water and food. The beauty of this legend is that it clearly describes a kind of alternative community, saying 'No!' to the madness of the battlefield: a group in which members of the warring nations live peacefully, their only enemy War itself. While they may appear as an image of War at its most crazy – outcasts living a wild life – they are simultaneously its self-negation, an island of peace between the front lines and the emergence of a universal fraternity that ignores these lines. Precisely by ignoring the official lines of division between Us and Them, they stand for the real division, the only one that matters, i.e., the negation of the entire space of imperialist warfare. They are the third element which subverts the opposition between Us and Them, our enemy – in short, they are the true Leninists in the situation, repeating Lenin's refusal to be drawn into patriotic fervour.

And this is our task, today more than ever: to discern the true division in the mêlée of secondary struggles. Here are two extreme cases of such false division.

The ideological struggle in Peru at the time of the Shining Path rebellion (1980–92) perfectly showed the country's political deadlock. On the one hand, 'the collective identity of the Shining Path was educational':[6] even their most brutal violence 'had the purpose of educating the people about the revolution and the state about its impending doom'.[7] This education was utterly authoritarian, exerted by those who believed they possessed the truth and claimed for themselves the right to have absolute power. On the other hand, the government's counter-strategy was even more ominous: a strategy of pure political demobilization and demoralization. The press, which was controlled and/or manipulated by the state, actively promoted what analysts called the 'mean world syndrome'. The government solicited an explosion of *prensa chicha*, tabloid newspapers specializing in celebrity gossip and crime stories, plus TV talk shows that focused on 'real cases' of drug addiction, family violence, adultery and so on. The goal of this strategy was to 'socially immobilize people through fear and [to] atomize the public sphere'[8] – the message was that the world was a dangerous place in which all one could do was look out for oneself, since there was no hope of solidarity, just envy of the rich and famous, and pleasure at their troubles. Rarely in modern history has the ideological space of a country been so neatly divided into 'totalitarian' educationalism, which submerges individuals into a political collective demanding total self-sacrifice, and atomized egotism, which impedes engaged solidarity, while traditional liberalism is reduced to a dwindling sideshow. Although this division is pure and radical, there is no place in it for authentic emancipatory politics.

Another false struggle concerns the status of anti-Semitism and Zionism today. For some pro-Muslim Leftists, Zionism is the exemplary case of today's neocolonial racism, which is why the Palestinian struggle against Israel is the paradigm for all other anti-racist and anti-imperialist struggles. In a strictly inverted way, for some Zionists anti-Semitism (which for them lurks in every critique of Zionism) is the exemplary case of today's racism, so that, in both cases, Zionism (or anti-Semitism) is the particular form of racism which colours all others. The true test of anti-racism today is to fight against anti-Semitism (or Zionism), i.e., if one doesn't fully endorse this particular struggle, one is accused by those who do of secretly playing the racist game (and, in a step further in the same direction, any critical remark about Islam is equated with 'Islamophobia'). While enough has been written about the deeply problematic nature of equating any critique of the State of Israel with anti-Semitism, one should also problematize the elevation of Zionism into the neo-imperialist racism par excellence. Critics of Israel often claim that we should see Zionism in this way, and Zionist oppression of the Palestinians as the paradigmatic case of today's imperialist oppression. When asked why Israel should hold this exceptional position when there are surely many cases of much more brutal oppression around the world, the standard reply is that this elevation is the result of the ongoing struggle for hegemony which no one can control – the Jews were chosen to be this exemplary case, and we have to follow this logic. This is what I find deeply problematic. When one specific ethnic group is 'chosen' as the symbol (or the personification) of a universal negative attitude, it is never a neutral operation but a choice within a well-defined space of ideological tradition. The Jews were already chosen twice in their history, first as the 'chosen people' by God himself (in their religious view), then as the target of anti-Semitism, as the personification of moral corruption, so any further 'choice' has to be read against the background of these previous choices.[9] If the Jewish state, doing things which are without doubt deeply problematic ethically and politically, is 'chosen' as the emblem of what is wrong in our world, then the surplus of libidinal energy that enables us to turn it into a universal symbol can only come from the (anti-Semitic) past. And what is wrong in this 'choice' is, again, the disavowal of class struggle.

Alessandro Russo has shown[10] how the Radical Left of the 1960s was defined by the vacillation between 'meta-classism' (adopting a position above class division: talking about the multitude, the people, the unity of all progressive or patriotic forces excluding only traitors[11]) and 'hyper-classism' (focusing on a part of the working class as the privileged revolutionary agent: 'the cognitariat', 'the precariat', illegal immigrants). It seems that, today, one can discern the same vacillation in Antonio Negri's work: multitude versus Empire *and* workers against capital. But does the first couple have anything to do with capital? Sometimes Negri implicitly identifies the two couples, talking about (capitalist) governance versus (proletarian) multitude; sometimes he discerns in the 'deterritorializing' functioning of today's most dynamic capitalism (up to financial speculations) the dimension of multitude, concluding that in the most advanced forms of capitalism we are 'almost there', almost in Communism – we just have to get rid of the capitalist form.

The problem that lurks beneath this vacillation is a crucial one: the problem of defining what really divides us today if it is no longer the traditional class conflict (the division between multitude and governance is not strong enough to play this role). What if it is still class struggle, but with the expansion of the scope of the proletariat, to find which we should no longer focus on the traditional working class but include all those who are exploited today: workers, the unemployed and the unemployable, the 'precariat', the 'cognitariat', illegal immigrants, slum dwellers, 'rogue states' excluded from 'civilized' space.[12] (We should bear in mind here that there is already a subtle subterranean difference between the working class and the proletariat discernible in Marx: the 'working class' is ultimately an empirical category designating a part of society (wage workers), while the proletariat is a more formal category designating the 'part of no-part' of the social body, the point of its symptomal torsion or, as Marx put it, the un-reason within reason – the rational structure of a society.) This is why, as Alain Badiou recently proposed[13] in a way that was both ironic and serious, today one should search for the 'principal contradiction' *within* the people (classes) themselves, not between the people and the enemies of the people, or between the people and the state: the primordial fact is a split/antagonism in the very heart of what we call the people.

DEATHS ON THE NILE

How, then, do we break through false divisions to reach the real one (real in the precise, Lacanian sense)? Let us take the case of Egypt. When, in the summer of 2013, the Egyptian army decided to break the stalemate and cleanse the public space of Islamist protesters, killing hundreds or maybe thousands, one should first just imagine what an uproar this would have caused if the same bloodbath were to happen in a country like Iran. However, it is more urgent to take a step back and focus on the absent third party in the ongoing conflict: where are the agents of the Tahrir Square protests from two years ago? Is their role now not weirdly similar to the role of the Muslim Brotherhood during the 2011 Arab Spring – that of the surprised, impassive observers? In June 2013, the Egyptian army, which was at first supported by the protesters who overthrew the Mubarak regime two years previously, deposed the democratically elected president and government. The protesters who toppled Mubarak and demanded democracy passively supported a military *coup d'état* which abolished democracy. What is going on?

The predominant interpretation, attuned to hegemonic ideology, was proposed by, among others, Fukuyama: the protest movement that toppled Mubarak was predominantly the revolt of the educated middle class, with the poor workers and farmers reduced to the role of (sympathetic) observers. But once the gates of democracy were open, the Muslim Brotherhood, whose social base is the poor majority, won democratic elections and formed a government dominated by Muslim fundamentalists, so that, understandably, the original core of secular protesters turned against them and was ready to endorse even a military coup as a way to stop them. However, such a simplified vision ignores a key feature of the protest movement: the explosion of heterogeneous organizations (of students, women workers, etc.) in the guise of which civil society began to articulate its interests outside the scope of state and religious institutions. This vast network of new social forms, much more than the overthrow of Mubarak, is the principal gain of the Arab Spring. It is an ongoing process, independent of big political changes like the army's coup against the Muslim Brotherhood government; it goes deeper than the religious/liberal divide.

The antagonism between the army and the Muslim Brotherhood is therefore not the ultimate antagonism of Egyptian society. Far from being a neutral, benevolent mediator and guarantor of social stability, the army stands for and embodies a certain social and political program – roughly speaking, integration into the global market, a pro-Western political stance and authoritarian capitalism. As such, the army's intervention is needed insofar as the majority is not ready to accept capitalism 'democratically'. In contrast to the army's secular vision, the Muslim Brotherhood endeavours to impose a fundamentalist-religious rule. Both these ideological visions exclude what the protesters actually stood for: universal social and political emancipation.

The ongoing events in Egypt provide yet another example of the basic dynamics of social revolts, which consists of two main steps traditionally designated by pairings like '1789/1793' (in the case of the French Revolution) or 'February/October' (in the case of the Russian Revolution). The first step, what Badiou recently called the 'rebirth of history', culminates in an all-popular uprising against a hated figure of power (Mubarak, in the case of Egypt, or the Shah, in the case of Iran three decades ago). People across all social strata assert themselves as a collective agent against the system of power which quickly loses its legitimacy, and all around the world we can follow on our TV screens those magic moments of ecstatic unity when hundreds of thousands of people gather on public squares for days on end and promise not to go anywhere until the tyrant steps down. Such moments stand for an imaginary unity at its most sublime: all differences, all conflicts of interest are forgotten as the whole society seems united in its opposition to the hated tyrant. In the late 1980s, something similar took place in the disintegrating Communist regimes, where all groups were united in their rejection of the Communist Party, although for different and ultimately even incompatible reasons: religious people hated it for its atheism, secular liberals for its ideological dogmatism, ordinary workers for causing them to live in poverty, potential capitalists for inhibitions on private property, intellectuals for the lack of personal freedom, nationalists for the betrayal of ethnic roots on behalf of proletarian internationalism, cosmopolitans for closed borders and the lack of intellectual contact with other countries, the youth for the regime's rejection of Western pop culture, artists for the limitations imposed on creative expression, and so on. However, once the old regime disintegrates, this imaginary unity is soon broken, and new (or, rather, old but oppressed) conflicts reappear with a vengeance: religious fundamentalists and nationalists versus secular modernizers, one ethnic group against the other, rabid anti-Communists against those suspected of sympathies with the old regime. This series of antagonisms tends to crystallize in one main political antagonism, in most cases along the axis of religious traditionalists versus secular pro-Western, multi-cultural, liberal-democratic capitalists, although the content of this dominant antagonism may vary (in Turkey, Islamists are more for the inclusion of Turkey into global capitalism than secular-nationalist Kemalists; ex-Communists can be allied with secular 'progressists' – as in Hungary or Poland – or with religious nationalists – as in Russia). Let us try to clarify this key point through a perhaps unexpected parallel with the Paulinian idea of passing from Law to love. In both cases (in Law and in love), we are dealing with division, with a 'divided subject'; however, the modality of the division is thoroughly different. The subject of Law is 'decentred', in the sense that it is caught in the self-destructive vicious cycle of sin and Law in which one pole engenders its opposite. Paul provided an unsurpassable description of this entanglement in Romans 7:

> We know that the law is spiritual; but I am carnal, sold into slavery to sin. What I do, I do not understand. For I do not do what I want, but I do what I hate. Now if I do what I do not want, I concur that the law is good. So now it is no longer I who do it, but sin that dwells in me. For I know that good does not dwell in me, that is, in my flesh. The willing is ready at hand, but doing the good is not. For I do not do the good I want, but I do the evil I do not want. Now if I do what I do not want, it is no longer I who do it, but sin that dwells in me. So, then, I discover the principle that when I want to do right, evil is at hand. For I take delight in the law of God, in my inner self, but I see in my members another principle at war with the law of my mind, taking me captive to the law of sin that dwells in my members. Miserable one that I am!

It is thus not that I am merely torn between the two opposites, Law and sin; the problem is that I cannot even clearly distinguish them: I want to follow the law, and I end up in sin. This vicious cycle is not so much overcome as broken. One breaks out of it with the experience of love, more precisely with the experience of the radical gap that separates love from Law. Therein resides the radical difference between the couple Law/sin and the couple Law/love. The gap that separates Law and sin is not a real difference: their truth is their mutual implication or confusion. Law generates sin and feeds on it. It is only with the couple Law/love that we see a real difference: these two moments are radically separate, they are not 'mediated', one is not the form of its opposite. It is therefore wrong to ask: 'Are we then forever condemned to the split between Law and love? What about the synthesis between Law and love?' The split between Law and sin is radically different from the split between Law and love: instead of a vicious cycle of mutual reinforcement, we get a distinction of two different domains which simply do not exist at the same level. This is why, once we become fully aware of the dimension of love in its radical difference from the Law, love has in a way already won, since this difference is visible only from the standpoint of love.

The point of this theological excursion should be clear now: the endless struggle between liberal permissiveness and fundamentalist intolerance functions in a way that is homologous to the split between Law and sin – in both cases, the two poles implicate and strengthen each other; their antagonism is constitutive of our predicament. Moreover, the distinction between Law and love is homologous to the distinction between the totality of the existing global capitalist universe (whose immanent political antagonism is the one between liberal democracy and fundamentalism) and the radical emancipatory (Communist) idea of stepping out of it.

The difference between liberalism and the radical Left is that, although they refer to the same three elements (the liberal centre, the populist Right, and the radical Left), they locate them in a different topology: for the liberal centre, the radical Left and Right are two forms of the same 'totalitarian' excess, while for the Left, the only true alternative is the one between itself and the liberal mainstream, with the populist 'radical' Right as nothing but the *symptom* of liberalism's inability to deal with the Leftist threat. When we hear today's politicians or ideologists offering us a choice between liberal freedom and fundamentalist oppression, and triumphantly asking a (purely rhetorical) question 'Do you want women to be excluded from public life and deprived of their elementary rights? Do you want everyone who mocks religion to be punished by death?', what should make us suspicious is the very self-evidence of the answer – who would ever want *that*? The problem is that such a simplistic liberal universalism lost its innocence long ago. This is why, for a true Leftist, the conflict between liberal permissiveness and fundamentalism is ultimately a *false* conflict – a vicious cycle of two poles generating and presupposing each other. One should take a Hegelian step back and question the very measure from which fundamentalism appears in all its horror. What Max Horkheimer said about Fascism and capitalism back in the 1930s (those who do not want to talk critically about capitalism should also keep quiet about Fascism) can be applied to today's fundamentalism: those who do not want to talk (critically) about liberal democracy and its noble principles should also keep quiet about religious fundamentalism.

How are we to understand this reversal of an emancipatory thrust into fundamentalist populism? Reacting to the well-known characterization of Marxism as 'the Islam of the twentieth century', which secularizes Islam's abstract fanaticism, Jean-Pierre Taguieff wrote that Islam is turning out to be 'the Marxism of the twenty-first century', prolonging, after the decline of Communism, its violent anti-capitalism.[14] But don't the recent vicissitudes of Muslim fundamentalism confirm Walter Benjamin's old insight that 'every rise of Fascism bears witness to a failed revolution'[15]? The rise of Fascism is not only the Left's failure, but also proof that there was a revolutionary potential, a dissatisfaction, which the Left was not able to mobilize. And does the same not hold for today's so-called 'Islamo-Fascism'? Is the rise of radical Islamism not exactly correlative to the disappearance of the secular Left in Muslim countries? When Afghanistan is portrayed as the utmost Islamic fundamentalist country, who still remembers that, forty years ago, it was a country with a strong secular tradition and a powerful Communist party which took power there independently of the Soviet Union?

Even in the case of clearly fundamentalist movements, one should be careful not to miss the social component. The Taliban are regularly presented as a fundamentalist Islamist group enforcing its rule with terror – however, when, in the spring of 2009, they took over the Swat valley in Pakistan, the *New York Times* reported that they engineered 'a class revolt that exploits profound fissures between a small group of wealthy landlords and their landless tenants'. The ideological bias of the *New York Times* article is discernible in how it speaks of the Taliban's 'ability to exploit class divisions', as if the Taliban's 'true' agenda is elsewhere – in religious fundamentalism – and they are merely 'taking advantage' of the plight of the poor landless farmers. To this, one should simply add two things. First, such a distinction between the 'true' agenda and instrumental manipulation is externally imposed on the Taliban – as if the poor landless farmers themselves do not experience their plight in 'fundamentalist religious' terms! Second, if, by 'taking advantage' of the farmers' plight, the Taliban are 'raising alarm about the risks to Pakistan, which remains largely feudal', what prevents liberal democrats in Pakistan as well as in the US similarly 'taking advantage' of this plight and trying to help the landless farmers? The sad implication of the fact that this obvious question is not raised in the *New York Times* report is that the feudal forces in Pakistan are the 'natural ally' of the liberal democracy.[16]

This is the truly ominous lesson of the Egyptian revolt: if moderate liberal forces continue to ignore the radical Left, they will generate an insurmountable fundamentalist wave. In order for the key liberal legacy to survive, liberals need the fraternal help of the radical Left. Although (almost) everyone enthusiastically supported these democratic explosions, there is a hidden struggle for their appropriation. Official circles and most of the media in the West celebrate them as the same thing as the 'pro-democracy' velvet revolutions in Eastern Europe: a desire for Western liberal democracy, a desire to become like the West. This is why uneasiness arises when one sees that there is something else at work in these protests: a demand for social justice. This struggle for re-appropriation is not only a question of interpretation, but has crucial practical consequences. We shouldn't be too fascinated by the sublime moments of national unity. The key question is: what happens the day after? How will this emancipatory explosion be translated into a new social order? As we have noted, in the last decades we witnessed a whole series of emancipatory popular explosions which were re-appropriated by the global capitalist order, either in its liberal form (from South Africa to Philippines) or in its fundamentalist form (Iran). We should not forget that none of the Arab countries where popular uprisings have happened is formally democratic: they were all more or less authoritarian, so that the demand for social and economic justice was spontaneously integrated into the demand for democracy, as if poverty was the result of the greed and corruption of those in power, and it was enough to get rid of them. What happens is that we get democracy, but poverty remains – what to do *then*?

This brings us back to the basic question: was the ecstatic unity of the people on Tahrir Square just an imaginary illusion mercilessly dispelled in the aftermath? Do the events in Egypt not confirm Hegel's claim that, when a political movement wins, the price of victory is that the movement splits into antagonistic factions? Was the anti-Mubarak unity a fiction that concealed the underlying true antagonism between pro-Western secular modernizers (members of the growing middle class) and Islamic fundamentalists with support mostly from the lower classes? In other words, are we seeing a class struggle with a twist?

It is true that there is something of an imaginary unity in the first climax of the revolt, when all groups are united in the rejection of the tyrant. However, there is more in this unity than imaginary ideological illusion – every radical revolt by definition contains a Communist dimension, a dream of solidarity and egalitarian justice that reaches beyond the narrow sphere of politics into economy, private life and culture, permeating the entire social edifice. There is a properly dialectical movement of reversals at work here. In the initial revolt, we have the all-encompassing unity of the people, and here already unity coincides with division (the division between the people and those who still work for the tyrant). Only when the tyrant is overthrown does the true work begin, the work of radical social transformation. In this period, everyone is formally for the revolution, but the efforts of those who want 'revolution without revolution' (Robespierre) are aimed at convincing people that the revolution is over, that, once the tyrant has fallen, life can return to normal (this is what the army in Egypt stands for today). At this moment, when everyone is for the revolution, one has to insist on the harsh division between those who really want a revolution and those who want a 'revolution without revolution'. Let us return to Martin Luther King: to put it in Badiou's terms, King followed the 'axiom of equality' well beyond the topic of racial segregation, and his readiness to pursue that work makes him a true fighter for emancipation. This is what Badiou means by his statement that a true Idea is something that divides, that permits us to draw a line of division: in a true Idea, universality and division are two sides of the same coin.

Communism is such an Idea that divides. In authoritarian right-wing countries, all those who fight (no matter how peacefully) for democracy, freedom, justice and other liberal goals, were (and in some cases still are) denounced as Communists or as gullible ignorants manipulated by Communists, the highest enemy of the state. The elementary liberal reaction to such accusations is denial: 'No, we are just sincere fighters for freedom and democracy, and since you (those in power) are really against freedom and democracy but are not ready to admit this publicly, you accuse us nonsensically of Communism.' But what if the Rightists who denounce those who fight for freedom as undercover Communists are ultimately right? What if, in a situation of intense emancipatory struggle when opportunists are afraid of the explosion of popular rage and tend to enact a compromise with the Right in power, the Communists are the only ones who unconditionally defend freedom and justice against authoritarian power? So, after rejecting such accusations ('Me, a Communist? Are you crazy? We are just consequent liberals!'), a moment arrives when the only consequent reaction is to accept the accusations: 'YES, so what, we *are* Communists, you pushed us into it!' Furthermore, when Communists have to resort to duplicitous language in conditions when direct self-designation as 'Communist' is impossible (censored), one should not fear and reject such displacements ('true democracy', 'justice', and so on, instead of 'Communism') as a dangerous compromise blurring the true line of struggle: they are useful because they expand the field of our struggle and allow us to appropriate/ hegemonize into it struggles for justice, freedom and equality.

This is why every revolution has to be repeated. It is only after the first enthusiastic unity disintegrates that true universality can be formulated, a universality no longer sustained by imaginary illusions. It is only after the initial unity of the people falls apart that the real work begins, the hard work of assuming all the implications of the struggle for an egalitarian and just society. It is not enough simply to get rid of the tyrant; the society which gave birth to the tyrant has to be thoroughly transformed. Only those who are ready to engage in this hard work remain faithful to the radical core of the initial enthusiastic unity. This hard work of fidelity is the process of dividing, of drawing the line that separates the Idea of Communism from those imaginary illusions about solidarity and unity that remain within the ideological confines of the existing order. Such patient clarification is the proper revolutionary work. While, for its opponents, such activity is an attempt to 'manipulate' people, to seduce well-meaning protesters into a dangerous violent radicalization, imputing to them what they never really wanted, for a proper revolutionary it is nothing more than the bringing out of the consequences and implications of the original ecstatic event: you want real justice and solidarity? Here is what you will have to do. No wonder that genuine revolutionary moments are so rare: no teleology guarantees them; they hinge on whether there is a political agent able to seize a (contingent, unpredictable) opening.

Back to Egypt, the parallel we should draw is between the Egyptian uprising and the failed Green Revolution that took place in Iran in 2011. The green colour adopted by the supporters of the illegally defeated presidential candidate Mousavi, the cries of 'Allahu akbar!' that resonated from the roofs of Tehran in the evening darkness, clearly indicated that they saw their activity as the repetition of the Khomeini revolution of 1979, as the return to its roots, the undoing of the revolution's later corruption. This return to the roots was not only programmatic. It it concerned even more the mode of activity of the crowds: the emphatic unity of the people, their all-encompassing solidarity, the creative self-organization, the improvisation of ways to articulate protest, the unique mixture of spontaneity and discipline, like the ominous march of thousands in complete silence. We were dealing with a genuine popular uprising of the deceived partisans of the Khomeini revolution: Mousavi's name stood for the genuine resuscitation of the popular dream that sustained the revolution. What this means is that the Khomeini revolution cannot be reduced to a hardline Islamist takeover – it was much more. The very fact that this explosion had to be stifled demonstrates that the Khomeini revolution was an authentic political event, a momentary *opening* that unleashed unheard-of forces of social transformation, a moment in which everything seemed possible. What followed was a gradual *closing*, through the take-over of political control by the Islamic establishment.

As we used to say almost half a century ago, one doesn't have to be a weatherman to know which way the wind blows in Egypt: towards Iran. Even if the army wins and stabilizes the situation, this very victory can breed an eruption similar to the Khomeini revolution which will sweep over Egypt in a couple of years – but will this one also be taken over by Muslim fundamentalists? What can save us from this prospect is only the unity of the struggle for freedom and democracy with the struggle for social and economic justice. This unity, and only this unity, is the universal goal.

DEMANDS . . . AND MORE

In his early writings, Marx described the German situation as one in which the solution of particular problems was possible only through the universal solution: radical global revolution. Therein resides the most succinct formula of the difference between a reformist and a revolutionary period: in a reformist period, global revolution remains a dream which in the best case sustains our attempts to enact local changes (and in the worst case prevents us from enforcing actual changes), while a revolutionary situation arises when it becomes clear that only a radical global change can resolve particular problems. In this purely formal sense, 1990 was a revolutionary year: it became clear that partial reforms of the Communist states would not do the job, that a radical global break was necessary to resolve even partial problems such as adequate food supply.

So where do we stand today with regard to this difference? The basic dilemma is a simple and brutal one: are the protests that have been taking place in the past few years signs of a global crisis that is gradually yet inexorably approaching, or are they just minor obstacles that can be contained, if not resolved, through precise interventions, merely local troubles in a global readjustment to a new progressive epoch?

The most uncanny and ominous thing about the protests is that they are not exploding only, or even primarily, at the weak points of the system, but in places which were until recently perceived as success stories. Trouble in hell seems understandable – we know why people are protesting in Greece or Spain; but why is there trouble in Paradise, in prosperous countries or at least fast-developing countries like Turkey, Brazil or even Sweden (where we've recently seen violent protests by immigrants who live in the suburbs)? In hindsight, we can now see that the original 'trouble in Paradise' was the Khomeini revolution in Iran, a country which was officially thriving, on the fast track to pro-Western modernization, and the West's staunchest ally in the region. Maybe there is something wrong with our notion of Paradise.

Before the current wave of protests, Turkey was hot – a model thriving liberal economy combined with moderate Islamism with a human face, fit for Europe, a welcome contrast to the more 'European' Greece caught in an old ideological quagmire and bent on economic self-destruction. True, there were some ominous signs here and there (the ongoing denial of the Armenian holocaust, the arrest and accusation of hundreds of journalists, the unresolved status of the Kurds, calls for a Great Turkey which would resuscitate the tradition of the Ottoman empire, the occasional imposition of religious legislation), but all these were dismissed as small stains that should not be allowed to taint the overall picture. This was a country in which the last thing one would have expected was widespread protests – they simply should not have happened.

Then, the unexpected happened – the Taksim Square protests exploded. Everyone knows that the planned transformation of a park that borders on Taksim Square in central Istanbul into a shopping centre was not what the protests were 'really about', that a much deeper unease was gaining strength beneath the surface. It is the same with the protests that erupted in Brazil in mid June 2013: what triggered those was a small rise in the price of public transport, but they went on even after this measure was rolled back. Again, the protests exploded in a country which – according to the media, at least – was in the midst of an economic boom, enjoying high confidence in its future. Adding to the mystery is the fact that the protests were immediately supported by the President, Dilma Rousseff, who said she was 'delighted' by them – so who are the true targets of the protesters' unease about corruption and disintegration of public services?

In short, hot Turkey all of a sudden became cold Turkey. So what were the protests really about? It is crucial not to limit the protests to the idea of the secular civil society rising against the Islamist authoritarian rule supported by the Muslim silent majority. What complicates the picture is the anti-capitalist thrust of the protests (privatization of public space) – the key axis of the Turkish protests was the link between authoritarian Islamism and free market privatization of public space. This link is what makes the case of Turkey so interesting and far reaching: the protesters intuitively sensed that market freedom and religious fundamentalism are not mutually exclusive, that they can work hand in hand – a clear sign that the 'eternal' marriage between democracy and capitalism is nearing divorce.

The paradox is that, precisely because it lacks democratic legitimacy, an authoritarian regime can sometimes be more responsible towards its subjects than one that was democratically elected: since it lacks democratic legitimacy, it has to legitimize itself by providing services to the citizens, with the underlying reasoning, 'True, we are not democratically elected, but as such, since we do not have to play the game of striving for cheap popularity, we can focus on citizens' real needs.' A democratically elected government, on the contrary, can fully exert its power for the narrow private interests of its members; they already have the legitimacy provided by elections, so they don't need any further legitimization and can feel safe doing what they want – they can say to those who complain, 'You elected us, now it's too late.'

One should avoid essentialism here: there is not a single 'real' goal pursued by protesters, something to which the general feeling of unease can be reduced. We cannot say that the protests are really against global capitalism, against religious fundamentalism, for civil freedoms and democracy. What the majority of those who have participated in the protests are aware of is a fluid feeling of unease and discontent which sustains and unites particular demands. Here again, Hegel's motto 'The secrets of the ancient Egyptians were secrets also for the Egyptians themselves' fully holds for today's Egyptians: the struggle for the interpretation of the protests is not just an 'epistemological' struggle, the struggle of journalists and theorists about the true content of the protests; it is also an 'ontological' struggle, a struggle which concerns the thing itself, a struggle that goes on in the very heart of the protests themselves: is it just a struggle against corrupt city administration? Is it a struggle against authoritarian Islamist rule? Is it a struggle against the privatization of public space? The outcome is open; it will be the result of the ongoing political process.

The same goes for the spatial dimension of protests. Already in 2011, when protests were erupting all around Europe and the Middle East, many observers insisted that one should not treat them as moments of the same global protest movement, that each of them reacted to a specific situation: in Egypt, protesters demanded freedom and democracy, something that societies in which the Occupy movement exploded already had; even in Muslim countries, the Arab Spring in Egypt was fundamentally different from the Green Revolution in Iran because the former was directed against a corrupted pro-Western authoritarian regime, while the latter was directed against authoritarian Islamism. It is easy to see how such a particularization of protests helps the defenders of the existing global order: there is no threat against the global order as such, just specific local problems.

Here, however, one should resuscitate the good old Marxist notion of *totality*, in this case, of the totality of global capitalism. Global capitalism is a complex process which affects different countries in different ways, and what unites protests in their multifariousness is that they are all reactions against different facets of capitalist globalization. The general tendency of today's global capitalism is towards further expansion of the reign of the market, combined with progressive enclosure of public space, diminishing of public services (health, education, culture) and rising authoritarianism. It is within this context that Greeks are protesting against the rule of international financial capital and their own corrupt and inefficient state, which is less and less able to provide basic social services, that Turks are protesting against the commercialization of public space and religious authoritarianism, that Egyptians protested against a corrupt authoritarian regime supported by Western powers, that Iranians protested against corrupt and inefficient religious fundamentalism, and so on. What unites these protests is that none of them can be reduced to a single issue: they all deal with a specific combination of (at least) two issues, a more or less radical economic one (from corruption and inefficiency to outright anti-capitalism) and a politico-ideological one (from demands for democracy to demands for overthrowing standard multiparty democracy). And does the same not hold already for the Occupy Wall Street movement? Beneath the profusion of (often confused) statements, the Occupy movement has had two basic insights: (1) the discontent with capitalism *as a system* – the problem is the capitalist system as such, not its particular corruption; (2) the awareness that the institutionalized form of representative multiparty democracy is not enough to fight capitalist excesses, i.e., that democracy has to be reinvented.

Global capitalism tends to reduce the commons to *res nullius*, which in Roman law designates anything that can be owned, even a slave (as opposed to a citizen), but which is not yet the object of the rights of any specific subject – such things are considered ownerless property, 'free to be owned'. The paradoxical expression 'ownerless property' indicates the ideological operation that underlies the notion of *res nullius*: it is as if things that are not yet owned are already potentially owned, as if being-a-property is already inscribed into their being (the same as in patriarchal ideology where a non-married woman is a kind of 'ownerless property' waiting to be 'owned' by a husband). In international law, *res nullius* is called *terra nullius*: a state may assert control of an unclaimed territory and gain control when one of its citizens (often on an exploratory and/or military expedition) enters it. This notion predictably justified colonization: already back in the early sixteenth century, the Church proclaimed large parts of America and Africa *terra nullius*, claiming that even though indigenous peoples resided in these newly discovered lands, it was the right of civilized Christian nations to occupy them and put them to good use.

This, of course, does not mean that, since the true underlying cause of the protests is global capitalism, the only solution is to overthrow it. The very alternative of pragmatically dealing with particular problems ('people are dying now in Rwanda, so forget about the anti-imperialist struggle, let us just prevent the slaughter') and patiently waiting for a radical transformation is a false one because it ignores the fact that global capitalism is necessarily inconsistent: market freedom goes hand in hand with the US supporting its own farmers, preaching democracy goes hand in hand with supporting Saudi Arabia. This inconsistency, this need to break one's own rules, opens up a space for genuine political interventions: since inconsistency is necessary, since the global capitalist system has to violate its own rules (free-market competition, democracy), to insist on consistency, i.e., on the principles of the system itself, at strategically selected points at which the system cannot afford to follow its principles, leads to a challenge to the entire system. In other words, the art of politics resides in insisting on a particular demand which, while thoroughly realistic, disturbs the very core of hegemonic ideology and implies a much more radical change because it may be definitely feasible and legitimate but it is *de facto* impossible. Obama's proposal for universal healthcare was such a case: although it was a modest, realistic proposal, it obviously disturbed the core of American ideology. In today's Turkey, a simple demand for actual multicultural tolerance (which is endorsed as a self-evident principle in most of Western Europe) has an explosive potential. In Greece, a reasonable call for a more efficient and non-corrupt state apparatus, if meant seriously, implies a total overhaul of the state. This is why there is no analytic value in blaming neoliberalism for our particular woes: today's world order is a concrete totality within which specific situations ask for specific acts. A measure (say, the defence of human rights) which is in general a liberal platitude, can lead to explosive developments in a specific context.

The motto of much of today's radical Left might be: 'We have to be outside. This is a postmodern idea. The idea is that I must subtract myself from the game of power.'[17] This stance is typical of contemporary French Leftist political thought, which is focusing on the state and its apparatuses: the radical emancipatory struggle is a struggle which should be led at a distance from the state, ultimately against it. (It is here that one should also apply Hegel's lesson about *absoluter Gegenstoss*: it is this very resistance to the state which constitutes the state as its point of reference.) What one tends to forget here is the Marxist insight, which holds today more than ever, that the basic antagonism that defines today's society is not the resistance against the state but the 'class struggle' *within society, at a distance from the state*. In short, the Marxist point is not directly against the state, but rather more concerned with how to change *society* so that it will no longer need a state.[18]

So, even if the emancipatory struggle begins as an opposition to state apparatuses, it has to change its target. Alain Badiou opposes a new 'affirmative' dialectics to (what he considers) the classic dialectical logic of negativity which engenders out of its own movement a new positivity. For him, the starting point of an emancipatory process should not be negativity, resistance, will to destruction, but a new affirmative vision disclosed in an Event – we oppose the existing order out of our fidelity to this event, drawing out its consequences. Without this affirmative moment, the emancipatory process ends up necessarily in imposing a new positive order which is an imitation of the old one, sometimes even radicalizing its worst features. But one should oppose to this 'affirmative' notion of dialectics the Hegelian notion of the dialectical *process* that begins with an affirmative idea towards which it strives, but in the course of which *the idea itself undergoes a profound transformation* (not just a tactical accommodation, but an essential redefinition), because the idea itself is caught in the process, (over)determined by its actualization.[19] Say we have a revolt motivated by a desire for justice: once people are truly engaged in it, they become aware that much more is needed to bring true justice than the limited requests with which they started (for instance, to repeal some laws). The problem is, of course, to know what precisely this 'much more' means. The liberal-pragmatic idea is that one can solve problems gradually, one by one. John Caputo recently wrote:

> I would be perfectly happy if the far left politicians in the United States were able to reform the system by providing universal healthcare, effectively redistributing wealth more equitably with a revised IRS code, effectively restricting campaign financing, enfranchising all voters, treating migrant workers humanely, and effecting a multilateral foreign policy that would integrate American power within the international community, etc., i.e., intervene upon capitalism by means of serious and far-reaching reforms ... If after doing all that Badiou and Zizek complained that some Monster called Capital still stalks us, I would be inclined to greet that Monster with a yawn.[20]

Mark Manolopoulos mischievously baptized this defence of capitalism 'Caputolism'.[21] The problem here is not Caputo's conclusion: if one can achieve all that within capitalism, why not stay there? The problem is the underlying premise that it is *possible* to achieve all that within the coordinates of the present global capitalism. What if the particular malfunctionings of capitalism enumerated by Caputo are not only accidental disturbances but structurally necessary? What if Caputo's dream is a dream of universality (the universal capitalist order) without its symptoms, without the critical points in which its 'repressed truth' articulates itself?

Today's protests and revolts are sustained by the overlapping of different levels, and this accounts for their strength: they fight for 'normal', parliamentary democracy against authoritarian regimes; against racism and sexism, especially against the hatred directed at immigrants and refugees; for the welfare state and against neoliberalism; against corruption in politics and economy (companies polluting the environment, for instance); and for new forms of democracy that reach beyond multi-party rituals. They question the global capitalist system as such and try to keep alive the idea of a non-capitalist society. Two traps are to be avoided here: false radicalism ('What really matters is the abolition of liberal-parliamentary capitalism, all other fights are secondary'), as well as false gradualism ('Now we fight against military dictatorship and for simple democracy, forget your socialist dreams, this comes later – maybe').

The situation is thus properly *overdetermined*, and one should shamelessly mobilize here the old Maoist distinctions between principal and secondary contradictions (or, rather, antagonisms), between the antagonism which is principal in the final analysis and the antagonism which dominates now. For example, there are concrete situations when to insist on the principal antagonism means to miss an opportunity to deal a blow for the current struggle. Only a politics which fully takes into account the whole complexity of overdetermination deserves the name of political *strategy*. When we have to deal with a specific struggle, the key question is: how will our engagement in it or disengagement from it affect other struggles? The general rule is that, when a revolt begins against an oppressive, half-democratic regime, as was the case in the Middle East in 2011, it is easy to

mobilize large crowds with slogans which one cannot but characterize as crowd-pleasers – for democracy, against corruption, and so on.
But then we gradually approach more difficult choices, when our
revolt succeeds in its direct goal, we come to realize that what really
bothered us (our unfreedom, humiliation, social corruption, lack of
the prospect of a decent life) goes on in a new guise. In Egypt, protesters got rid of the oppressive Mubarak regime, but corruption did not
disappear, and the prospect of a decent life moved even further away.
After the overthrow of an authoritarian regime, the last vestiges of
patriarchal care for the poor can fall away, so that the newly gained
freedom is *de facto* reduced to the freedom to choose the preferred
form of one's misery – the majority not only remain poor, but, to
add insult to injury, they are told that, since they are now free, poverty
is their own responsibility. In such a predicament, we have to
admit that there was a flaw in the goal itself, that this goal was not
specific enough – say, that standard political democracy can also serve
as the very form of unfreedom: political freedom can easily provide
the legal frame for economic slavery, with the underprivileged 'freely'
selling themselves into servitude. We are thus brought to demand
more than just political democracy: we need a democratization of
social and economic life. In short, we have to admit that what we
first took as the failure fully to realize a noble principle of democratic freedom is a failure inherent to this principle itself. Learning
how the distortion of a notion, its incomplete realization, is grounded
in the distortion immanent to this notion is a big step in political
education.

The ruling ideology mobilizes its entire arsenal to prevent us from
reaching this radical insight. Our rulers tell us that democratic freedom brings its own responsibility, that it comes at a price, that we are
not yet mature if we expect too much from democracy. In this way,
they blame us for our predicament: in a free society, so we are told, we
are all capitalists investing in our lives, deciding to put more into our
education than into having fun if we want to succeed. At a more directly political level, US foreign policy elaborated a detailed strategy of
how to exert damage-control by way of re-channelling a popular
uprising into acceptable parliamentary-capitalist constraints, as was
done successfully in South Africa after apartheid, in the Philippines

after the fall of Marcos, in Indonesia after the fall of Suharto, and so on. At this precise conjuncture emancipatory politics faces its greatest challenge: how to push things further after the first enthusiastic stage is over, how to take the next step without succumbing to the catastrophe of 'totalitarian' temptation – in short, how to move further from Mandela without becoming Mugabe.

In the last two decades of his life, Nelson Mandela was celebrated as a model of how to liberate a country from colonial rule without succumbing to the temptation of dictatorial power and anti-capitalist posturing. In short, Mandela was not Mugabe, and South Africa remained a multi-party democracy with a free press and a vibrant economy that was well integrated into the global market and immune to hasty socialist experiments. When his death was announced on 5 December 2013, his stature as a saintly wiseman seemed confirmed for eternity: there are Hollywood movies about him – he has been played by Morgan Freeman, whose other roles have included God and at least one US president – and rock stars and religious leaders, sportsmen and politicians, from Bill Clinton to Fidel Castro, are all united in his beatification.

But is this the whole story? Two key facts are hidden by this celebratory portrait. In South Africa, the miserable life of the poor majority remains the same as under apartheid, and the rise of political and civil rights is counterbalanced by growing insecurity, violence and crime. The main change is that the old white ruling class is joined by the new black elite. Secondly, people remember that the old African National Congress promised not only the end of apartheid, but also social justice, even a kind of socialism. This much more radical ANC past is gradually obliterated from our memory. No wonder that anger is growing among the poor black population.

South Africa is just one version of the recurrent story of the contemporary Left. A leader or a party is elected with universal enthusiasm, promising a 'new world' – but then, sooner or later, stumbles upon the key dilemma: does one dare to touch capitalist mechanisms, or does one decide to play the game? If one disturbs these mechanisms, one is very swiftly 'punished' by market perturbations, economic chaos, and the rest. This is why it is all too simple to criticize Mandela for abandoning the socialist perspective after the end of apartheid: did he really have a choice? Was the move towards socialism a real option? It is easy to ridicule Ayn Rand, but there is a grain of truth in the famous 'hymn to money' from her *Atlas Shrugged*: 'Until and unless you discover that money is the root of all good, you ask for your own destruction. When money ceases to become the means by which men deal with one another, then men become the tools of other men. Blood, whips and guns – or dollars. Take your choice – there is no other.'[22] Did Marx not say something similar when he noted that relations between people assume the guise of relations between things?[23] In the market economy, relations between people can appear as relations of mutually recognized freedom and equality: domination is no longer directly enacted and visible as such. What is problematic is Rand's underlying premise: that the only choice is between direct and indirect relations of domination and exploitation, with any alternative dismissed as utopian. However, one should nonetheless bear in mind the moment of truth in Rand's otherwise ridiculously ideological claim: the great lesson of state socialism is that the direct abolition of private property and market-regulated exchange without concrete forms of social regulation of the process of production necessarily resuscitates relations of servitude and domination. If we merely abolish the market (inclusive of market exploitation) without replacing it with a proper form of Communist organization of production and exchange, domination returns with a vengeance, and with it direct exploitation.

This obliterated dimension did emerge in the midst of the funeral ceremonies for Mandela. Our daily lives are mostly a mixture of drab routine and bad surprises – however, from time to time, something unexpected happens which cracks like lightning and makes life worth living. Something of this order occurred at the funeral ceremony for Nelson Mandela on 10 December 2013, at the big FNB stadium in Johannesburg, where tens of thousands were listening to world leaders making statements. And then ... it happened (or, rather, it was going on for some time before we noticed it). Standing alongside world dignitaries, including Barack Obama, was a black man in formal attire, an interpreter for the deaf, who was seen by millions of television viewers worldwide translating Nelson Mandela's memorial service into sign language. Those versed in sign language gradually became aware that something strange was going on: the man was a fake, he was making up his own signs, flapping his hands around, and there was no meaning in what he was doing.

A day later, an official inquiry disclosed that the man, Thamsanqa Jantjie, 34, was a qualified interpreter hired by the African National Congress. In an interview with the Johannesburg *Star*, Jantjie put his behaviour down to a sudden attack of schizophrenia, for which he takes medication. He told the newspaper that a schizophrenic episode was to blame for him gesticulating nonsense during the entire service – he couldn't focus, and started hearing voices and hallucinating. 'There was nothing I could do. I was alone in a very dangerous situation,' he said. 'I tried to control myself and not show the world what was going on. I am very sorry. It's the situation I found myself in.' Jantjie none-theless defiantly insisted that he was happy with his performance: 'Absolutely! Absolutely. What I have been doing, I think I have been a champion of sign language.' The following day brought a new, sur-prising twist: the media reported that Jantjie had been arrested at least five times since the mid 1990s, but he allegedly dodged jail because he was mentally unfit to stand trial. He was accused of rape, theft, housebreaking and malicious damage to property; his most recent brush with the law occurred in 2003 when he faced charges of murder, attempted murder and kidnapping.

Reactions to this weird episode were a mixture of laughter (which was gradually suppressed as undignified) and outrage. There were, of course, security concerns: how was it possible, despite strict security measures, for such a person to move in the proximity of world lead-ers? What lurked behind these concerns was the feeling that Jantjie's appearance was a kind of miracle, as if he popped up from nowhere, or from another dimension of reality. This feeling seemed further con-firmed by suspiciously repetitive assurances from mute and deaf organizations that Jantjie's signs had no meaning, that they corre-sponded to no existing sign language, as if to quell the suspicion that, maybe, there *was* some hidden message delivered through his ges-tures. What if he was signalling to aliens in an unknown language? Or what if – since most of the time he just stood immobile and only 'translated' speakers with rather short performances, which seemed uncannily similar to each other – he was repeatedly making a quite accurate statement in sign language: 'The speaker is just reiterating the usual pathetic *blah blah*, no need to translate the details!' Jantjie's very appearance seemed to point in this direction: there was no vivacity in his gestures, no trace of being involved in a practical joke – he was going through the motions with expressionless, almost robotic, calm.

Jantjie's performance was not meaningless – precisely because it delivered no particular meaning, it directly rendered meaning as such, the pretence of meaning. Those of us who hear well and do not understand sign language assumed that Jantjie's gestures had meaning, although we were not able to understand them. And this brings us to the crux of the matter: are sign language translators for the deaf really meant for those who cannot hear the spoken word? Are they not much more intended for us – it makes us feel good to see the interpreter for the deaf next to the speaker, giving us the politically correct satisfaction that we are doing the right thing, taking care of the underprivileged. I remember how, in the first 'free' elections in Slovenia in 1990, one of the Leftist parties produced a TV spot where the politician delivering the message was accompanied by an interpreter (a gentle young woman) translating his message into sign language. We all knew that the true addressees of her translation were not the deaf but those who could hear: the true message was that the party stood for the disabled. It was like great charity spectacles that are not really about children with cancer or victims of a flooding, but about making us, the public, aware that we are doing something good and displaying solidarity.

Now we can see why Jantjie's gesticulations had such an uncanny effect once it became clear that they were meaningless: what he confronted us with was the truth of sign-language translation – it doesn't really matter if there are any deaf people watching; the translator is here to make those of us who do not understand sign language feel good. And was this also not the truth about the Mandela funeral ceremony? All the crocodile tears of the dignitaries were a self-congratulatory exercise, and Jantjie translated them into what they actually were: nonsense. What world leaders celebrated was the successful postponement of the true crisis which will explode when the black South Africans who continue to be deprived become a collective political agent. These poor black crowds were the Absent One to whom Jantjie was signalling, and his message was: the dignitaries really don't care about you. Through his fake translation, Jantjie rendered palpable the deceptiveness of the entire ceremony.

If we want to remain faithful to Mandela's legacy, we should forget about celebratory crocodile tears and focus on the unfulfilled promises that his leadership gave rise to. We can safely surmise that, on account of his doubtless moral and political greatness, he was well aware of how his very political triumph and his elevation into a universal hero masked a bitter defeat. His universal glory is also a sign that he really didn't disturb the global order of power.

Here again, the problem is to know what, precisely, this 'much more' (to change society more than just by making it a liberal democracy) means. Everyone knows Winston Churchill's quip about democracy, usually rendered: 'Democracy is the worst possible system, except for all others.' What Churchill actually said (in the House of Commons on 11 November 1947) was slightly less paradoxical and scintillating: 'Many forms of Government have been tried, and will be tried in this world of sin and woe. No one pretends that democracy is perfect or all-wise. Indeed it has been said that democracy is the worst form of Government except for all those other forms that have been tried from time to time.'[24] The underlying logic is most clearly expressed if one applies to Churchill's dictum Lacan's 'formulae of sexuation' and rephrases it as follows: 'Democracy is the worst of all systems; however, compared to it, any other system is worse.' If one takes all possible systems as a whole and ranges them with regard to their worth, democracy is the worst and finishes at the bottom; if, however, one compares democracy one to one with all other systems, it is better than any of them.[25] Does something similar not hold (or seem to hold) for capitalism? If one analyses it in an abstract way, trying to locate it in the hierarchy of all possible systems, it appears to be the worst – chaotic, unjust, destructive. However, if one compares it in a concrete, pragmatic way to every alternative, it is still better than any of them.

This 'illogical' imbalance between the universal and the particular is a direct indication of the efficiency of ideology. An opinion poll in the US at the end of June 2012, just before the Supreme Court decision about Obama's healthcare reform, showed that 'strong majorities favour most of what is in the law': 'Most Americans oppose President Barack Obama's healthcare reform even though they strongly support most of its provisions, a Reuters/Ipsos poll showed on Sunday, with the Supreme Court set to rule within days on whether the law should stand. The survey results suggest that Republicans are convincing voters to reject Obama's reform even when they like much of what is in it, such as allowing children to stay on their parents' insurance until age 26.'[26] Here we encounter ideology at its purest: the majority wants to have its (ideological) cake and eat it too. They want the real profits of the healthcare reform, while rejecting its ideological form (which they perceive as a threat to 'freedom of choice') – they reject water, but accept H_2O, or, rather, they reject (the concept of) fruit, but they want apples, plums and strawberries.

THE FASCINATION OF SUFFERING

One way to resolve (or neutralize, at least) these confusions is by means of a direct reference to human suffering: surely we can intervene to alleviate it? However, all that is false in the idea and practice of humanitarian interventions was laid bare when it came to the example of Syria. There is a bad dictator who is using poisonous gases against his own people – but who is opposing his regime? It seems that whatever remained of the democratic-secular resistance is now more or less drowned in the mess of fundamentalist Islamist groups supported by Turkey and Saudi Arabia, with a strong presence of al-Qaida in the shadows. (Recall that, a year ago, a top Saudi cleric urged Muslim girls to go to Syria and support the rebels by offering themselves to be gang raped, since the rebels lacked sexual satisfaction!)

As to Assad, his Syria at least pretended to be a secular state, so no wonder that Christian and other minorities now tend to take his side against Sunni rebels. In short, we are dealing with an obscure conflict, vaguely resembling the Libyan revolt against Gaddafi – there are no clear political stakes, no signs of a broad emancipatory-democratic coalition, just a complex network of religious and ethnic alliances overdetermined by the influence of superpowers (the US and Western Europe on the one side, Russia and China on the other). In such conditions, any direct military intervention means political madness with incalculable risks. What if radical Islamists take over after Assad's fall? Will the US repeat their Afghanistan mistake of arming the future al-Qaida and Taliban cadres?

In such a messy situation, military intervention can only be justified by short-term, self-destructive opportunism. The moral outrage that could provide a rational cover for the compulsion to intervene ('We cannot allow the use of poisonous gases on civilians!') is fake and obviously doesn't even take itself seriously. (As we now know, the US more than tolerated the use of poisonous gases against the Iranian army by Saddam Hussein, providing him with satellite shots of the enemies to help him – where were moral concerns then?) Faced with the weird ethics that justifies taking the side of one fundamentalist criminal group against another, one cannot but sympathize with Ron Paul's reaction to John McCain's advocacy of strong intervention: 'With politicians like these, who needs terrorists?'[27]

The struggle in Syria is thus ultimately a false one, a conflict towards which one should remain indifferent. The only thing to keep in mind is that this pseudo-struggle thrives because of the absent Third, a strong radical-emancipatory opposition, whose elements were clearly perceptible in Egypt. Nothing really special is going on in Syria, except that China is one step closer to becoming the world's new superpower while her competitors are eagerly weakening each other.

But, again, what about the humanitarian aspect, the suffering of millions? Often, one cannot but be shocked by the excessive indifference towards suffering, even and especially when this suffering is widely reported in the media and condemned, as if it is the very outrage at suffering which turns us into its immobilized, fascinated spectators. Recall, in the early 1990s, the three-year-long siege of Sarajevo, with the population starving, exposed to permanent shelling and snipers' fire. The big enigma here is: although the media was full of pictures and reports, why did the UN forces, NATO, or the US not accomplish just the small act of *breaking the siege of Sarajevo*, of imposing a corridor through which people and provisions could move freely? It would have cost nothing: with a little bit of serious pressure on Serbian forces, the prolonged spectacle of an encircled Sarajevo, exposed to a daily dose of terror, would have been over. (In a similar case, Radovan Karadzic once mentioned in an interview how surprised he was that NATO forces did not cut the Serbian territory in Bosnia in two: the only passage between the eastern and the western part was a narrow track which could have been easily occupied by a small paratroop unit of NATO, and the much larger western part of the Serb territory in Bosnia would have been suffocated and lost. One should also note what Karadzic said at the beginning of the post-Yugoslav war: what Serbs in Bosnia want is half the territory with less than 10 per cent of non-Serbs in it – and that's what they got in Dayton!) There is only one answer to this enigma, the one proposed by Rony Brauman who, on behalf of the Red Cross, coordinated the help to Sarajevo: the very presentation of the crisis of Sarajevo as 'humanitarian', the very recasting of the political-military conflict into humanitarian terms, was sustained by an eminently *political* choice (basically, taking the Serb side in the conflict):

> The celebration of 'humanitarian intervention' in Yugoslavia took the place of a political discourse, disqualifying in advance all conflicting debate ... It was apparently not possible, for François Mitterand, to express his analysis of the war in Yugoslavia. With the strictly humanitarian response, he discovered an unexpected source of communication or, more precisely, of cosmetics, which is a little bit the same thing ... Mitterand remained in favour of the maintenance of Yugoslavia within its borders and was persuaded that only a strong Serbian power was in the position to guarantee a certain stability in this explosive region. This position rapidly became unacceptable in the eyes of the French people. All the bustling activity and the humanitarian discourse permitted him to reaffirm the unfailing commitment of France to the Rights of Man in the end, and to mimic an opposition to Greater Serbian fascism, all in giving it free rein.[28]

This kind of sympathy for victims, which politically implies support for those who made them victims, is far from a rare exception: our very fascination with their plight immobilizes us, turning us into impassive observers and thus blocking our ability to intervene politically. Again, how are we to break the spell of such morbid fascination?

RAGE AND DEPRESSION IN
THE GLOBAL VILLAGE

A century ago, G. K. Chesterton made some useful comments about movements for radical social change:

> Let us ask ourselves first what we really do want, not what recent legal decisions have told us to want, or recent logical philosophies proved that we must want, or recent social prophecies predicted that we shall someday want ... If there is to be Socialism, let it be social; that is, as different as possible from all the big commercial departments of today. The really good journeyman tailor does not cut his coat according to his cloth; he asks for more cloth. The really practical statesman does not fit himself to existing conditions, he denounces the conditions as unfit.[29]

Such (perhaps too idealized and therefore false) consequentiality is what is conspicuously absent from the rage exploding all around Europe today – this rage, says Franco Bifo Berardi,

> is impotent and inconsequential, as consciousness and coordinated action seem beyond the reach of present society. Look at the European crisis. Never in our life have we faced a situation so charged with revolutionary opportunities. Never in our life have we been so impotent. Never have intellectuals and militants been so silent, so unable to find a way to show a new possible direction.[30]

Berardi locates the origin of this impotence in the exploding speed of the functioning of the big Other (the symbolic substance of our lives) and the slowness of human reactivity (due to culture, corporeality, diseases, and so on): 'the long-lasting neoliberal rule has eroded the cultural bases of social civilization, which was the progressive core of modernity. And this is irreversible. We have to face it.'[31] Outbursts of

impotent rage bear witness to the devastating effects of a global capitalist ideology that combines individualist hedonism with frantic,
competitive work, thereby closing the space for coordinated collective
action. Recall the great wave of protests that erupted all over Europe
in 2011, from Greece and Spain to London and Paris. Even if there
was hardly any consistent political programme mobilizing the protesters, these demonstrations did function as part of a large-scale
educational process: the protesters' misery and discontent were transformed into a great collective act of mobilization – hundreds of
thousands gathered in public squares, proclaiming that they had had
enough, that things could not go on like that. However, although such
protests constitute as universal political subjects the individuals who
participate in them, they remain at the level of purely formal universality. What these protests stage is a purely negative gesture of angry
rejection and an equally abstract demand for justice, lacking the ability to translate this demand into a concrete political programme. In
short, these protests were not yet proper political acts, but rather
abstract demands addressed at an Other who is expected to act. What
can be done in such a situation, where demonstrations and even
democratic elections are of no use? Only withdrawal, passivity, and
abandonment of illusions can open a new way: 'Only self-reliant
communities leaving the field of social competition can open a way to
a new hope.'[32]

One cannot but note the cruel irony of this contrast between
Berardi and Hardt/Negri. Hardt/Negri celebrate 'cognitive capitalism'
as opening up a path towards 'absolute democracy,' since the object,
the 'stuff', of immaterial work, is increasingly made up of social relations: 'What the multitude produces is not just goods or services; the
multitude also and most importantly produces cooperation, communication, forms of life, and social relationships.'[33] In short, immaterial
production is directly biopolitical, the production of social life. Marx
has emphasized that material production is always also the (re)pro-
duction of the social relations within which it occurs; with today's
capitalism, however, the production of social relations is the immediate end/goal of production: 'Such new forms of labour . . . present
new possibilities for economic self-management, since the mechanisms of cooperation necessary for production are contained in the

labour itself.'[34] The wager of Hardt and Negri is that this directly socialized, immaterial production not only renders owners progressively superfluous (who needs them when production is directly social, both in form and content?); the producers also master the regulation of social space, since social relations (politics) *is* the stuff of their work: economic production becomes political production, the production of society itself. This opens the way for 'absolute democracy', allowing the producers directly to regulate their social relations, bypassing democratic representation. The illusion at work here was succinctly formulated by Althusser when he noted how Marx never managed to relinquish the 'mythical idea of Communism as *a mode of production without relations of production*; in Communism, the free development of individuals takes the place of social relations in the mode of production.'[35] Is this idea of Communism 'as a mode of production without relations of production' also not what motivates Negri and Hardt? When social relations (inclusive of relations of production) are directly produced by social production, they are no longer social relations proper (i.e., a structural frame, given in advance, within which social production takes place), but become directly planned and produced and, as such, totally transparent. This stance finds its clearest expression in the accelerationist movement based on the premise that the only radical political response to capitalism is not to protest, disrupt or critique it, not to resist it on behalf of ancient forms of communal life threatened by the capitalist disruptive power, not to await its demise at the hands of its own contradictions, but to accelerate its uprooting, alienating, decoding, abstractive tendencies.[36]

Berardi's conclusion is exactly the opposite: far from bringing out the potential transparency of social life, today's 'cognitive capitalism' makes it more impenetrable than ever, undermining the very subjective conditions of any form of collective solidarity of the 'cognitariat'.[37] What is symptomatic here is the way the same conceptual apparatus leads to two radically opposed conclusions. Berardi warns us against what he calls the Deleuzian 'gospel of hyper-dynamic deterritorialization' – for him, if we are not able to step outside the compulsion of the system, the gap between the frantic dynamics imposed by the system and our corporeal and cognitive limitations sooner or later can lead to depression.

Berardi makes this point apropos Felix Guattari, his friend who preached the theoretical gospel of hyper-dynamic deterritorialization while personally suffering long bouts of depression:

> Actually the problem of depression and of exhaustion is never elaborated in an explicit way by Guattari. I see here a crucial problem of the theory of desire: the denial of the problem of limits in the organic sphere ... The notion of the 'body without organs' hints at the idea that the organism isn't something that you can define, that the organism is a process of exceeding, of going beyond a threshold, of 'becoming other'. This is a crucial point, but it's also a dangerous point ... What body, what mind is going through transformation and becoming? Which invariant lies under the process of becoming other? If you want to answer this question you have to acknowledge death, finitude, and depression.[38]

Depression, finitude, and exhaustion are not empirico-psychological categories, but indications of a basic ontological limitation. When Berardi talks of depression, it is with regard to interpellation proper, i.e. a reaction of the human animal to the Cause which addresses us, specifically with regard to late-capitalist interpellation, but *also* with regard to emancipatory mobilization. The critique of political representation as a passivizing alienation (instead of allowing others to speak for them, people should directly organize themselves into associations) reaches here its limit. The idea of organizing society in its entirety as a network of associations is a utopia which obfuscates a triple impossibility:[39]

– there are numerous cases in which representing (speaking for) others is a necessity; it is cynical to say that victims of mass violence from Auschwitz to Rwanda (and the mentally ill, children, etc., not to mention the suffering animals) should organize themselves and speak for themselves;
– when we effectively get a mass mobilization of hundreds of thousands of people self-organizing themselves horizontally (Tahrir Square, Gezi Park ...), we should never forget that they remain a minority, and that the silent majority remains outside, non-represented

(This is how, in Egypt, this silent majority defeated the Tahrir Square crowd and elected the Muslim Brotherhood);

– permanent political engagement has a limited time-span: after a couple of weeks or, rarely, months, the majority disengages, and the problem is to safeguard the results of the uprising at this moment, when things return to normal.

Does this imply a resigned surrender to the hegemonic power structure? No. There is nothing inherently 'conservative' in being tired of the usual radical Leftist demands for permanent mobilization and active participation, demands which follow the superego logic – the more we obey them, the more we are guilty. The battle has to be won *here*, in the domain of citizens' passivity, when things return back to normal the morning after ecstatic revolts; it is (relatively) easy to have a big ecstatic spectacle of sublime unity, but how will ordinary people feel the difference in their daily lives? No wonder conservatives like to see sublime explosions from time to time – they remind people that nothing can really change, that things return to normal the day after.

And there's more: nature itself is today in disorder, not because it overwhelms our cognitive capacities but primarily because we are not able to master the effects of our own interventions in its course – who knows what the ultimate consequences of our biogenetic engineering or of global warming will be? The surprise comes from ourselves and it concerns the opacity of how we fit into the picture. It is against this background that one should understand Jacques-Alain Miller's thesis: '*Il y a un grand désordre dans le réel*' ('There is a great disorder in the real').[40] That's how Miller characterizes the way reality appears to us as we experience the full impact of two fundamental agents: modern science and capitalism. Nature as the real in which everything, from the stars to the sun, always returns to its proper place, as the realm of large, reliable cycles and of stable laws regulating them is being replaced by a thoroughly contingent real, a real outside the Law, a real that is permanently revolutionizing its own rules, a real that resists any inclusion into a totalized World (universe of meaning), which is why Badiou characterized capitalism as the first world-less civilization.

How should we react to this constellation? Should we assume a defensive approach and search for a new limit, a return to (or, rather, the invention of) some new balance? This is what bioethics endeavours to do with regard to biotechnology and why the two form a couple: biotechnology pursues new possibilities of scientific interventions (genetic manipulations, cloning), and bioethics imposes moral limitations on what biotechnology enables us to do. As such, bioethics is not immanent to scientific practice; it intervenes into this practice from the outside, imposing external morality onto it. But isn't bioethics precisely the betrayal of the ethics immanent to scientific endeavour, the ethics of 'do not compromise your scientific desire, but inexorably follow its path'? The slogan of the Porto Allegro protesters, 'A new world is possible', also proposes a new limit and, at this point, even ecology offers itself as the provider of a new limit ('We cannot go further in our exploitation of nature, nature will not tolerate it, it will collapse'). Or should we follow the above-mentioned opposite path (of Deleuze and Negri, among others) and posit that capitalist disorder is still too much order, obeying the capitalist law of the surplus-value appropriation, so that the task is not to limit it but to push it beyond its limitation? In other words, should we risk a paraphrase of Mao's well-known motto: there is disorder in the real, so the situation is excellent? Perhaps the path to follow is this one, although not in exactly the sense advocated by Deleuze and Negri in their celebration of deterritorialization? Miller claims that the pure lawless Real resists symbolic grasp, so that we should always be aware that our attempts to conceptualize it are mere semblances, defensive elucubrations – but what if there is still an underlying *order* that generates this disorder, a matrix that provides its coordinates? This is what also accounts for the repetitive sameness of the capitalist dynamics: the more things change, the more they stay the same. And this is also why the obverse of breathtaking capitalist dynamics is a clearly recognizable order of hierarchic domination.

MAMIHLAPINATAPEI

We should follow T. J. Clark[41] in his rejection of the eschatological notion of the Future which Marxism inherited from the Christian tradition, and whose most concise version is rendered by Hölderlin's well-known lines: 'But where danger is, grows the saving power also.' Perhaps, therein resides the lesson of the terrifying experiences of the Left in the twentieth century, the experience which compels us to return from Marx back to Hegel, i.e., from Marxist revolutionary eschatology back to Hegel's tragic vision of a history which forever remains radically open, since the historical process always redirects our activity in an unexpected direction. Perhaps the Left should learn fully to assume the basic 'alienation' of the historical process: we cannot control the consequences of our acts – not because we are just puppets in the hands of some secret Master or Fate which pulls the strings, but for precisely the opposite reason: there is no big Other, no agent of total accountability that can take into account the consequences of our own acts. This acceptance of 'alienation' in no way entails a cynical distance; it implies a fully engaged position aware of the risks involved – there is no higher historical Necessity whose instruments we are and which guarantees the final outcome of our interventions. From this standpoint, our despair at the present deadlock appears in a new light: we have to renounce the very eschatological scheme which underlies our despair. There will never be a Left that magically transforms confused revolts and protests into one big consistent Project of Salvation; all we have is our activity, open to all the risks of contingent history. Franco Berardi made this point poignantly apropos the ongoing events in Greece: 'I reject every consideration of ongoing events. In a way I consciously reject the possibility that the present world can be rendered better since we have to be without any hope if we want to see new possibilities.'[42]

Does this mean that we should simply abandon the topic (and experience) of 'living in the end time', of approaching the apocalyptic point of no return when 'things cannot go on like this any longer'? That we should replace it with the happy, liberal-progressive, 'post-metaphysical' view of modest, risky but cautious pragmatic interventions? No, the thing to do is to separate apocalyptic experience from eschatology: we are now approaching a certain zero-point – ecologically, economically, socially – things will change, and the change will be most radical if we do nothing, but there is no eschatological turn ahead pointing towards the act of global Salvation. In politics, an authentic Event is not the Event traditional Marxists are waiting for (the big Awakening of the revolutionary Subject), but something that occurs as an unexpected side-event. Remember how, just months before the 1917 revolutionary upheaval in Russia, Lenin gave a speech to the Swiss socialist youth where he told them that their generation may be the first one to witness a socialist revolution, in a couple of decades.

So let us conclude by going back to the protests in two neighbouring countries, Greece and Turkey. At first glance, they may seem to be entirely different: Greece is caught in the ruinous politics of austerity, while Turkey enjoys an economic boom and is emerging as a new regional superpower. But what if each Turkey generates and contains its own Greece, its own islands of misery? In one of his 'Hollywood Elegies', Brecht wrote about this village, as he calls it:

> The village of Hollywood was planned according to the notion
> People in these parts have of heaven. In these parts
> They have come to the conclusion that God
> Requiring a heaven and a hell, didn't need to
> Plan two establishments but
> Just the one: heaven. It
> Serves the unprosperous, unsuccessful
> As hell.[43]

Does the same not hold for today's global village, exemplarily for villages like Qatar or Dubai, with glamour for the rich and near-slavery for the immigrant workers? No wonder, then, that a closer look reveals the underlying similarity between Turkey and Greece: privatization, enclosure of public spaces, dismantling of social services, the rise of authoritarian politics (compare the threat of closing down the public TV in Greece to signs of censorship in Turkey). At this elementary level, Greek and Turkish protesters are engaged in the same struggle. The true event would thus have been to coordinate the two struggles, to reject 'patriotic' temptations, to refuse to worry about the other's worries (about Greece and Turkey as historical enemies), and to organize common manifestations of solidarity.

Perhaps, the very future of the protests depends on the ability to organize such global solidarity. The Fuengian language spoken in parts of Chile has the wonderful word *mamihlapinatapei*: a shared look between two people – say, in our case, a protesting Greek and a protesting Turk – who are both interested in contact yet neither is willing to make the first move. But someone will have to take a risk and do it. And the current events in Ukraine should also be interpreted in this light.

LENIN IN UKRAINE

In television reports on the mass protests in Kiev against the Yanukovich government, we saw again and again how enraged protesters were tearing down statues of Lenin. These furious attacks were understandable insofar as Lenin's statues functioned as a symbol of Soviet oppression, and Putin's Russia is perceived as continuing the Soviet policy of subjecting neighbouring countries to Russian domination. One should also bear in mind the precise historical moment when Lenin's statues started to proliferate throughout the Soviet Union: before 1956, Stalin's statues were much more numerous, and only in 1956, after Stalin's denunciation at the 20th Congress of the Communist Party, were Stalin's statues *en masse* replaced by Lenin's. Lenin was literally a stand-in for Stalin, as made clear by a weird thing that happened in 1962 to the front page of *Pravda*, the official Soviet daily newspaper:

> Lenin appeared on the masthead of *Pravda* in 1945 (one might speculatively suggest that he appeared there to reassert Stalin's authority over the Party – in light of the potentially disruptive force of returning soldiers, who have seen both death and bourgeois Europe, and in light of circulating myths that Lenin had warned against him on his deathbed). In 1962 – when, at the 22nd congress of the Communist Party, Stalin was publicly denounced – two images of Lenin suddenly appear on the masthead, as if the strange double-Lenin covered the missing 'other leader' who was actually never there![44]

Why then two identical profiles of Lenin printed side by side? In this weird repetition, Stalin was in a way more present than ever in his absence, since his shadowy presence was the answer to the obvious question: 'Why have two Lenins rather than one?'

There was nonetheless a deep irony in watching Ukrainians tearing down Lenin's statues as a sign of their will to break with Soviet domination and assert their national sovereignty: the golden era of Ukraine's national identity was not Tsarist Russia (where Ukrainian self-assertion as a nation was thwarted), but the first decade of the Soviet Union when they established their full national identity. Here is the Wikipedia passage on Ukraine in the 1920s:

> The civil war that eventually brought the Soviet government to power devastated Ukraine. It left over 1.5 million people dead and hundreds of thousands homeless. In addition, Soviet Ukraine had to face the famine of 1921. Seeing an exhausted Ukraine, the Soviet government remained very flexible during the 1920s. Thus, under the aegis of the Ukrainization policy pursued by the national Communist leadership of Mykola Skrypnyk, Soviet leadership encouraged a national renaissance in literature and the arts. The Ukrainian culture and language enjoyed a revival, as Ukrainization became a local implementation of the Soviet-wide policy of 'korenization' (literally *indigenization*) policy. The Bolsheviks were also committed to introducing universal healthcare, education and social-security benefits, as well as the right to work and housing. Women's rights were greatly increased through new laws designed to wipe away centuries-old inequalities. Most of these policies were sharply reversed by the early 1930s after Joseph Stalin gradually consolidated power to become the *de facto* communist party leader.

This 'indigenization' followed the principles formulated by Lenin in quite unambiguous terms:

> The proletariat cannot but fight against the forcible retention of the oppressed nations within the boundaries of a given state, and this is exactly what the struggle for the right of self-determination means. The proletariat must demand the right of political secession for the colonies and for the nations that 'its own' nation oppresses. Unless it does this, proletarian internationalism will remain a meaningless phrase; mutual confidence and class solidarity between the workers of the oppressing and oppressed nations will be impossible.[45]

Lenin remained faithful to this position to the end: immediately after the October Revolution, he engaged in a polemic with Rosa Luxemburg, who advocated allowing small nations to be given full sovereignty only if progressive forces predominated in the new state, while Lenin was for the unconditional right to secede, even if the 'bad guys' were in power in the new state. In his last struggle against Stalin's project for a centralized Soviet Union, Lenin again advocated the unconditional right of small nations to secede (in this case, Georgia was at stake), insisting on the full sovereignty of the national entities that composed the Soviet state. No wonder that, on 27 September 1922, in a letter to the members of the Politburo, Stalin openly accused Lenin of 'national liberalism'. The direction in which Stalin's wind was already blowing is clear from how Stalin proposed to enact the decision simply to proclaim the government of Soviet Russia as the government of the other five republics (Ukraine, Belarus, Azerbaijan, Armenia and Georgia):

> If the present decision is confirmed by the Central Committee of the RCP, it will not be made public, but communicated to the Central Committees of the Republics for circulation among the Soviet organs, the Central Executive Committees or the Congresses of the Soviets of the said Republics before the convocation of the All-Russian Congress of the Soviets, where it will be declared to be the wish of these Republics.[46]

The interaction of the higher authority (the Central Committee) with its base was abolished so that the higher authority could impose its will, and, to add insult to injury, this relationship was turned on its head: the Central Committee decided what the base would ask the higher authority to enact, as if it were its own wish. Recall the most conspicuous case of such re-staging from 1939, when the three Baltic states freely asked to join the Soviet Union, which granted their wish. What Stalin did in the early 1930s was thus simply a return to the pre-revolutionary policy (for example, as part of this turn, the Russian colonization of Siberia and Muslim Asia was no longer condemned as imperialist expansion, but was celebrated as the introduction of

progressive modernization that set in motion the inertia of these traditional societies). And Putin's foreign policy is a clear continuation of
this tsarist-Stalinist line. According to Putin, after the Russian Revolution of 1917 it was the turn of the Bolsheviks to damage Russian
interests:

> The Bolsheviks, for a number of reasons – may God judge them –
> added large sections of the historical South of Russia to the Republic of
> Ukraine. This was done with no consideration for the ethnic makeup of
> the population, and today these areas form the southeast of Ukraine.[47]

No wonder we now see Stalin's portraits again during military parades
and public celebrations, while Lenin has been obliterated. In a large
opinion poll from a couple of years ago, Stalin was voted the third
greatest Russian of all time, while Lenin was nowhere to be seen.
Stalin is not celebrated as a Communist, but as a restorer of Russia's
greatness after Lenin's anti-patriotic 'deviation'. Putin has recently
used the term *Novorussiya* (New Russia) for the south-eastern coun-
ties of Ukraine, resuscitating a term that had not been used since
1917. The Leninist undercurrent, although repressed, continued to
exist in the Communist underground opposition to Stalin. Communist critics of Stalinism were certainly full of illusions but, as Christopher
Hitchens has pointed out, long before Solzhenytsin 'the crucial questions about the Gulag were being asked by left oppositionists, from
Boris Souvarine to Victor Serge to C. L. R. James, in real time and at
great peril. Those courageous and prescient heretics have been somewhat written out of history (they expected far worse than that, and
often received it).'[48] This large-scale critical movement was inherent
to the Communist movement, in clear contrast to Fascism. Hitchens
writes: 'nobody can be bothered to argue much about whether fascism might have turned out better, given more propitious circumstances.
And there were no dissidents in the Nazi Party, risking their lives on
the proposition that the Führer had betrayed the true essence of
National Socialism.'[49] Precisely because of this immanent tension at
the very heart of the Communist movement, the most dangerous
place to be at the time of the terrible 1930s purges in the Soviet Union
was at the top of the *nomenklatura*: within a few years, 80 per cent of

the Central Committee and Red Army Headquarters members were shot.[50] Furthermore, one should not underestimate the totalitarian potential, as well as the outright brutality, of the White, counter-revolutionary forces during the Civil War. If they had won, says Hitchens (repeating a point already made by Trotsky),

> the common word for fascism would have been a Russian one, not an Italian one. *The Protocols of the Elders of Zion* was brought to the West by the White emigration ... Major General William Graves, who commanded the American Expeditionary Force during the 1918 invasion of Siberia (an event thoroughly airbrushed from all American textbooks), wrote in his memoirs about the pervasive, lethal anti-Semitism that dominated the Russian right wing and added, 'I doubt if history will show any country in the world during the last fifty years where murder could be committed so safely, and with less danger of punishment, than in Siberia during the reign of Kolchak.[51]

No wonder that Kolchak was recently celebrated as an honourable Russian patriot and soldier in a big biopic, *Admiral* (2008), directed by Andrei Kravchuk. And, as if echoing this dark past, the entire European neo-Fascist Right (in Hungary, France, Italy and Serbia) is firmly supporting Russia in the ongoing Ukrainian crisis, belying the official Russian presentation of the Crimean referendum as a choice between Russian democracy and Ukrainian Fascism. The ongoing events in Ukraine – the massive protests which toppled Yanukovich and his government – are thus to be understood as a defence against this dark legacy resuscitated by Putin: they were triggered by the Ukrainian government's decision to give priority to good relations with Russia over the integration of Ukraine into the European Union. Predictably, many anti-imperialist Leftists reacted to the news with their usual patronizing of the poor Ukrainians: how deluded they are, still idealizing Europe, not being able to see that Europe is in decline, and that joining the European Union would just turn Ukraine into an economic colony of Western Europe, sooner or later pushed into the position of Greece. What these Leftists ignore is that the Ukrainians were far from blind about the reality of the European Union, and were fully aware of its troubles and disparities – their message was simply that their own situation is much worse. Europe's problems are still a rich man's problems – remember that, in spite of the terrible predicament of Greece, African refugees are still arriving there *en masse*, causing the ire of self-proclaimed patriots.

Should we, then, simply support the Ukrainian side of the conflict? There is even a 'Leninist' reason to do it. In Lenin's very last writings, long after he renounced the utopia of *State and Revolution*, we can discern the contours of a modest, 'realistic' project for what the Bolshevik government should do. The economic underdevelopment and cultural backwardness of the Russian masses meant there was no way for Russia to 'pass directly to socialism'; all the Soviet power could do was to combine the moderate politics of 'state capitalism' with an intense cultural education of the inert peasant masses – *not* 'Communist propaganda' brainwashing, but simply a patient, gradual imposition of developed, civilized standards. Facts and figures reveal, writes Lenin, 'what a vast amount of urgent spadework we still have to do to reach the standard of an ordinary West European civilized country ... We must bear in mind the semi-Asiatic ignorance from which we have not yet extricated ourselves.'[52] Could we not see the Ukrainian protesters' reference to 'Europe' as the sign that their goal is also 'to reach the standard of an ordinary West European civilized country'?

But here is where things quickly get complicated: what, exactly, does the 'Europe' the Ukrainian protesters are referring to stand for? It cannot be reduced to a single idea: it includes nationalist and even Fascist elements and also the idea of what Étienne Balibar calls *égaliberté*, freedom-in-equality, the unique contribution of Europe to the global political imaginary, even if it is today more and more betrayed by European institutions and people themselves. Between these two poles, there is also a naive trust in European liberal-democratic capitalism. What Europe should see in the Ukrainian protests is its best and its worst aspects. But to see this clearly, Europe has to look outside itself, towards Ukraine.

The Ukrainian nationalist Right is one example of what is going on today from the Balkans to Scandinavia, from the US to Israel, from central Africa to India: a new Dark Age is looming, with ethnic and religious passions exploding, and Enlightenment values receding.

These passions were lurking in the dark all the time, but what is new now is the outright shamelessness of their display. In the middle of 2013, two public protests were announced in Croatia, a country in deep economic crisis, with high unemployment rates and a deep sense of despair among the population: trade unions tried to organize a rally in support of workers' rights, while right-wing nationalists started a protest movement against the use of Cyrillic letters on public buildings in cities with a Serb minority. Trade unions brought a couple of hundred people to a big square in Zagreb, whereas the nationalists succeeded in mobilizing hundreds of thousands, which happened again for protests against gay marriage. It is crucial to see this ethical regression as the obverse of the explosive development of global capitalism – they are the two sides of the same coin.

The German expression *rückgängig machen* ('retroactive undoing', making it as if it didn't happen) suits this process perfectly. Imagine a society which has fully integrated into its ethical substance the great modern axioms of freedom, equality, democratic rights, the duty of a society to provide for the education and basic healthcare of all its members, making racism or sexism simply unacceptable and ridiculous. There would be no need to argue against racism, since anyone who openly advocated racism would be immediately perceived as a weird eccentric not to be taken seriously. But then, step by step, although society continues to pay lip service to these axioms, they would be *de facto* deprived of their substance. Here is a recent example: in the Summer of 2012, Viktor Orbán , the right-wing Hungarian prime minister, said that a new economic system had to be built in Central Europe:

> and let us hope that God will help us and we will not have to invent a new type of political system instead of democracy that would need to be introduced for the sake of economic survival . . . Cooperation is a question of force, not of intention. Perhaps there are countries where things don't work that way, for example in the Scandinavian countries, but such a half-Asiatic rag-tag people as we are can unite only if there is force.[53]

The irony of these lines was not lost on some old Hungarian dissidents: when the Soviet army moved into Budapest to crush the

1956 anti-Communist uprising, the message repeatedly sent by the beleaguered Hungarian leaders to the West was: 'We are defending Europe here.' (Against the Asiatic Communists, of course.) Now that Communism has collapsed, the Christian-conservative government paints as its main enemy the multi-cultural consumerist liberal democracy for which today's Western Europe stands, and calls for a new, more organic communitarian order to replace the 'turbulent' liberal democracy of the last two decades. Orbán has already expressed his sympathy for 'capitalism with Asian values', so if the European pressure on Orbán continues, we can easily imagine him sending a message to the East: 'We are defending Asia here!'

Today's anti-immigrant populism has replaced direct barbarism with barbarism with a human face. It is a regression from the Christian love of the neighbour back to the pagan privileging of our tribe (Greeks, Romans) versus the barbarian Other. Even if it is cloaked as a defence of Christian values, it is itself the greatest threat to Christian legacy. A century ago G. K. Chesterton clearly depicted the fundamental deadlock in which critics of religion find themselves: 'Men who begin to fight the Church for the sake of freedom and humanity end by flinging away freedom and humanity if only they may fight the Church ... The secularists have not wrecked divine things; but the secularists have wrecked secular things, if that is any comfort to them.'[54] Doesn't the same hold for the advocates of religion? How many fanatical defenders of religion started by ferociously attacking contemporary secular culture and ended up forsaking any meaningful religious experience? In a similar way, many liberal warriors are so eager to fight anti-democratic fundamentalism that they will end by flinging away freedom and democracy themselves if only they may fight terror. If the 'terrorists' are ready to wreck this world for love of another, our warriors on terror are ready to wreck their own democratic world out of hatred for the Muslim other. Some of them love human dignity so much that they are ready to legalize torture – the ultimate degradation of human dignity – to defend it. And doesn't the same hold for the recent rise of the defenders of Europe against the immigrant threat? In their zeal to protect Judeo-Christian legacy, the new zealots are ready to forsake the true heart of the Christian legacy. They, the anti-immigrant defenders of Europe, not the crowds of immigrants supposedly waiting to invade it, are the true threat to Europe.

One of the signs of this regression is the demand from the new European Right for a more 'balanced' view of the two 'extremisms', the Right and the Left: we are repeatedly told that one should treat the extreme Left (Communism) much like Europe was treating the extreme Right after the Second World War (the defeated Fascists and Nazis). But this new 'balance' is heavily unbalanced: the equation of Fascism and Communism secretly privileges Fascism, as can be seen from a series of arguments, such as the idea that Fascism copied Communism, which preceded it: before becoming a Fascist, Mussolini was a socialist, and even Hitler was a National Socialist; concentration camps and genocides could be found in the Soviet Union a decade before the Nazis used the same means; the annihilation of the Jews has a clear precedent in the annihilation of the class enemy, and so on. The point of this argumentation is that a moderate Fascism was a justified response to the Communist threat (a claim made long ago by Ernst Nolte in his defence of Heidegger's involvement with Nazism in 1933). In Slovenia, the Right is arguing for the rehabilitation of the anti-Communist Home Guard which fought the partisans during the Second World War: they made the difficult choice to collaborate with the Nazis in order to prevent the much greater absolute Evil of Communism. But the same could be said for the Nazis (or the Fascists, at least): they did what they did to prevent the absolute Evil of Communism.[55]

What are we to do in such a situation? Mainstream liberals tell us that, when basic democratic values are under threat by ethnic or religious fundamentalists, we should all unite behind the liberal-democratic agenda of cultural tolerance, save what can be saved, and put aside dreams of a more radical social transformation. There is, however, a fatal flaw in this call for solidarity: it ignores how liberal permissiveness and fundamentalism are caught in a vicious cycle as the two poles generate and presuppose each other.

So what is the fate of the liberal-democratic capitalist European dream in Ukraine? One cannot be sure what awaits the country should it join the EU. Recall the Rabinovitch joke quoted in Chapter 1 – we can easily imagine a similar exchange between a critical

Ukrainian and a financial administrator working for the European Union. The Ukrainian complains: 'There are two reasons we are panicking here in Ukraine. First, we are afraid that the EU will simply abandon us and let our economy collapse.' The EU administrator interrupts him: 'But you can trust us, we will not abandon you, we will tightly control you and advise you what to do!' 'Well,' responds the Ukrainian calmly, 'that's our second reason.'

So the question is not whether Ukraine is worthy of Europe or good enough to join the EU, but whether today's Europe is worthy of the deepest aspirations of the Ukrainians. If Ukraine ends up with a mixture of ethnic fundamentalism and liberal capitalism, with oligarchs pulling the strings, it will be as European as Russia (or Hungary) is today. (And, incidentally, it would be crucial to tell the full story of the conflict between different groups of oligarchs – the 'pro-Russian' ones and the 'pro-Western' ones – that forms the background to current events in Ukraine.) Political commentators have claimed that the EU has not done enough to support Ukraine in its conflict with Russia, that the EU response to the Russian occupation and annexation of Crimea has been half-hearted. But there is something else the EU has been unable or unwilling to do: offer Ukraine a feasible strategy for breaking out of this deadlock. To do this, Europe should first transform itself and renew its pledge to the emancipatory core of its legacy.

To put it bluntly, if the emerging New World Order is our non-negotiable destiny, then Europe is lost, so the only solution for Europe is to take the risk and break this spell. Only in such a new Europe could Ukraine find its place. It is not the Ukrainians who should learn from Europe; Europe itself has to learn to incorporate the dream that motivated the Maidan protesters. Today, more than ever, fidelity to the emancipatory core of the European legacy is needed. The lesson that the frightened liberals should learn is this: only a more radicalized Left can save what is worth saving of the liberal legacy today.

How, then, are we to proceed? We don't have to look far from Croatia. In February 2014, cities were burning in the Bosnian Federation. It all began in Tuzla, a city with a Muslim majority; the protests then spread to Sarajevo, Zenica, Mostar (with a large segment of Croat population) and Banja Luka (the capital of the Serb part of Bosnia). Thousands of enraged protesters occupied, devastated and set fire to government buildings, including the Presidency of the Bosnian Federation. The events immediately gave rise to conspiracy theories (according to one scenario, the Serb government had organized the protests to topple the Bosnian leadership), but one should safely ignore them, since it is clear that whatever lurks 'behind' the protesters' despair is authentic. Here, again, one is tempted to paraphrase Mao Zedong's famous phrase: there is chaos in Bosnia, the situation is excellent! Why? The protesters' demands were as simple as they can be: we want jobs, the chance of a decent life, an end to corruption. But they mobilized people *in Bosnia*, a country which, in the last decades, came to symbolize ferocious ethnic cleansing, leading to hundreds of thousands of dead. In one of the photos from the protests, we see the demonstrators waving three flags side by side: Bosnian, Serbian and Croatian – expressing the will to ignore ethnic differences. In short, we are dealing with a rebellion against nationalist elites. The people of Bosnia finally understand who their true enemy is: not other ethnic groups but their own nationalist elites pretending to protect them from the others. It is as if the old and much abused Titoist motto of the 'brotherhood and unity' of Yugoslav nations has now become relevant.

One of the protesters' targets was the European Union administration which oversees the Bosnian state, enforcing peace between the three nations, and providing significant financial help, enabling the state to function. This may come as a surprise, since the goals of the protesters are nominally the same as the goals of the EU administration: prosperity, the end of ethnic tensions and of corruption. However, while the EU administration pretends to act to overcome ethnic hatreds and to promote multicultural tolerance, the way it effectively governs Bosnia entrenches partitions: the EU deals with nationalist elites as their privileged partners, mediating within them.

What the Bosnian outburst confirms is that one cannot really overcome ethnic passions by imposing the liberal agenda. What brought the protesters together is a radical programme of justice. The next and most difficult step would have been to organize the protests into a new social movement that ignored ethnic divisions and to stage further protests – can we imagine enraged Bosnians and Serbs manifesting together in Sarajevo? Even if the protests gradually lose their power, they will remain a brief spark of hope, something like the enemy soldiers fraternizing across the trenches in the First World War. Authentic emancipatory events always involve ignoring particular identities as irrelevant. And the same holds for the recent visit of the two Pussy Riot members to New York: in a big gala show, they were introduced by Madonna in the presence of Bob Geldof, Richard Gere and other celebrities – the usual human rights gang. What they should have done there was just one thing: to express their solidarity with Edward Snowden, to assert that Pussy Riot and Snowden are part of the same global movement. Without such gestures, bringing together groups that seem incompatible (Muslims, Serbs and Croats in Bosnia; Turkish secularists and anti-capitalist Muslims in Turkey, and so on), protest movements will always be manipulated by one superpower in its struggle against the other.

And the same goes for Ukraine. Yes, the Maidan protesters were heroes, but the true fight begins now, the fight for what the new Ukraine will be, and this fight will be much tougher than the fight against Putin's intervention. A new and much more risky heroism will be needed here.[56] The model for this is the Russians who courageously oppose their country's nationalism and denounce it as a tool of those in power. What is needed today is the *rejection of the very terms of the conflict* and the *solidarity* of Ukrainians and Russians. One should begin by organizing events of fraternization across the imposed divisions, establishing shared organizational networks between the authentic emancipatory core of Ukrainian political agents and the Russian opposition to Putin's regime. This may sound utopian, but only such 'crazy' acts can lead to emancipation. Otherwise, we will get just a conflict of nationalist passions manipulated by oligarchs. Such geopolitical games for spheres of influence are of no interest whatsoever to authentic emancipatory politics.

4

EPIGNOSIS *J'ai hâte de vous servir!*

The original title of Julien Gracq's novel *The Opposing Shore* is *Le rivage des Syrtes*, which refers to the southern-most region of Orsenna, a fictional stand-in for Italy, where there are cars but no electricity, a country ruled by the ancient and decadent city of the same name which seems to be – but isn't quite – Venice. Almost all the characters in the novel have Italian names. For the last 300 years, Orsenna has been in a state of suspended war with Farghestan, the barbarian desert country across the sea to the south. With its two main cities on the coast and endless sand dunes, Farghestan seems a great deal like Libya, although some of the places change sides: Mount Etna moves to Libya and becomes the Tängri; the ruins of Sabratha leave Libya for Italy and become Sagra; and Sirt goes to Italy and becomes Syrtes. Aldo, the novel's narrator and protagonist, belongs to one of the ruling families of Orsenna. Sent as a state observer to Orsenna's dilapidated naval base of Syrtes, Aldo surrenders to his fascination with Farghestan; he crosses the forbidden line dividing the dead sea, sailing to the city of Rhages on the enemy shore. There, his ship is welcomed with three cannon shots. Having by this irreparable act rekindled the war that will destroy Orsenna, Aldo accomplishes the suicidal gesture that a whole people secretly yearned for: when he returns from Syrtes to Orsenna, he discovers that the ruling elite of Orsenna is using the pretence of a war with Farghestan to whip up nationalist patriotism. Danielo, one of the masters of Orsenna, explains how Aldo's actions have proven useful:

When you rule, nothing is worse than *losing hold*. Once the Thing came to me, it was a strange discovery to realize that this was the only way to hold on to Orsenna. Everything that focused on Syrtes again, everything that led to the renewal of your ... episode made the old gears turn with almost phantasmagorical ease, everything that failed to concern it met with a wall of inertia and unconcern. The Thing took advantage of every instance – the gestures to accelerate it and the gestures to slow it down – like a man sliding down the slope of a roof. Once the question was raised – how can I put this to you? – everything was *mobilized* of its own accord.[1]

(Note how the first sentence – 'When you rule, nothing is worse than *losing hold*' – echoes Mao's warning to the revolutionary power: 'Above all, hold on to [state] power, never allow [state] power to slide out of your hands.') However, beyond the obvious reproach that Gracq is depicting a descent of Orsenna into Fascism (evoking an external threat to create a state of emergency, and so on), one should discern here a deeper existential dilemma: what is more desirable, a still, inert life of small satisfactions, not a true life at all, or taking a risk that may well end in a catastrophe? This choice is the core of what Badiou is aiming at with his formula *mieux vaut un désastre qu'un désêtre*: better a disaster (the catastrophic outcome of an event) than a non-eventful survival in a hedonist-utilitarian universe – or, to put it in brutal political terms, better the worst of Stalinism than the best of the liberal-capitalist welfare state. Why?

Since, today, capitalism defines and structures the totality of the human civilization, every 'Communist' territory was and is – again, in spite of its horrors and failures – a kind of 'liberated territory', as Fred Jameson put it apropos of Cuba. What we are dealing with here is the old structural notion of the gap between the Space and the positive content that fills it. Although, as far as their positive content was concerned, the Communist regimes were mostly a dismal failure, generating terror and misery, they at the same time opened up a certain space, the space of utopian expectations, which among other things enabled us to measure the failure of the 'really existing socialism' itself. (What the anti-Communist dissidents as a rule tend to overlook is that the very space from which they themselves criticized and denounced the everyday terror and misery was opened and sustained by the Communist breakthrough, by its attempt to escape the logic of capital.) This, again, is how one should understand Badiou's *mieux vaut un désastre qu'un désêtre*, an idea so shocking to liberal sensitivities: better the worst Stalinist terror than the most liberal capitalist democracy. Of course, the moment one compares the positive content of the two, the welfare state-driven capitalist democracy is incomparably better, but what redeems Stalinist 'totalitarianism' is the formal aspect, the *space* it opens up. Can one imagine a utopian point at which this subterranean level of the utopian Other Space unites with the positive space of 'normal' social life? The key political question is this: is there in our 'postmodern' time still a space for such communities? Are they limited to the undeveloped outskirts (favelas, ghettos), or is a space for them emerging in the very heart of the 'postindustrial' landscape? Can one make a wild wager that the dynamics of 'postmodern' capitalism, with its rise of new eccentric geek communities, provide a new chance here? That, perhaps for the first time in history, the logic of alternative communities can be grafted onto the latest state of technology?

But perhaps it is not enough to say this. First, is Gracq's example not misleading? The hedonist-decadent non-being of Orsenna society has a false class-biased appearance which obfuscates the underlying social antagonisms – an obfuscation continued by the pseudo-event of the war with Farghestan.[2] So there are three terms and not two: the event (which may end up in disaster), the pseudo-event (Fascism or, in this case, war), and the hedonist-utilitarian bio-politics of non-being, of regulating animal-human life.[3] The difficulty today is how to distinguish the first from the second, since they often share many features. In short, even if we agree with the formula *mieux vaut un désastre qu'un désêtre*, what about *mieux vaut un pseudo-événement qu'un désêtre*? Is a Fascist 'event' also better than a non-eventful capitalist survival?

BACK TO THE ECONOMY OF GIFT

In principle, the answer may appear simple. Every historical situation contains its own unique utopian perspective, an immanent vision of what is wrong with it, an ideal representation of how, with some changes, the situation could be rendered much better. When the desire for radical social change emerges, it is thus logical that it first endeavours to actualize this immanent utopian vision – and this endeavour is what characterizes every authentic emancipatory struggle. Here, however, problems begin: why have all attempts hitherto to do this, to actualize the utopian potential immanent to a historical situation, end in catastrophe?

It is at this level that we should also discern a mistake of Marx. He perceived how capitalism unleashed the breathtaking dynamics of self-enhancing productivity – witness his fascinated descriptions of how, in capitalism, 'all things solid melt into thin air', of how capitalism is the greatest revolutionizer in the entire history of humanity. He also clearly perceived how this capitalist dynamics is propelled by its own inner obstacle or antagonism; that the ultimate limit of capitalism (of capitalism's self-propelling productivity) is Capital itself – the incessant capitalist development and revolutionizing of its own material conditions, the mad dance of its unconditional spiral of productivity. Capital is ultimately engaged in nothing but a desperate flight forwards in an attempt to escape its own debilitating inherent contradiction. Marx's fundamental mistake was to conclude from these insights that a new, higher social order (Communism) is possible that would not only maintain, but even raise to a higher degree and effectively fully release, the potential of the self-increasing spiral of productivity which, in capitalism – on account of its inherent obstacle (contradiction) – is again and again thwarted by socially destructive economic crises.

In short, what Marx overlooked is, to put it in standard Derridean terms, that this inherent obstacle/antagonism as the 'condition of impossibility' of the full deployment of the productive forces is simultaneously its 'condition of possibility': if we abolish the obstacle, the inherent contradiction of capitalism, we do not get the fully unleashed drive to productivity finally delivered of its impediment, we lose precisely this productivity that seemed to be generated and simultaneously thwarted by capitalism. If we take away the obstacle, the very potential thwarted by this obstacle dissipates (herein resides Lacan's critique of Marx, which focuses on the ambiguous overlapping of surplus-value and surplus-enjoyment). So the critics of Communism were in a way right when they claimed that Marxian Communism is an impossible fantasy. What they did not perceive is that Marxian Communism, this notion of a society of pure unleashed productivity outside the frame of Capital, was a fantasy inherent to capitalism itself, the capitalist inherent transgression at its purest, a strictly ideological fantasy of maintaining the thrust to productivity generated by capitalism, while getting rid of the 'obstacles' and antagonisms that were – as the sad experience of 'really existing capitalism' demonstrates – the only possible framework for the effective material existence of a society of permanently self-enhancing productivity. This is why a revolution has to be repeated: only the catastrophic experience can make the revolutionary agent aware of the fateful limitation of the first attempt. Marx (especially in his youthful texts) provides the basic formula of the illusion on which this fatal limitation is based, in a series of 'instead of' theses: their implicit (sometimes explicit) line of reasoning begins with 'instead of' (which stands for the alleged 'normal' state of things), and goes on to describe the alienated inversion of this 'normal' state. Here is a long passage from his *Economic and Philosophic Manuscripts of 1844*:

> So much does labour's realization appear as loss of realization that the worker loses realization to the point of starving to death.
>
> So much does the appropriation of the object appear as estrangement that the more objects the worker produces the less he can possess and the more he falls under the sway of his product, capital.
>
> All these consequences are implied in the statement that the worker is related to the *product of labour* as to an *alien* object. For on this premise it is clear that the more the worker spends himself, the more powerful becomes the alien world of objects which he creates over and against himself, the poorer he himself – his inner world – becomes, the less belongs to him as his own. It is the same in religion. The more man puts into God, the less he retains in himself. The worker puts his life into the object; but now his life no longer belongs to him but to the object. Hence, the greater this activity, the more the worker lacks objects. Whatever the product of his labour is, he is not. Therefore, the greater this product, the less is he himself.
>
> (According to the economic laws the estrangement of the worker in his object is expressed thus: the more the worker produces, the less he has to consume; the more values he creates, the more valueless, the more unworthy he becomes; the better formed his product, the more deformed becomes the worker; the more civilized his object, the more

barbarous becomes the worker; the more powerful labour becomes, the more powerless becomes the worker; the more ingenious labour becomes, the less ingenious becomes the worker and the more he becomes nature's slave.)

As a result, therefore, man (the worker) only feels himself freely active in his animal functions – eating, drinking, procreating, or at most in his dwelling and in dressing-up, etc.; and in his human functions he no longer feels himself to be anything but an animal. What is animal becomes human and what is human becomes animal.[4]

It would be easy to rephrase this passage in the 'instead of' formulation: instead of being the realization of the worker, labour appears as the loss of his realization; instead of appearing as what it is, the appropriation of the object through labour appears as its estrangement; instead of possessing more of what he produces the more he produces, the worker possesses less; instead of civilizing himself through producing civilized objects, the more civilized his object, the more barbarous the worker becomes; and so on. The desire to fully actualize this 'normal' state is ideology at its purest and cannot but end in a catastrophe. One form this catastrophic reversal can take is the unexpected practical interpretation of the Communist ideal which turns its realization into a nightmare. During the Great Leap Forward of the late 1950s, Chinese Communists decided that China should bypass socialism and directly enter Communism. They referred to Marx's famous formula of Communism: 'From each according to his abilities, to each according to his needs!' The catch was the reading given to it in order to legitimize the total militarization of life in agricultural communes: the Party cadre who commands a commune knows what every farmer is able to do, so he sets the plan and specifies the individuals' obligations according to their abilities, plus he knows what farmers really need for survival and organizes accordingly the distribution of food and other necessaries for life to be sustained. The condition of militarized extreme poverty thus becomes the actualization of Communism, and, of course, it is not sufficient to claim that such a reading falsifies a noble idea – one should rather say that it lies dormant in Communism as a possibility.

So, again, how are we to break out of this trap, if we have to renounce the expectation of a Great Rupture which will actualize the innermost tendency of our epoch and bring about the reversal of which we dream? One possible path is outlined by Kojin Karatani, whose basic premise is the use of modes of exchange (instead of modes of production, as in Marxism) as the tool with which to analyse the history of humanity.[5] Karatani distinguishes four progressive modes of exchange: (A) gift exchange, which predominates in pre-state societies (clans or tribes exchanging gifts); (B) domination and protection, which predominates in slave and feudal societies (here, exploitation is based on direct domination, plus the dominating class has to offer something in exchange, say protecting its subjects from danger); (C) commodity exchange of objects, which predominates in capitalism (free individuals exchange not only their products but also their own labour power); (X) a further stage to come, a return to the gift-exchange at a higher level. This X is a Kantian regulative idea, a vision that has assumed different guises in the history of humanity, from egalitarian religious communities reliant on communal solidarity to anarchist cooperatives and Communist projects. Karatani introduces here two further complications. (1) There is a crucial rupture, the so-called 'sedentary revolution', which takes place in pre-state early societies: the passage from nomadic hunter-groups to permanently settled groups organized in tribes or clans. At the level of exchange, we pass from 'pure' gift to the complex web of gift and counter-gift. This distinction is crucial insofar as the forthcoming passage to X will enact at a higher level the return to the nomadic mode of social existence. (2) In the passage from A to B and so on, the previous stage does not disappear; although it is 'repressed', the repressed returns in a new form. With the passage from A to B, gift-exchange survives as the spirit of religious reconciliation and solidarity; with the passage from B to C, A survives as nation, national community, and B (domination) survives as the state power. For this reason, capitalism is for Karatani not a 'pure' reign of B, but a triad (or, rather, a Borromean knot) of Nation–State–Capital: nation as the form of communal solidarity, state as the form of direct domination, capital as the form of economic exchange. All three of them are necessary for the reproduction of capitalist society.

The exemplary cases of such a 'return of the repressed' are the radical millenarian religious communities that we find in Christianity (Canudos in Brazil, say) and in Islam (for example, Alamut). No wonder that, as soon as a religion establishes itself as an ideological institution legitimizing existing power relations, it has to fight against its own innermost excess. The Christian church faced a common problem from the fourth century onwards, when it became the state religion: how does one reconcile feudal class society, in which rich lords ruled over impoverished peasants, with the egalitarian poverty of the collective of believers as described in the Gospels? The solution of Thomas Aquinas is that, while, in principle, shared property is better, this holds only for perfect humans; for the majority of us, who dwell in sin, private property and difference in wealth are natural, and it is even sinful to demand the abolition of private property or to promote egalitarianism in our fallen societies, i.e., to demand for imperfect people what befits only the perfect. This is the immanent contradiction at the core of the Church's identity, making the established Church the main anti-Christian force today. The subversive core of the authentic religious experience does not point towards the standard Marxist notion of an illusory religious unity masking actual divisions, but aims at something much stronger: the foundation of a new form of actual social life in solidarity. Maybe we should rehabilitate Heidegger's idea that 'only a god can save us' – not, of course, that a god who now dwells somewhere in the beyond will decide to intervene, but in the sense that something like a proper religious engagement can happen again – 'god happens', almost in the same sense that 'shit happens'. Maybe, we should also turn around the old logic of MAD (Mutually Assured Destruction) that helped us survive the Cold War: today, it is no longer that there will not be a global war *except for some unforeseen accident* – it is rather that we are condemned to catastrophe *except for some unforeseen miracle that can save us*. Was it not Nietzsche, that great critic of religion, who played with the idea of such a miracle? As a rule, one ignores how Nietzsche's celebrations of war and ruthless struggle as the only path towards the greatness of man are accompanied by a continuous stream of 'pacifist' statements, most famous among them the call for a unilateral 'breaking of the sword' – the call for an authentic political act, if there ever was one:

And perhaps the great day will come when a people, distinguished by wars and victories and by the highest development of a military order and intelligence, and accustomed to make the heaviest sacrifices for these things, will exclaim of its own free will, 'We break the sword', and will smash its entire military establishment down to its lowest foundations. Rendering oneself unarmed when one had been the best-armed, out of a height of feeling – that is the means to real peace, which must always rest on a peace of mind; whereas the so-called armed peace, as it now exists in all countries, is the absence of peace of mind. One trusts neither oneself nor one's neighbour and, half from hatred, half from fear, does not lay down arms. Rather perish than hate and fear, and twice rather perish than make oneself hated and feared – this must someday become the highest maxim for every single commonwealth too.[6]

This line of thought culminates in a note of Nietzsche's from 1883: 'To dominate? To impose onto others my type? Disgusting! Does my luck not reside precisely in contemplating many others?'[7] And we should imagine a series of similar gifts: what if Brazil were to renounce the depletion of the Amazon rainforest as a gift to humanity, what if Microsoft were to renounce the property rights on its software, and so on and so on? Such gifts should not be interpreted as 'aid' to the undeveloped and poor or any other kind of redistributive justice:

aid serves to generate further accumulation of capital in the advanced countries. In this, the aid resembles the case of domestic social-welfare policies within those countries: in both cases, redistribution simply functions as another link in the process of capitalist accumulation. Far from eliminating inequality, redistributive justice actually proliferates inequality.[8]

But is such a vision of gift-society not a utopia with no chances of success in actual life? Here, things are much more ambiguous and open: signs which point towards a new economy of gift abound in our societies.[9] For example, the strange thing about Peter Sloterdijk's attempt to assert (as the solution to what one is tempted to call the 'antinomies of the welfare state') an 'ethics of gift'[10] beyond mere egotist-possessive market exchange is one that brings us unexpectedly close to the Communist vision. Sloterdijk is guided by the elementary lesson of dialectics: sometimes, the opposition between maintaining the old and changing things does not cover the entire field, i.e., sometimes the only way to maintain what is worth keeping in the old is to intervene and change things radically. If, today, one wants to save the core of the welfare state, one should precisely abandon any nostalgia for twentieth-century Social Democracy. What Sloterdijk proposes is a kind of new cultural revolution, a radical psycho-social change based on the insight that today, the exploited productive stratum is no longer the working class, but the (upper-)middle class: they are the true 'givers' whose heavy taxation finances the education, health, and so on of the majority. In order to accomplish this change, one should leave behind statism, this absolutist remainder which strangely survived in our democratic era: the idea, surprisingly strong even among the traditional Left, that the state has the unquestionable right to tax its citizens, to determine and seize (through legal coercion, if necessary) part of their product. It is not that citizens give part of their income to their state; they are treated as if they are *a priori* indebted to the state. This attitude is sustained by a misanthropic premise which is strongest in the very Left which otherwise preaches solidarity: people are basically egotists; they have to be forced to contribute something for the common welfare, and it is only the state which, by means of its coercive legal apparatus, can do the job of assuring the necessary solidarity and redistribution.

One should thus learn, Sloterdijk continues, to treat those who are productive of wealth not as a group which is *a priori* suspicious for refusing to pay its debt to society, but as the true givers whose contribution should be fully recognized, so that they can be proud of their generosity. The first step is the shift from proletariat to voluntariat: instead of taxing the rich excessively, one should give them the (legal) right to decide voluntarily what part of their wealth they will donate to common welfare. To begin with, one should, of course, not radically lower taxes, but open up at least a small domain in which the freedom is given to givers to decide how much and for what they will donate. Such a beginning, modest as it is, would gradually change the entire ethics on which social cohesion is based. Do we not get caught here into the old paradox of freely choosing what we are anyway obliged to do? That is to say, is it not that the freedom of choice accorded to the 'voluntariat' of 'achievers' is a false freedom which relies on a forced choice? If society is to function normally, the 'achievers' are free to choose (to give money to society or not) only if they make the right choice (to give it)?

There is a series of problems with this idea, but the fundamental retort to Sloterdijk should be: why does he assert generosity only within the constraints of capitalism, which is *the* order of possessive competition? Within these constraints, every generosity is *a priori* reduced to the obverse of this brutal possessiveness, a benevolent Dr Jekyll to the capitalist Mr Hyde. Here, just recall the first model of generosity mentioned by Sloterdijk: Carnegie, the man of steel with a heart of gold, as they say. First, Carnegie used Pinkerton detective agents and a private army to crush workers' resistance, and then displayed generosity by way of (partially) giving back what he had (not created but) grabbed. Even with Bill Gates, how can one forget his brutal tactics to crush competitors and gain monopoly (tactics which made US authorities set in motion multiple legal proceedings against Microsoft)? The key question is therefore: is there no place for generosity outside the capitalist frame? Is each and every such project a case of sentimental moralist ideology?

The traps of imagining a possible change are clearly perceptible in Thomas Piketty's *Capitalism in the Twenty-First Century*,[11] a kind of 'realist' counterpoint to Sloterdijk's speculations, the result of more than a decade of research into historical changes in the concentration of income and wealth. In the eighteenth and nineteenth centuries Western European society was highly unequal: private wealth dwarfed national income and was concentrated in the hands of the rich families within a rigid class structure. This state persisted even as industrialization slowly contributed to rising wages for workers, and the trend towards higher inequality was only reversed between 1930 and 1975 on account of a series of unique circumstances. The two World Wars, the Great Depression, as well as the rise of the Communist states, prompted governments in developed capitalist states to enforce measures towards redistributing income. (Note the weirdness of this fact: egalitarianism and universal welfare were conditioned by the unimaginable catastrophes of world wars and crisis.) From 1975 onwards, and especially after the fall of Communism, the trend towards inequality returned; if the global capitalist system is allowed to follow its immanent logic, Piketty predicts a world of low economic growth, dismissing the idea that bursts of technological advances will bring growth back to the levels of the twentieth century. Only a strong political intervention can counteract the exploding inequality – Piketty proposes an annual global wealth tax of up to 2 per cent, combined with a progressive income tax reaching as high as 80 per cent. An obvious question arises here: if capitalism's immanent logic pushes it towards growing inequality and a weakening of democracy, why should we not aim at overcoming capitalism itself? For Piketty, the problem is the no-less-obvious fact that the twentieth-century alternatives to capitalism didn't work: capitalism has to be accepted as the only game in town. The only feasible solution is thus to allow the capitalist machinery to do its work in its proper sphere, and to impose egalitarian justice politically, by a democratic power which regulates the economic system and enforces redistribution. One should not underestimate Piketty here: in a typically French way, the naivety (of which he is fully aware) of his proposal is part of his strategy to paint the bleak picture of our situation – here is the obvious solution, and we all know it cannot happen . . .

Although this solution is superficially opposed to Sloterdijk's, they share an underlying premise: the capitalist machinery should be kept since it is the only efficient way to produce wealth, and inequality should be corrected by re-distributing wealth to those underprivileged. Instead of transforming the capitalist mode of production, one should limit oneself to a change in distribution. They differ on how to achieve this: Piketty advocates direct massive state regulation through high taxes, while Sloterdijk counts on voluntary contributions of the wealthy. And both solutions are for this reason *utopian* in the proper sense of the term. Piketty is well aware that the model he proposes would only work if enforced globally, beyond the confines of nation states (otherwise capital would flee to the states with lower taxes); such a global measure presupposes an already existing global power with the strength and authority to enforce it. However, such a global power is unimaginable within the confines of today's global capitalism and the political mechanisms it implies – in short, if such a power were to exist, *the basic problem would already have been resolved*. We can thus repeat, apropos of this notion of a global power, the same thing Freud says about psychoanalysis: in a situation in which conditions for psychoanalytic practice are fully met, psychoanalysis would no longer be needed.

It is here that one should analyse the capitalist system as a *totality* of interdependent links and, when imagining a measure, always focus on what are its presuppositions and implications: under what conditions is it possible to imagine the measures proposed by Piketty? What further measures would the global imposition of high taxes proposed by Piketty necessitate? Of course, the only way out of this vicious cycle is simply to cut the Gordian knot and act. There are never perfect conditions for an act – every act by definition comes too early; one has to begin somewhere, with a particular intervention, and bear in mind the further complications that such an act will lead to. In other words, the true utopianism is to imagine global capitalism as we know it today, still functioning the way it does, but with the high tax rate proposed by Piketty. Perhaps, then, Sloterdijk does have a point, and we should imagine a more radical change, a move towards gift-economy. We often hear that the Communist vision relies on a dangerous idealization of human beings, attributing to them a kind of 'natural goodness' that is simply alien to our (egotist, and so on) nature. However, in his book *Drive*,[12] Daniel Pink refers to a body of behavioral-science research that suggests that sometimes, at least, external incentives (money reward) can be counterproductive: optimal performance comes when people find intrinsic meaning in their work. Incentives may be useful in getting people to accomplish boring routine work; but with more intellectually demanding tasks, the success of individuals and organizations increasingly depends on being nimble and innovative, so there is more and more need for people to find intrinsic value in their work. Pink identifies three elements underlying such intrinsic motivation: autonomy, the ability to choose what and how tasks are completed; mastery, the process of becoming adept at an activity; and purpose, the desire to improve the world. Here is Pink's report on a study done at MIT:

They took a whole group of students and they gave them a set of challenges. Things like memorizing strings of digits, solving word puzzles, other kinds of spatial puzzles, even physical tasks like throwing a ball through a hoop. To incentivize their performance they gave them three levels of rewards: if you did pretty well, you got a small monetary reward; if you did medium well, you got a medium monetary reward; if you did really well, if you were one of the top performers, you got a large cash prize. Here's what they found out. As long as the task involved only mechanical skill, bonuses worked as they would be expected: the higher the pay, the better their performance. But once the task calls for even rudimentary cognitive skill a larger reward led to poorer performance. How can that possibly be? This conclusion seems contrary to what a lot of us learned in economics which is that the higher the reward, the better the performance. And they're saying that once you get above rudimentary cognitive skill it's the other way around which seems like the idea that these rewards don't work that way seems vaguely Left-Wing and Socialist, doesn't it? It's this kind of weird Socialist conspiracy. For those of you who have these conspiracy theories I want to point out the notoriously left-wing socialist group that financed the research: The Federal Reserve Bank. Maybe that 50 dollars or 60 dollars prize isn't sufficiently motivating for an MIT student – so they went to Madurai in rural India, where 50 or 60 dollars is a significant sum of money. They replicated the experiment in India and what happened was that the people offered the medium reward did no better than the people offered the small reward but this time around, the people offered the top reward did worst of all: higher incentives led to worse performance. This experiment has been replicated over and over and over again by psychologists, by sociologists and by economists: for simple, straight-forward tasks, those kinds of incentives work, but when the task requires some conceptual, creative thinking those kind of motivators demonstrably don't work. The best use of money as a motivator is to pay people enough to take the issue of money off the table. Pay people enough, so they are not thinking about money and they're thinking about the work. You get a bunch of people who are doing highly skilled work but they're willing to do it for free and volunteer their time 20, sometimes 30 hours a week; and what they create, they give it away, rather than sell it. Why are these people, many of whom are technically sophisticated highly skilled people who have jobs, doing equally, if not more, technically sophisticated work not for their employer, but for someone else for free! That's a strange economic behaviour.[13]

This 'strange behaviour' is that of a Communist who follows Marx's well-known motto 'From each according to his abilities, to each according to his needs' – *this* is the only 'ethics of gift' that has any authentic utopian dimension. Karatani emphasizes that such a shift towards the economy of gift can only occur at a global level; he refers to Kant who, in his essay on permanent peace, outlines a vision of a world-wide federation of states: 'The only principle that can ground the establishment of a federation of nations as a new world system is the reciprocity of the gift.'[14] Before we dismiss this idea as a vain and empty utopia, we should bear in mind how all the global problems we are dealing with today – ecology, intellectual property, the welfare state – cry out for global intervention. Ecological threat can – if at all – only be contained through a world-wide coordination of measures; 'intellectual property' is more and more undermined through uncontrolled circulation of data; the welfare state is threatened by the competition of underpaid labour from poor countries, and so on.

This lack of global coordination is acutely felt: the problem is that today, in our emerging multi-centred world, we are still searching for the rules which would regulate the relations between these multiple centres.[15] To know a society is not only to know its explicit rules. One should also know *how to apply these rules*: when to use them or not use them; when to violate them; when not to use a choice that is offered; when to recognize one's obligation to do something but pretend one is doing it as a free choice. Recall the paradox of offers-meant-to-be-refused: it is a habit to refuse such an offer, and anyone who accepts such an offer commits a vulgar blunder. When I am invited to a restaurant by a rich uncle, we both know that he will cover the bill, but I nonetheless have to insist a little bit that we share the bill – imagine the surprise if my uncle were simply to say: 'OK, then you pay it!'

During the chaotic post-Soviet Yeltsin era in Russia, the problem could be located at this level: although the legal rules were known (and were largely the same as under the Soviet Union), what disinte-grated was the complex network of implicit unwritten rules that sustained the entire social edifice. Say if, in the Soviet Union, you wanted to get better hospital treatment or a new apartment, if you had a complaint against the authorities, if you were summoned to a court or you wanted your child to be accepted in a top school, if a factory manager needed raw materials but they weren't delivered on time by the state contractors, and so on, everyone knew what you really had to do, whom to address, whom to bribe, what you could do and what you could not do. After the collapse of the Soviet power, one of the most frustrating aspects of ordinary people's daily existence was that these unwritten rules largely got blurred. People simply no longer knew what to do, how to react, how to relate to explicit legal regula-tions: what can you ignore? when does bribery work, etc? (One of the functions of organized crime was to provide a kind of *ersatz*-legality: if you owned a small business and a customer owed you money, you turned to your mafia-protector, who dealt with the problem since the state legal system was inefficient.) The stabilization under the reign of Putin mostly amounts to the newly established transparency of these unwritten rules: now, again, people mostly know how to act or react in the complex cobweb of social interactions.

In international politics, we have not yet reached this stage. Back in the 1990s, a silent pact regulated the relationship between the Western great powers and Russia: Western states treated Russia as a great power on condition that Russia effectively didn't act as one. Of course, the problem here is: what if the person to whom the offer-to-be-rejected is made actually accepts it? What if Russia really starts to act as a great power? A situation like this is properly cata-strophic. It threatens to tear apart the entire fabric of existing relations. Indeed, something like this happened only a few years ago in Georgia: tired of being only treated as a superpower, Russia acted as one. How did it come to this?

The 'American century' is over and we are entering a period of the formation of multiple centres of global capitalism: the US, Europe, China, maybe Latin America. Each of them stands for capitalism with a specific twist: US for neoliberal capitalism; Europe for what remains of the welfare state; China for the 'Eastern Values' authoritarian capitalism; Latin America for populist capitalism. After the failure of the US attempt to impose itself as the sole superpower (the universal policeman), there is now the need to establish the rules of interaction between these local centres, in the case of their conflicting interests.

This is one of the reasons why the US and Israel, the two exemplary nation states obsessed with sovereignty, are natural allies, and this is why at some deep and often obfuscated level they perceive the European Union as *the* enemy. This perception, kept under control in the public political discourse, explodes in its underground obscene double, the extreme-Right Christian-fundamentalist political vision with its obsessive fear of the New World Order (Obama is in secret collusion with the United Nations, international forces will intervene in the US and put all true American patriots in concentration camps – a couple of years ago, there were rumours that Latin American troops were already in the Midwest plains, building concentration camps . . .). This vision is deployed in the hard-line Christian fundamentalism exemplified in the works of Tim laHaye *et consortes*. The title of one of laHaye's novels points in this direction: *The Europa Conspiracy*. The true enemies of the US are not Muslim terrorists – they are merely puppets secretly manipulated by the European secularists, the true forces of the anti-Christ who want to weaken the US and establish the New World Order under the domination of the United Nations . . . In a way, they are right in this perception: Europe is not just another geopolitical power bloc, but a global vision which is ultimately incompatible with nation-states. This dimension of the EU provides the key to the so-called European 'weakness': there is a surprising correlation between European unification and its loss of global military-political power. If, however, the European Union is more and more an impotent trans-state confederacy in need of US protection, why then is the US so obviously ill at ease with it? Recall the indications that the US financially supported those forces in Ireland that organized the 'No' campaign in the referendum on the new European treaty.

This is why our times are potentially more dangerous than it may at first appear. During the Cold War, the rules of international behaviour were clear, guaranteed by the superpowers' MAD-ness (Mutually Assured Destruction). When the Soviet Union violated these unwritten rules by invading Afghanistan, it paid dearly for this infringement – the war in Afghanistan was the beginning of its end. Today, the old and new superpowers are testing each other, trying to impose their own version of global rules, experimenting with them through proxies, which, of course, are other small nations and states. Karl Popper once praised the scientific testing of hypotheses, saying that, in this way, we allow our hypotheses to die instead of us. In today's testing, small nations get hurt instead of big ones – Georgians, as usual, are paying the price for such testing and, although the official justifications for it are highly moral (human rights and freedoms, etc.), the nature of the game is clear.

And are the events in Ukraine that began in early 2014 not the next stage of this geopolitical struggle for control in a non-regulated, multi-centred world, something like 'the crisis in Georgia, part two'? It is definitely time to teach the superpowers some manners – but who will do it? Obviously, only a trans-national entity can manage it. More than 200 years ago, Kant saw the need for a trans-national legal order grounded in the rise of a global society. 'Since the narrower or wider community of the peoples of the earth has developed so far that a violation of rights in one place is felt throughout the world, the idea of a law of world citizenship is no high-flown or exaggerated notion.'[16] This, however, brings us to what is arguably the 'principal contradiction' of the New World Order: the structural impossibility of finding a global political order that corresponds to the global capitalist economy. What if, for structural reasons – and not only due to empirical limitations – there cannot be a world-wide democracy or a representative world government? The structural problem (antinomy) of global capitalism resides in the impossibility (and, simultaneously, necessity) of a socio-political order that would fit it: the global market economy cannot be directly organized as a global liberal democracy with worldwide elections and so on. In politics, the 'repressed' of the economy returns: archaic fixations, particular substantial (ethnic, religious, cultural) identities. This embarrassing supplement is the condition of impossibility and of possibility for the global economy. This tension defines our predicament today: the global free circulation of commodities, accompanied by the growing separations in the social sphere proper. How, then, can we pass from the globalism of commodities to a more radical political globalism?

THE WOUND OF EUROCENTRISM

When anti-globalists and other fighters for radical emancipation engage in their struggle, they as a rule endorse a set of axioms concerning their ideas and organization that seem to form a kind of summary of the *a priori* of today's Left. First, they emphasize anti-Eurocentrism, the urgent need to break out of the confines of the Western thought that gave birth to capitalist modernization. Second, in criticizing the becoming-passive of our lives (the more we seem to be frantically active, the more we are passive elements regulated by an anonymous order), they insist on the need for active engagement against mere political representation. Finally, they claim that the era of hierarchic orders dominated by a Master figure is over: we are entering a new universe of multitudes, of dynamic lateral links, of molecular self-organizations which cannot ever be totalized.

But what if it is precisely this triad that forms the principal 'epistemological obstacle' to the renewal of the Left?

With regard to global capitalism – which, although it originated in Europe, is today a system in which Europe is more and more losing its leading role – one should be especially careful not to succumb to the non-reflective anti-Eurocentrism which can sometimes serve as the ideological cover for the rejection of what is worth fighting for in the European legacy. An exemplary case of someone who does precisely this is Walter D. Mignolo, in his recent critique of my defence of Leftist Eurocentrism:

> As a non-European thinker, my senses reacted to the first sentence of Zizek's article: *When one says Eurocentrism, every self-respecting postmodern leftist intellectual has as violent a reaction as Joseph Goebbels had to culture – to reach for a gun, hurling accusations of proto-fascist*

*Eurocentrist cultural imperialism. However, is it possible to imagine a
leftist appropriation of the European political legacy?* ... My response
to that paragraph, published in a couple of places, is the following:
*When one says Eurocentrism, every self-respecting decolonial intellec-
tual has not as violent a reaction as Joseph Goebbels had to culture – to
reach for a gun, hurling accusations of proto-fascist Eurocentrist cultural imperialism. A self-respecting decolonial intellectual will reach
instead to Frantz Fanon: 'Now, comrades, now is the time to decide to
change sides. We must shake off the great mantle of night, which has
enveloped us, and reach for the light. The new day, which is dawning,
must find us determined, enlightened and resolute. So, my brothers,
how could we fail to understand that we have better things to do than
follow that Europe's footstep'* ... we, decolonial intellectuals, if not
philosophers, 'have better things to do' as Fanon would say, than being
engaged with issues debated by European philosophers.[17]

What Mignolo proposes is thus a version of Baudrillard's battle cry
'Forget Foucault!': forget Europe, we have better things to do than
deal with European philosophy, even better things than endlessly
deconstructing it. The irony here is that this battle cry obviously did
not hold for Fanon himself who dealt extensively and intensively with
Hegel, psychoanalysis, Sartre and even Lacan. So when I read lines
like Mignolo's, I also reach for Fanon – this Fanon:

I am a man, and what I have to recapture is the whole past of the
world. I am not responsible solely for the slave revolt in Santo Domingo.
Every time a man has contributed to the victory of the dignity of the
spirit, every time a man has said no to an attempt to subjugate his fel-
lows, I have felt solidarity with his act. In no way does my basic
vocation have to be drawn from the past of peoples of colour. In no way
do I have to dedicate myself to reviving a black civilization unjustly
ignored. I will not make myself the man of any past ... My black skin
is not a repository for specific values ... Haven't I got better things to
do on this earth than avenge the Blacks of the seventeenth century? ...
I as a man of colour do not have the right to hope that in the white man
there will be a crystallization of guilt toward the past of my race. I as a
man of colour do not have the right to seek ways of stamping down the

pride of my former master. I have neither the right nor the duty to demand reparations for my subjugated ancestors. There is no black mission; there is no white burden . . . I do not want to be the victim of the Ruse of a black world . . . Am I going to ask today's white men to answer for the slave traders of the seventeenth century? Am I going to try by every means available to cause guilt to burgeon in their souls? . . . I am not a slave to slavery that dehumanized my ancestors . . . it would be of enormous interest to discover a black literature or architecture from the third century before Christ. We would be overjoyed to learn of the existence of a correspondence between some black philosopher and Plato. But we can absolutely not see how this fact would change the lives of eight-year-old kids working in the cane fields of Martinique or Guadeloupe . . . I find myself in the world and I recognize that I have one right alone: that of demanding human behaviour from the other.'[18]

What Fanon clearly saw is that today's global world is capitalist, and as such cannot be effectively problematized from the standpoint of local pre-capitalist cultures. This is why the lesson of Marx's two short 1853 articles on India ('The British rule in India', 'The Future Results of British Rule in India'), usually dismissed by postcolonial studies as embarrassing cases of Marx's 'Eurocentrism', are today more relevant than ever. Marx admits without restraint the brutality and exploitative hypocrisy of the British colonization of India, including the systematic use of torture prohibited in the West but 'outsourced' to Indians (really, there is nothing new under the sun – there were Guantanamos in the midst of nineteenth-century British India): 'The profound hypocrisy and inherent barbarism of bourgeois civilization lies unveiled before our eyes, turning from its home, where it assumes respectable forms, to the colonies, where it goes naked.'[19] All Marx adds is that

England has broken down the entire framework of Indian society, without any symptoms of reconstitution yet appearing. This loss of his old world, with no gain of a new one, imparts a particular kind of melancholy to the present misery of the Hindoo, and separates Hindostan, ruled by Britain, from all its ancient traditions, and from the whole of its past history . . . England, it is true, in causing a social revolution in Hindostan, was actuated only by the vilest interests, and was stupid in her manner of enforcing them. But that is not the question. The question is, can mankind fulfil its destiny without a fundamental revolution in the social state of Asia? If not, whatever may have been the crimes of England she was the unconscious tool of history in bringing about that revolution.[20]

One should not dismiss the talk of the 'unconscious tool of history' as the expression of a naive teleology, of a trust in the Cunning of Reason which makes even the vilest crimes instruments of progress. The point is simply that the British colonization of India created conditions for the double liberation of India: from the constraints of its own tradition as well as from colonization itself. This is why the quoted passage does *not* display the same dismissive attitude towards 'unhistorical nations' as the one clearly discernible in 'The Magyar Struggle', an article written by Friedrich Engels and published in *Neue Rheinische Zeitung* on 13 January 1849. The historical context of this text is the approaching defeat of the 1848 revolution, when the small Slavic nations (with the exception of the Poles) militarily supported the Austrian emperor in his effort to crush the Hungarian uprising (something which explains Engels's furious aggression):

> Among all the large and small nations of Austria, only three standard-bearers of progress took an active part in history, and still retain their vitality – the *Germans*, the *Poles* and the *Magyars*. Hence they are now revolutionary.
>
> All the other large and small nationalities and peoples are destined to perish before long in the revolutionary world storm. For that reason they are now counter-revolutionary ... There is no country in Europe which does not have in some corner or other one or several ruined fragments of peoples, the remnant of a former population that was suppressed and held in bondage by the nation which later became the main vehicle of historical development. These relics of a nation mercilessly trampled under foot in the course of history, as Hegel says, these *residual fragments of peoples*, always become fanatical standard-bearers of counter-revolution and remain so until their complete extirpation or loss of their national character, just as their whole existence in general is itself a protest against a great historical revolution ... But at the first

victorious uprising of the French proletariat, which Louis Napoleon is striving with all his might to conjure up, the Austrian Germans and Magyars will be set free and wreak a bloody revenge on the Slav barbarians. The general war which will then break out will smash this Slav Sonderbund and wipe out all these petty hidebound nations, down to their very names.

The next world war will result in the disappearance from the face of the earth not only of reactionary classes and dynasties, but also of entire reactionary peoples. And that, too, is a step forward.[21]

These lines sound like Mao's distinction between bourgeois and proletarian nations, but in the inverted sense: the struggle is not just about classes within nations; it also goes on between progressive and reactionary nations, with all that this implies, namely, the destruction of 'these petty hidebound nations, down to their very names', in the revolutionary process. Engels' line of thought relies on a simplified pseudo-Hegelianism: there is historical progress, there are nations that are part of this progress ('historical nations') and nations which are inert bystanders or even actively oppose it, and the latter are destined to perish. (Engels further embellishes this line of thought with a Hegelian-sounding reflexive twist: how could these nations not be reactionary when their existence itself is a reaction, a remainder of the past?) Engels stuck to his position to the end, convinced that, with the exception of Poles, small Slavic nations were all looking towards Russia, the bulwark of reaction, for their liberation. In 1882, he wrote to Bernstein (who had sympathies for Southern Slavs): 'We must cooperate in the work of setting the West European proletariat free and subordinate everything else to that goal. No matter how interesting the Balkan Slavs, etc., might be, the moment their desire for liberation clashes with the interests of the proletariat they can go hang for all I care.' And in a letter to Kautsky from the same year, he again asserts the opposition of progressive and reactionary nations:

Thus I hold the view that there are *two* nations in Europe which do not only have the right but the duty to be nationalistic before they become internationalists: the Irish and the Poles. They are internationalists of the best kind if they are very nationalistic. The Poles have understood this in all crises and have proved it on the battlefields of all revolutions. Take away their expectation to re-establish Poland; or persuade them that the new Poland will soon fall into their laps by itself, and they are finished with their interest in the European Revolution.[22]

As for the Southern Slavs:

> Only when with the collapse of Tsarism the nationalist ambitions of these dwarfs of peoples will be freed from association with Panslavist tendencies of world domination, only then we can let them take their fate in their own hands. And I am certain that six months of independence will suffice for most Austro-Hungarian Slavs to bring them to a point where they will beg to be readmitted. But these tiny nations can never be granted the right, which they now assign to themselves in Serbia, Bulgaria and Eastern Rumelia, to prevent the extension of the European railroad net to Constantinople.[23]

As we have already seen, the great opponent of Engels is here none other than Lenin; yet Marx's texts on India also diverge radically from Engels' position. Marx's point is not that Indians 'are destined to perish before long in the revolutionary world storm', but almost the exact opposite: getting caught in the dynamics of universal capitalism will enable Indians to get rid of their traditional constraints and engage in a modern struggle for liberation from the British colonial yoke. Lenin also stuck to this view: when the failure of the European revolution in early 1920s had become clear, he saw that the main task of Soviet power was to bring European modernity to Russia: instead of talking about big goals like building socialism, one should patiently engage in spreading (bourgeois) culture and civilization, in total opposition to 'socialism in one country'. The modesty of this ambition is sometimes surprisingly openly expressed, as when Lenin mocks all attempts to 'build socialism' in the Soviet Union. How different is this stance from Mignolo's view of the anti-capitalist struggle:

> As we know from history, the identification of the problem doesn't mean that there is only one solution. Or better yet, we can coincide in the prospective of harmony as a desirable global future, but

Communism is only one way to move toward it. There cannot be only one solution simply because there are many ways of being, which means of thinking and doing. Communism is an option and not an Abstract Universal ... In the non-European World, Communism is part of the problem rather than the solution. Which doesn't mean that if you are not Communist, in the non-European world, you are Capitalist ... So the fact that Žižek, and other European intellectuals, are seriously rethinking Communism means that they are engaging in one option (the reorientation of the Left) among many, today, marching toward the prospect of harmony overcoming the necessity of war; overcoming success and competition which engender corruption and selfishness, and promoting the plenitude of life over development and death.[24]

Mignolo relies here on an all-too-naive distinction between problem and solution. If there is a thing we really know from history, it is that, while 'the identification of the problem doesn't mean that there is only one solution,' there is also not just one single identification of the problem. When we encounter a problem (like a global economic crisis), we get a multitude of formulations concerning in what this problem resides and what its causes are (or, to put it in a more postmodern vein, we get a multitude of narratives): too much state regulation, not enough state regulation, moral failings, the overwhelming power of financial capital, capitalism as such, and so on. These different identifications of the problem form a dialectical unity with the proposed solutions – or, one could even say that the identification of a problem is already formulated from the standpoint of its alleged/imagined solution. Communism is therefore not just one of the solutions but, first of all, a unique formulation of the problem as it appears within the Communist horizon. Mignolo's identification of the problem, as well as his formulation of the common goal shared by all proposed solutions, is a proof of his limitation, and as such he is worth reading carefully: the common goal – '*marching* toward the prospect of harmony, promoting the plenitude of life'; the problem – 'the necessity of war ... success and competition that engender corruption and selfishness ... development and death'. His goal – harmony, plenitude of life – is a true Abstract Universal if there ever was one, an empty container that can mean many incompatible things (depending on what we understand by 'plenitude of life' and 'harmony'). (One can also add in an acerbic mode that many anti-capitalist movements have achieved great results in 'overcoming success'.) The easy equation of development and death, as well as the abstract rejection of war, corruption and selfishness, are no less meaningless abstractions. (And, incidentally, the abstract opposition of war and harmony is especially suspicious, since it can be also read as a call against aggravating social antagonisms, for a peaceful harmony of the social organism. If this is the direction taken, I much prefer to be called a 'Left Fascist', insisting on the emancipatory dimension of struggle.)

What Mignolo offers are not alternative modernities, but a kind of alternative postmodernity, i.e., different ways to overcome European (capitalist) modernity. Against such an approach, one should definitely defend the European universalist legacy – but in what precise sense? According to some Indian cultural theorists, the fact that they are compelled to use the English language is a form of cultural colonialism that censors their true identity. Their line of argument is: 'We have to speak in an imposed foreign language to express our innermost identity, and does this not put us in a position of radical alienation – even our resistance to colonization has to be formulated in the language of the colonizer?' The answer to this is: yes – but this imposition of English (a foreign language) created the very X which is 'oppressed' by it: that is, what is oppressed is not pre-colonial India, but the authentic dream of a new universalist democratic India.

Was Malcolm X not following the same insight when he adopted X as his family name? The point of choosing X – and thereby signaling that the slave traders who brought the enslaved Africans from their homeland brutally deprived them of their family and ethnic roots, of their entire cultural life-world – was not to mobilize the blacks to fight for the return to some primordial African roots, but precisely to seize the opening provided by X, an unknown new (lack of) identity engendered by the very process of slavery which rendered the African roots forever lost. The idea is that this X, which deprives the blacks of their particular traditions, offers a unique chance to redefine (reinvent) themselves, to freely form a new identity that is much more universal than white people's professed universality. (Malcolm X, of course, found this new identity in the universalism of Islam.)

So, back to India, 'reconciliation' means reconciliation with the English language, which is to be accepted not as the obstacle to a new India, to be discarded for some local language, but as an enabling medium, as the positive condition of liberation. The true victory over colonization is not the return to any 'authentic' pre-colonial existence, even less any 'synthesis' between modern civilization and pre-modern origins – but, paradoxically, the *fully accomplished loss of these pre-modern origins*. In other words, colonialism is not overcome when the intrusion of the English language as a medium is abolished, but when the colonizers are, as it were, beaten at their own game – when the new Indian identity is effortlessly formulated in English, i.e., when English language is 'denaturalized', when it loses its privileged link to 'native' Anglo-Saxon English-speakers. It is crucial to point out that this role of the English language was clearly perceived by many intellectuals among the Dalits or 'untouchables', the lowest caste: a large proportion of Dalits welcomed English and in fact even the colonial encounter as a whole. For Ambedkar (the foremost political figure of the Dalit caste) and his legatees, British colonialism — unwittingly and incidentally — gives scope for the so-called rule of law and formal equality for all Indians. Before that, Indians only had caste laws, which gave Dalits almost no rights and only duties.[25] Furthermore, in India today, the genuinely endangered tribal groups (like those in the jungles around Hyderabad) do not fight for their traditional values and ties; they engage much more strongly in Maoist struggle (the Naxalite guerilla movement), which is formulated in the universal aim of overcoming capitalism. It is high-class and high-caste (mostly Brahmin) post-colonial theorists, not those who really belong to indigenous tribal groups, who celebrate the perseverance of local traditions and communal ethics as constituting resistance to global capitalism.

At a more general level, one should bear in mind that global capitalism does not automatically push all its subjects towards hedonist/permissive individualism, and also the fact that, in many countries which have recently set off on the road of rapid capitalist modernization (like India), many individuals stick to so-called traditional (pre-modern) beliefs and ethics (family values, rejection of unbridled hedonism, strong ethnic identification, giving preference to community ties over individual achievement, respect for elders and so on). This in no way proves that they are not fully 'modern', as if people in the liberal West can afford direct and full capitalist modernization, while those from less-developed Asian, Latin American and African countries can only survive the onslaught of capitalist dynamics through the help of the crutches of traditional ties, i.e., as if traditional values are needed when local populations are not able to survive capitalism by way of adopting its own liberal-hedonist individualist ethics. Post-colonial 'subaltern' theorists, who detect in the persistence of pre-modern traditions the resistance to global capitalism and its violent modernization, are here thoroughly wrong: on the contrary, fidelity to pre-modern ('Asian') values is paradoxically *the* very feature which allows countries like China, Singapore and India to follow the path of capitalist dynamics even more radically than Western liberal countries. Reference to traditional values enables individuals to justify their ruthless engagement in market competition in ethical terms ('I am really doing it to help my parents, to earn enough money so that my children and cousins will be able to study,' and so on).[26]

There is a nicely vulgar joke about Christ: the night before he is arrested and crucified, his followers start to worry – Christ is still a virgin, wouldn't it be nice to have him experience a little bit of pleasure before he dies? So they ask Mary Magdalene to go to the tent where Christ is resting and seduce him. Mary willingly agrees and goes in, but five minutes later runs out screaming, terrified and furious. The followers asked her what went wrong, and she explained: 'I slowly undressed, spread my legs and showed Christ my pussy; he looked at it, said "What a terrible wound! It should be healed!" and gently put his palm on it.' So beware of people too intent on healing other people's wounds – what if one enjoys one's wound? In exactly the same way, directly healing the wound of colonialism (effectively returning to the pre-colonial reality) would be a nightmare: if today's Indians were to find themselves in a pre-colonial reality, they would undoubtedly utter the same terrified scream as Mary Magdalene. It is precisely apropos of the wound of colonialism that the final message of Richard Wagner's *Parsifal* holds: 'The wound can be healed only by the spear that smote it' (*Die Wunde schliesst der Speer nur der Sie schlug*). The very disintegration of traditional forms opens up the space of liberation. As was clear to Nelson Mandela and the ANC, white supremacy and the temptation of returning to tribal roots are two sides of the same coin.[27]

According to the standard liberal myth, the universality of human rights brings peace: it establishes the conditions of peaceful co-existence between the multiplicity of particular cultures. From the standpoint of the colonized, on the other hand, liberal universality is false: it functions as the violent intrusion of a foreign culture dissolving our particular roots. Even if he or she admits some truth in this reproach, a liberal would continue to strive for 'universality without wounds', for a universal frame which would not impinge violently on particular cultures. From a properly dialectical perspective, we should strive for (or, rather, endorse the necessity of) an exactly inverted approach: the wound as such is liberating – or, rather, contains a liberating potential – so, while we should definitely problematize the positive content of the imposed universality (the particular content it secretly privileges), we should fully endorse the liberating aspect of the wound (to our particular identity) as such.[28]

To put it in yet another way, what the experience of the English language as an oppressive imposition obfuscates is that the same holds for *every* language: language is as such a parasitic foreign intruder. Throughout his work, Lacan varies Heidegger's motif of language as the house of being: language is not man's creation and instrument, it is man who 'dwells' in language. 'Psychoanalysis,' he states, 'should be the science of language inhabited by the subject.'[29] Lacan's 'paranoiac' twist, his additional Freudian turn of the screw, comes from his characterization of this house as a *torture-house*: 'From the Freudian point of view man is the subject captured and tortured by language.'[30] Not only does man dwell in the 'prison-house of language' (the title of Fredric Jameson's early book on structuralism), he dwells in a torture-house of language: the entire psychopathology deployed by Freud, from conversion-symptoms inscribed in the body up to total psychotic breakdowns, are scars of this permanent torture, so many signs of an original and irremediable gap between subject and language, so many signs that man cannot ever be at home in his own home. This is what Heidegger ignores: this dark torturing other side of our dwelling in language – and this is why there is also no place for the Real of *jouissance* in Heidegger's edifice, since the torturing aspect of language concerns primarily the vicissitudes of libido.

A, NOT G FLAT

So if we discard the obscene notion that it is better to be 'authentically' tortured by one's 'own' language than by a foreign imposed one, we should first emphasize the liberating aspect of being compelled to use a foreign 'universal' language. There was a certain historical wisdom in the fact that, from medieval times until recently, the *lingua franca* of the West was Latin, a 'secondary' inauthentic language, a 'fall' from Greek, and not Greek with all its authentic burden: it was this very emptiness and 'inauthenticity' of Latin that allowed Europeans to fill it with their own particular contents, in contrast to the full-to-bursting overbearing nature of Greek. Learning precisely this lesson, Samuel Beckett started to write in French, a foreign language, leaving behind the 'authenticity' of his roots. So, to recapitulate: the function of experiencing the foreign language as an oppressive imposition is to obfuscate this oppressive dimension in our own language, i.e., to retroactively elevate our own maternal tongue into a lost paradise of full authentic expression. The move to be accomplished when we experience the imposed foreign language as oppressive, as out of sync with our innermost life, is thus to transpose this discord into our own maternal tongue. Such a move is, of course, an extremely painful one: it equals the loss of the very substance of our being, of our concrete historical roots. It means that, as George Orwell put it, I have in a way to 'alter myself so completely that at the end I should hardly be recognizable as the same person.' Are we ready to do this? Back in 1937, Orwell deployed the ambiguity of the predominant Leftist attitude towards class difference:

> We all rail against class-distinctions, but very few people seriously want to abolish them. Here you come upon the important fact that every revolutionary opinion draws part of its strength from a secret conviction that nothing can be changed ... The fact that has got to be faced is that to abolish class-distinctions means abolishing a part of yourself.

Here am I, a typical member of the middle class. It is easy for me to say that I want to get rid of class-distinctions, but nearly everything I think and do is a result of class-distinctions. All my notions – notions of good and evil, of pleasant and unpleasant, of funny and serious, of ugly and beautiful – are essentially *middle-class* notions; my taste in books and food and clothes, my sense of honour, my table manners, my turns of speech, my accent, even the characteristic movements of my body, are the products of a special kind of upbringing and a special niche about half-way up the social hierarchy.[31]

So where is Orwell himself here? He rejects patronizing compassion or any attempt to 'become like workers' – indeed, he wants workers to wash more, and so on. But does this mean he wants to remain middle-class and therefore accepts that class differences are to remain? The problem is that the way Orwell formulates the alternative – 'sticking to one's middle-class values or becoming like workers' – is a false one: being an authentic revolutionary has nothing whatsoever to do with 'becoming like workers', with imitating the lifestyle of the poor classes. The goal of revolutionary activity is, on the contrary, to change the entire social situation so that workers themselves will no longer be 'workers'. In other words, both poles of Orwell's dilemma – sticking to middle-class values or effectively becoming like workers – are typical middle-class options. Indeed, Robespierre and Lenin were distinctly middle-class in their private sensibility, but this is neither here nor there – the point is not to become like workers, but to change the workers' lot. Orwell's insight holds only for a certain kind of 'bourgeois' Leftist. There are Leftists who do have the courage of their convictions, who do not want only a 'revolution without revolution', as Robespierre put it – Jacobins and Bolsheviks, among others. The starting point of these true revolutionaries can in fact be the very position of the 'bourgeois' Leftists: what happens is that, in the middle of their pseudo-radical posturing, they get wrapped up in their own game, and start truly to question their subjective position. It is difficult to imagine a more trenchant political example of the weight of Lacan's distinction between the 'subject of the enunciated' and the 'subject of the enunciation': first, in a direct negation, you start by wanting to 'change the world' without endangering the subjective position from which you are ready to enforce the change; then, in the 'negation of the negation', the subject enacting the change is ready to pay the subjective price for it, to change himself, or, to quote Gandhi's formula, to be himself the change he wants to see in the world.

Is 'to alter myself so completely that at the end I should hardly be recognizable as the same person' not an event of radical self-transformation comparable to rebirth? Orwell's point is that radicals invoke the need for revolutionary change as a kind of superstitious token that should achieve the opposite, i.e., *prevent* the change from really occurring, in the sense that today's academic Leftist who criticizes capitalist cultural imperialism is in reality horrified at the idea that his field of study would break down. Think about the world of the big international art biennales, a true capitalist venture that as a rule is sustained by an 'anti-capitalist' ideology whose predominant form is a mixture of anti-Eurocentrism, critiques of modernity ('we live in a post-Kantian universe'), and warnings on how even art events are moments of the circulation of capital – to which one cannot but reply with a version of the old Marx brothers' quip: 'They say today's art scene is part of capitalist machinery, but this shouldn't deceive you – it really is part of capitalist machinery!' The famous lines from Act II of *Othello*, 'O gentle lady, do not put me to't, / for I am nothing if not critical', seem to render perfectly the stance of today's art critic: the moment he is put to his job, he cannot but thoroughly denounce the way art production, distribution, consumption and critique are determined by global capitalist coordinates. In the morass of such ideological denegations, it is refreshing, subversive even, to find a direct assertion of 'bourgeois' values, as with Robert Pippin, who recently claimed that his entire philosophical project is to defend the bourgeois way of life. If one is consequent enough in this assertion, one soon discovers inconsistencies in the bourgeois way of life, inconsistencies which compel one to move beyond this way of life precisely in order to save what is worth saving in it.

Is then a conference on the idea of Communism, such as the one held in Seoul from 24 to 29 September 2013, also destined to become a similar kind of pseudo-event, a Communist biennale? Or are we setting in motion something that has the potential to develop into an actual force of social transformation? It may appear that one cannot act today, that all we can really do is just state things. But in a situation like today's, to state what is can be much stronger than calls to action, which are as a rule just so many excuses *not* to do anything. Let me quote Alain Badiou's provocative thesis: 'It is better to do nothing than to contribute to the invention of formal ways of rendering visible that which Empire already recognizes as existent.' Better to do nothing than to engage in localized acts whose ultimate function is to make the system run more smoothly (acts like providing space for the multitude of new subjectivities, etc.). The threat today is not passivity, but pseudo-activity, the urge to 'be active', to 'participate', to mask the Nothingness of what goes on. People intervene all the time, 'do something', while academics participate in meaningless 'debates', and so on, and the truly difficult thing is to step back, to withdraw from all this. Those in power often prefer even a 'critical' participation, an exchange of whatever kind, to silence – just in order to engage us in a 'dialogue', to make sure our ominous passivity is broken. This is why the title of the fourth 'Idea of Communism' meeting in Seoul, in September 2013, was fully justified: 'Stop to think!'

Events point in this direction even in a country like South Korea, with its explosive economic development. There is in Korea a widespread workers' resistance to the rapid passage into a post-historical society, and this resistance reaches far beyond a simple workers' struggle for better wages and working conditions – it is a struggle for an entire way of life, the resistance of a *world* threatened by the rapid modernization of South Korea. 'World' stands here for a specific horizon of meaning, for an entire civilization or, rather, *culture*, with its everyday rituals and manners, which are threatened by post-historical commodification. Is then this resistance conservative? Today's mainstream self-declared political and cultural conservatives are not really conservatives: fully endorsing capitalist continuous self-revolutionizing, they just want to make it more efficient by supplementing it with some traditional institutions (such as religion) to contain its destructive consequences for social life and maintain social cohesion. A true conservative today is the one who fully admits the antagonisms and deadlocks of global capitalism, the one who rejects simple progressivism, and is attentive to the dark obverse of progress. In this sense, only a radical Leftist can be today a true conservative. Such a stance was described long ago by John Jay Chapman (1862–1933), today a half-forgotten American political activist and essayist[32] who wrote about political radicals:

> The radicals are really always saying the same thing. They do not change; everybody else changes. They are accused of the most incompatible crimes, of egoism and a mania for power, indifference to the fate of their own cause, fanaticism, triviality, want of humour, buffoonery and irreverence. But they sound a certain note. Hence the great practical power of consistent radicals. To all appearance nobody follows them, yet everyone believes them. They hold a tuning-fork and sound A, and everybody knows it really is A, though the time-honoured pitch is G flat. The community cannot get that A out of its head. Nothing can prevent an upward tendency in the popular tone so long as the real A is kept sounding.[33]

One should emphasize here the moment of passivity and immobility: in Kierkegaard's terms, a radical is not a creative genius but an apostle who just embodies and delivers a truth – he just goes on and on repeating the same message ('class struggle goes on'; 'capitalism engenders antagonisms'; and so on), and although it may appear that nobody follows him, everyone believes him, i.e., everybody secretly knows he is telling the truth – which is why he is constantly accused 'of the most incompatible crimes, of egoism and a mania for power, indifference to the fate of their own cause, fanaticism, triviality, want of humour, buffoonery and irreverence.' And what this means is that, in the choice between dignity and the risk of appearing a buffoon, a true political radical easily renounces dignity.

The motto that united the Turks who protested on Istanbul's Taksim Square in 2013 was 'Dignity!' – a good but ambiguous slogan. The term 'dignity' is appropriate insofar as it makes it clear that protests are not just about particular material demands, but about the protesters' freedom and emancipation. In the case of the Taksim Square protests, the call for dignity referred not only to institutional corruption and venality, but was also – crucially – directed against the patronizing ideology of the Turkish prime minister, Recep Tayyip Erdoğan. The direct target of the Taksim Square protests was neither neoliberal capitalism nor Islamism, but the personality of Erdoğan: the demand was for *him* to step down – but why? What was it about him that made Erdoğan the target of secular educated protesters as well as of anti-capitalist Muslim youth, the object of a hatred that fused them together? Here is Bülent Somay's explanation:

> Everybody wanted PM Erdoğan to resign. Because, many activists explained both during and after the Resistance, he was constantly meddling with their lifestyles, telling women to have at least three children, telling them not to have C-sections, not to have abortions, telling people not to drink, not to smoke, not to hold hands in public, to be obedient and religious. He was constantly telling them what was best for them ('shop and pray'). This was probably the best indication of the neoliberal ('shop') soft-Islamic ('pray') character of the JDP rule: PM Erdoğan's utopia for Istanbul (and we should remember that he was the Mayor of Istanbul for four years) was a huge shopping mall and a huge mosque in Taksim Square and Gezi Park. He had become 'Daddy Knows Best' in all avenues of life, and tried to do this in a clumsy patronizing disguise, which was quickly discarded during Gezi events to reveal the profoundly authoritarian character behind the image.[34]

Is 'shop and pray' not a perfect late-capitalist version of the old Christian *ora et labora*, with the identity of a worker (toiling peasant) replaced by a consumer? The underlying wager is, of course, that praying (a codename for the fidelity to old communal traditions) makes us even better 'shoppers', i.e., participants in the global capitalist market. However, the call for dignity is not only a protest against such a patronizing injunction; dignity is also the appearance of dignity, and in this case the demand for dignity means that I want to be duped and controlled in such a way that proper appearances are maintained, that I don't lose face. Is this not a key feature of our democracies? Walter Lippmann, that icon of twentieth-century American journalism, played a key role in the self-understanding of US democracy; in *Public Opinion* (1922),[35] he wrote that a 'governing class' must rise to face the challenge – he saw the public as Plato did, a great beast or a bewildered herd, floundering in the 'chaos of local opinions'. So the herd of citizens must be governed by 'a specialized class whose interests reach beyond the locality', and this elite class is to act as a machinery of knowledge that circumvents the primary defect of democracy, the impossible ideal of the 'omni-competent citizen'. This is how our democracies function – with our consent. There is no mystery in what Lippmann was saying: it is an obvious fact. The mystery is that, knowing it, we nevertheless play the game. We act *as if* we are free and freely deciding, silently not only accepting but even *demanding* that an invisible injunction (inscribed into the very form of our free speech) tells us what to do and think. As Marx realized long ago, the secret is in the form itself. In this sense, in a democracy, every ordinary citizen effectively is a king – but a king in a constitutional democracy, a king who only formally decides, whose function is to sign measures proposed by an executive administration. This is why the problem of democratic rituals is homologous to the big problem of constitutional democracy: how to protect the dignity of the king? How to maintain the appearance that the king effectively decides, when we all know this is not true? What we call a 'crisis of democracy' does not occur when people stop believing in their own power but, on the contrary, when they stop trusting the elites, those who are supposed to know for them and provide the guidelines, when they experience the anxiety signalling that 'the (true) throne is empty', that the decision is now *really* theirs. There is thus in 'free elections' always a minimal aspect of politeness: those in power politely pretend that they do not really hold power, and ask us to freely decide if we want to give them power – in a way which mirrors the logic of the offer-meant-to-be-refused, as mentioned above. So, back to Turkey, is it only this type of dignity that the protesters want, tired as they are of the primitive and openly direct way they are cheated and manipulated? Is their demand in fact, 'We want to be cheated in a proper way – at least make an honest effort to cheat us without insulting our intelligence!', or is it really more? If we aim at more, then we should be aware that the first step of liberation is to get rid of the appearance of false freedom and to openly proclaim our unfreedom. Say, the first step towards female liberation is to throw off the appearance of respect for women and to proclaim openly that women are oppressed – more than ever, today's master doesn't want to appear as a master.[36]

TOWARDS A NEW MASTER

In the very last pages of his monumental *Second World War*, Winston Churchill ponders on the enigma of a military decision. After the specialists (economic and military analysts, psychologists, meteorologists ...) propose their multiple, elaborated and refined analysis, somebody must assume the simple and for that very reason most difficult act of transposing this complex multitude – where for every reason for there are two reasons against – into a simple 'Yes' or 'No': we shall attack; we continue to wait. This gesture, which can never be fully grounded in reason, is that of a Master. It is for the experts to present the situation in its complexity, and it is for the Master to simplify it into a point of decision.

Such a Master figure is needed especially in situations of deep crisis. The function of a Master is here to enact an authentic division – a division between those who want to drag on within the old parameters and those who are aware of the change that is necessary. President Obama is often accused of dividing the American people instead of bringing them all together to find broad bi-partisan solutions – but what if this, precisely, is what is good about him? Such a division, not the opportunistic compromises, is the only path to true unity. Let us take an example which surely is not problematic: France in 1940. Even Jacques Duclos, the second man of the French Communist Party, admitted in a private conversation that if, at that time, free elections were to be held in France, Marshal Pétain would have won with 90 per cent of the votes. When de Gaulle, in his historic act, refused to acknowledge Pétain's capitulation to Germany and continued to resist, he claimed that it was only he, not the Vichy regime, who spoke on behalf of true France (on behalf of true France as such, not only on behalf of the 'majority of the French'!) what he was saying was deeply true, even if it was 'democratically' not only without legitimization, but clearly opposed to the opinion of the majority of the French people. And Margaret Thatcher, the 'lady who is not for turning', was also such a Master, sticking to her plan of economic liberalism which was at first perceived as crazy, gradually elevating her singular madness into an accepted norm. When Thatcher was asked about her greatest achievement, she promptly answered: 'New Labour.' And she was right: her triumph was that even her political enemies adopted her basic economic policies. The true triumph is not victory over the enemy; it occurs when the enemy itself starts to use your language, so that your ideas form the foundation of the entire field.

So what remains of Thatcher's legacy today? Neoliberal hegemony is clearly falling apart. The only solution is to repeat Thatcher's gesture in the opposite direction. Thatcher was perhaps the only true Thatcherite – she clearly believed in her ideas. Today's neoliberalism, on the contrary, 'only imagines that it believes in itself and demands that the world should imagine the same thing' (to quote Marx). In short, today, cynicism is openly on display. Recall again the already-mentioned cruel joke from Lubitsch's *To Be Or Not to Be*: when asked about the German concentration camps in occupied Poland, the responsible Nazi officer, 'concentration camp Erhardt', snaps back: 'We do the concentrating, and the Poles do the camping.' Does the same not hold for the Enron bankruptcy in January 2002 (as well as for all the financial meltdowns that followed), which can be interpreted as a kind of ironic commentary on the notion of the risk society? The thousands of employees who lost their jobs and savings were certainly exposed to risk, but without any true choice: the risk appeared to them as blind fate. Those, on the contrary, who effectively did have an insight into the risks as well as a possibility to intervene in the situation (the top managers), minimized their risks by cashing in their stocks and options before the bankruptcy – so it is true that we live in a society of risky choices, but some (the Wall Street managers) do the choosing, while others (the common people paying mortgages) do the risking.

As we have already pointed out, one of the weird consequences of the financial meltdown and the measures taken to counteract it (enormous sums of money to help banks) was a revival in the works of Ayn Rand, the closest that one can come to an ideologist of radical 'greed is good' capitalism – the sales of her magnum opus *Atlas Shrugged* exploded again. According to some reports, there are already signs that the scenario described in *Atlas Shrugged* – the creative capitalists themselves going on strike – has been enacted. John Campbell, a Republican congressman, said in support of the Tea Party movement:

'The achievers are going on strike. I'm seeing, at a small level, a kind of protest from the people who create jobs . . . who are pulling back from their ambitions because they see how they'll be punished for them.' The absurdity of this reaction is that it totally misreads the situation: most of the gigantic sums of bailout money went precisely to the deregulated Randian 'titans' who failed in their 'creative' schemes and thereby brought about the meltdown. It is not the great creative geniuses who are now helping lazy ordinary people but the ordinary taxpayers who are helping the failed 'creative geniuses'.

The other aspect of Thatcher's legacy targeted by her Leftist critics was her 'authoritarian' form of leadership, her lack of a sense for democratic coordination. Here, however, things are more complex than they may appear. The ongoing popular protests around Europe converge in a series of demands which, in their very spontaneity and directness, form a kind of 'epistemological obstacle' to any proper confrontation with the ongoing crisis of our political system. These demands effectively read as a popularized version of Deleuzian politics: people know what they want, they are able to discover and formulate this but only through their own continuous engagement and activity, so we need active participatory democracy, not just representative democracy with its electoral ritual which every four years interrupts the voters' passivity; we need the self-organization of the multitude, not a centralized Leninist Party with its Leader.

But is this myth of non-representative direct self-organization not the last trap, the deepest illusion that is most difficult to renounce? Yes, there are, in every revolutionary process, ecstatic moments of group solidarity, when thousands, hundreds of thousands, together occupy a public place, like on Cairo's Tahrir Square in 2011; yes, there are moments of intense collective participation in which local communities debate and decide, when people live in a kind of permanent emergency state, taking things into their own hands, with no Leader guiding them. But such states don't last – and 'tiredness' is here not a simple psychological fact, it is a category of social ontology. The large majority – me included – *wants* to be passive and to rely on an efficient state apparatus to guarantee the smooth running of the entire social edifice, so that I can pursue my work in peace.

Following the spirit of today's ideology, which demands the shift from traditional hierarchy, a pyramid-like subordination to a Master, to pluralizing rhizomatic networks, political analysts like to point out that the new anti-globalist protests all around Europe and the US, from Occupy Wall Street (OWS) to Greece and Spain, have no central agency, no Central Committee, coordinating their activity. Rather, there are just multiple groups interacting, mostly through new media like Facebook or Twitter, and coordinating their activity spontaneously. This is why, when the apparatuses of police power look for the secret organizing committees, they miss the point – in the Slovenian capital Ljubljana, 10,000 protesters gathered in front of the Parliament in February 2014 and proudly proclaimed: 'The protest is attended by 10,000 organizers.' But is this 'molecular' spontaneous self-organization really the most efficient new form of 'resistance'? Is it not that the opposite side, especially capital, already acts more and more as what Deleuzian theory calls the post-Oedipal multitude?[37] Power itself has to enter a dialogue at this level, answering tweet with tweet – indeed, now Pope and prime ministers are on Twitter. We should not be afraid to pursue this line of reasoning to its conclusion: the opposition between centralized-hierarchic vertical power and horizontal multitudes is inherent in the existing social and political order; none of the two is *a priori* 'better' or more 'progressive'.[38]

Furthermore, as far as concerns the molecular self-organizing multitude against the hierarchic order sustained by reference to a charismatic Leader, it is worth noting the irony that Venezuela, a country praised by many for its attempts to develop modes of direct democracy (local councils, cooperatives, workers running factories), is also a country whose president was Hugo Chavez, a strong charismatic Leader if there ever was one. It is as if the Freudian rule of transference is at work here also: in order for the individuals to 'reach beyond themselves', to break out of the passivity of representative politics and become direct political agents themselves, reference to a Leader is necessary, a Leader who allows them to pull themselves out of the swamp like Baron Münchhausen, a Leader who is 'supposed to know' what they want. This is why, in their book of dialogues, Alain Badiou and Elisabeth Roudinesco were right to point out how, while horizontal networking does undermine the classic Master, it simultaneously breeds new forms of domination that are much stronger than the classic Master. Badiou's thesis is that a subject needs a Master to elevate itself above the 'human animal' and to practise fidelity to a Truth-Event:

> ROUDINESCO: In the last resort, what was lost in psychoanalytic societies is the position of the Master to the benefit of the position of small bosses.
>
> AESCHIMANN: What do you mean by 'master'?
>
> ROUDINESCO: The position of the master allows transference: the psychoanalyst is 'supposed to know' what the analysand will discover. Without this knowledge attributed to the psychoanalyst, the search for the origin of suffering is quasi impossible.
>
> AESCHIMANN: Do we really have to go through the restoration of the master?
>
> BADIOU: The master is the one who helps the individual to become subject. That is to say, if one admits that the subject emerges in the tension between the individual and the universality, then it is obvious that the individual needs a mediation, and thereby an authority, in order to progress on this path. The crisis of the master is a logical consequence of the crisis of the subject, and psychoanalysis did not escape it. One has to renew the position of the master; it is not true that one can do without it, even and especially in the perspective of emancipation.
>
> ROUDINESCO: When the master disappears, he is replaced by the boss, by his authoritarianism, and sooner or later this always ends in fascism – unfortunately, history has proven this to us.[39]

And Badiou is not afraid to oppose the necessary role of the Master to our 'democratic' sensitivity:

> I am convinced that one has to re-establish the capital function of leaders in the Communist process, whichever its stage. Two crucial episodes in which the leadership was insufficient were the Paris Commune (no worthy leader, with the exception of Dombrowski in the strictly military domain) and the Great Proletarian Cultural Revolution (Mao too

old and tired, and the 'group of the GPCR' infected by ultra-Leftism). This was a severe lesson.

This capital function of leaders is not compatible with the predominant 'democratic' ambience, which is why I am engaged in a bitter struggle against this ambience (after all, one has to begin with ideology). When I am dealing with people whose jargon is Lacanian I say 'a figure of Master'. When they are militants I say 'dictatorship' (in the sense of Carl Schmitt). When they are workers I say 'leader of a crowd', and so on. It is so that I am quickly understood.[40]

But is this effectively the case? Is the only alternative to the Master the (potentially 'totalitarian') 'boss'? In psychoanalysis, the Master is by definition an impostor, and the whole point of the analytic process is to dissolve the transference to the Master *qua* 'subject supposed to know' – the conclusion of analysis involves the fall of the subject-supposed-to-know. While Jacques-Alain Miller (as an analyst) endorses this fall, he nonetheless agrees with Badiou that the domain of politics is the domain of the discourse of the Master. Their difference resides in the fact that, while Badiou opts for full engagement, Miller advocates a cynical distance towards the Master: a psychoanalyst

occupies the position of ironist who takes care not to intervene into the political field. He acts so that semblances remain at their places while making it sure that subjects under his care do not take them for *real* . . . one should somehow bring oneself to remain *taken in by them* (fooled by them). Lacan could say that 'the non-duped err': if one doesn't act as if semblances are real, if one doesn't leave their efficiency undisturbed, things turn for the worse.[41]

One should reject this shared premise: an axiom of radical emancipatory politics is that the Master is *not* the ultimate horizon of our social life, that one can form a collective not held together by a Master figure. Without this axiom, there is no Communist politics proper, but just pragmatic ameliorations of the existing order. However, we should at the same time follow the lesson of psychoanalysis: the only path to liberation leads through transference, and this is why the figure of a Master is unavoidable. So we should fearlessly follow Badiou's

suggestion: in order to effectively awaken individuals from their dogmatic 'democratic slumber', from their blind reliance on institutionalized
forms of representative democracy, appeals to direct self-organization
are not enough: a new figure of the Master is needed. Recall the famous lines from Arthur Rimbaud's '*À une raison*' ('To a Reason'):

> A tap of your finger on the drum releases all sounds and initiates
> the new harmony.
> A step of yours is the conscription of the new men and their
> marching orders.
> You look away: the new love!
> You look back — the new love![42]

There is absolutely nothing inherently 'Fascist' in these lines. The
supreme paradox of political dynamics is that a Master is needed to
pull individuals out of the quagmire of their inertia and motivate
them towards the self-transcending emancipatory struggle for freedom. What we need today, in this situation, is thus a Thatcher of the
Left: a leader who would repeat Thatcher's gesture in the opposite
direction, transforming the entire field of presuppositions shared by
today's political elite of all main orientations. This is also why we
should reject the ideology of what Saroj Giri called 'anarchic horizontalism', the distrust of all hierarchic structures – we should shamelessly
reassert the idea of 'vanguard', when one part of a progressive movement assumes leadership and mobilizes other parts:

> If consensus and horizontalism are not to remain stuck in nursing
> quasi-liberal egos, then we must be able to delineate how they can con-
> tribute towards a more substantive notion of politics – one which
> involves a verticalism. Perhaps this would be a better way to revive a
> communist politics instead of taking politically correct vows of hori-
> zontalism and consensus.[43]

Giri takes the example of the Spokes Council in Oakland's OWS
movement, a body separate from the General Assembly,

> a separate body, which was not to be confused with the movement,
> taking key decisions and implementing them: was this (incipient)

verticalism violating democratic decision making or was it the natural working of horizontalism, giving us a verticalism whih is the unfolding of horizontalism, horizontalism's truth? ... *the minority providing the line of march to the movement does not amount to a reified subjectivity.*'[44]

The same goes for so-called 'extreme' tactics, which can be counter-productive, but can also radicalize a broad circle of supporters: 'such practices that are the actions of a radical minority do not lead to dis-unity but to a higher revolutionary unity.'[45]

'THE RIGHT OF DISTRESS'

So what is the elementary gesture of this Master? Surprisingly, Hegel pointed out the way here. Let us begin with his account of the 'right of distress (*Notrecht*)':[46]

§ 127 The particularity of the interests of the natural will, taken in their entirety as a single whole, is personal existence or life. In extreme dan-ger and in conflict with the rightful property of someone else, this life may claim (as a right, not a mercy) a right of distress [*Notrecht*], because in such a situation there is on the one hand an infinite injury to a man's existence and the consequent loss of rights altogether, and on the other hand only an injury to a single restricted embodiment of free-dom, and this implies a recognition both of right as such and also of the injured man's capacity for rights, because the injury affects only this property of his.

Remark: The right of distress is the basis of *beneficium competentiae* whereby a debtor is allowed to retain of his tools, farming implements, clothes, or, in short, of his resources, i.e. of his creditor's property, so much as is regarded as indispensable if he is to continue to support life – to support it, of course, on his own social level.

Addition: Life as the sum of ends has a right against abstract right. If for example it is only by stealing bread that the wolf can be kept from the door, the action is of course an encroachment on someone's prop-erty, but it would be wrong to treat this action as an ordinary theft. To refuse to allow a man in jeopardy of his life to take such steps for self-preservation would be to stigmatize him as without rights, and since he would be deprived of his life, his freedom would be annulled altogether . . .

§ 128 This distress reveals the finitude and therefore the contingency of both right and welfare of right as the abstract embodiment of free-dom without embodying the particular person, and of welfare as the sphere of the particular will without the universality of right.

Hegel is not talking here about the humanitarian considerations that should temper our legalistic zeal (if an impoverished father steals bread to feed his starving child, we should show mercy and under-standing even if he breaks the law). The partisans of such an approach, which constrains its zeal to fighting suffering while leaving intact the economico-legal edifice within which this suffering takes place, 'only demonstrate that, for all their bloodthirsty, mock-humanist yelping, they regard the social conditions in which the bourgeoisie is domin-ant as the final product, the *non plus ultra* of history'[47] – Marx's characterization, which perfectly fits today's humanitarians like Bill Gates. What Hegel talks about is a basic legal right, a right which is *as a right* superior to other particular legal rights. In other words, we are not dealing simply with the conflict between the demands of life and the constraints of the legal system of rights, but with a right (to life) that overcomes all formal rights, i.e., with *a conflict inherent to the sphere of rights*, a conflict which is unavoidable and *necessary* insofar as it serves as an indication of the finitude, inconsistency and 'abstract' character of the system of legal rights as such. 'To refuse to allow a man in jeopardy of his life to take such steps for self-preservation [like stealing the food necessary for his survival] would be to *stigma-tize him as without rights*.' So, again, the point is not that the punishment for justified stealing would deprive the subject of his life, but that it would exclude him from the domain of rights, i.e., that it would reduce him to a bare life outside the domain of law, of the legal order. In other words, this refusal deprives the subject of his very *right to have rights*. Furthermore, the quoted *Remark* applies this logic to the situation of a debtor, claiming that he should be allowed to retain of his resources so much as is regarded as indispensable if he is to continue with his life not just at the level of bare survival, but 'on his own social level' – a claim that is today fully relevant with regard to the situation of the impoverished majority in indebted states like Greece. However, the key question here is: can we universalize this 'right of distress', extending it to an entire social class and its acts against the property of another class? Although Hegel does not directly address this question, a positive answer imposes itself from Hegel's description of the 'rabble' as a group or class whose exclusion from the domain of social recognition is *systematic*:

> § 244 *Addition*: Against nature man can claim no right, but once society is established, poverty immediately takes the form of a wrong done to one class by another.

In such a situation, in which a whole class of people is systematically pushed beneath the level of dignified survival, to refuse to allow them to take 'steps for self-preservation' (which, in this case, can only mean open rebellion against the established legal order) is to *stigmatize them as without rights*. In short, what we get in such a reading of Hegel is nothing less than a Maoist Hegel, a Hegel who is telling us what Mao was telling the young at the outset of the Cultural Revolution: '*It is right to rebel!*' This is the lesson of a true Master.

A true Master is not an agent of discipline and prohibition. His message is not 'You cannot!', nor 'You have to . . . !', but a liberating 'You can!' But 'can' what? Do the impossible, i.e., what appears impossible within the coordinates of the existing constellation – and today, this means something very precise: you can think beyond capitalism and liberal democracy as the ultimate framework of our lives. A Master is a vanishing mediator who gives you back to yourself, who delivers you to the abyss of your freedom: when we listen to a true leader, we discover what we want (or, rather, what we always-already wanted without knowing it). A Master is needed because we cannot accede to our freedom directly – in order to gain this access we have to be pushed from outside, since our 'natural state' is one of inert hedonism, of what Badiou calls the 'human animal'. The underlying paradox is here that the more we live as 'free individuals with no Master', the more we are effectively non-free, caught within the existing frame of possibilities: we have to be pushed/disturbed into freedom by a Master.

In Udi Aloni's documentary *Art/Violence*, a tribute to Juliano Mer Khamis, the founder of the Jenin Freedom Theatre, a young Palestinian actress describes what Juliano meant to her and her colleagues: he gave them their freedom, i.e., he made them aware of what they can do, he opened up a new possibility to them, homeless kids from a refugee camp. This is the role of an authentic Master: when we are afraid of something (and fear of death is the ultimate fear that makes us slaves), a true friend will say something like: 'Don't be afraid, look, I'll do it, what you're so afraid of, and I'll do it for free – not because I have to, but out of my love for you; I'm not afraid!' He does it and in this way sets us free, demonstrating *in actu* that it can be done, that we can do it too, that we are not slaves . . .

There was a trace of this authentic Master's call in Obama's slogan from his first presidential campaign: 'Yes, we can!', a phrase that thereby opened a new possibility. But, one might say, did Hitler also not do something formally similar? Wasn't his message to the German people 'Yes, we can' kill the Jews, squash democracy, act in a racist way, attack other nations? A closer analysis immediately brings out the difference: far from being an authentic Master, Hitler was a populist demagogue who carefully played upon people's obscure desires. It may seem that, in doing this, Hitler followed Steve Jobs' infamous motto: 'A lot of times, people don't know what they want until you show it to them.' However, in spite of all one has to criticize in Jobs' activities, he was close to an authentic Master in how he understood his motto. When he was asked how much Apple inquires into what customers want, he replied: 'None. It's not the customers' job to know what they want . . . we figure out what we want.'[48] Note the surprising turn of this argument: after denying that customers know what they want, Jobs doesn't go on with the expected direct reversal – 'It is our task (the task of creative capitalists) to figure out what customers want and then "show it to them" on the market.' Instead, he continues: 'we figure out what *we* want'. This is how a true Master works. He doesn't try to guess what people want; he simply obeys his own desire so that it is up to the people to decide if they will follow him. In other words, his power stems from his fidelity to his desire, from not compromising it. Therein resides the difference between a true Master and, say, a Stalinist leader who pretends to know (better than the people themselves) what people really want (what is really good for them), and is then ready to enforce this on them even against their will.

Hegel's solution to the deadlock of the Master – to have a Master (like a king) reduced to its Name, a purely symbolic authority totally dissociated of all actual qualifications for his job, a monarch whose only function is to sign his name on proposals prepared by experts – should not be confused with the cynical stance of 'Let's have a master who we know to be an idiot.' One cannot cheat in this way since one has to make a choice: either we really don't take the master figure seriously (and in this case the Master simply doesn't function performatively), or we take the Master seriously in the way we act, in spite of our direct conscious irony (which can develop to the point of actually despising the Master). In the latter case, we are simply dealing with a case of disavowal, of 'I know very well, but': our ironic distance is part of the transferential relation to the master figure; it functions as a subjective illusion enabling us effectively to endure the Master – which is to say, we pretend not to take the Master seriously so that we can endure the fact that the Master really is our master.

A similar mechanism of cheating is to accept the need for the figure of a political Master, but to claim that such a figure should only be allowed to rise up after a process of collective deliberation: the Master cannot directly be called on to bring the solution when people find themselves in a deadlock. In such a case we only get a dictator who doesn't really know what to do. People first have to unite their will around a determinate project, and only then can they allow a Master-like figure to lead them along the way outlined in their project. Logical as it may appear, such a notion puts the cart ahead of the horse: as discussed, true leaders do not do what people want or plan; they tell the people what they want, and it is only through them that they realize what they want. Therein resides the act of a true political leader: after listening to him or her, people all of a sudden realize what they always-already knew they wanted – listening to the Master clarifies to them their own position, enables them to recognize themselves, their own innermost need, in the project proposed to them.

But an authentic Master does not need to be a leader. Marek Edelman (1919–2009) was a Jewish-Polish political and social activist. Before the Second World War, he had been active in the Leftist General Jewish Labor Bund (which opposed the Zionist project); during the war, he co-founded the Jewish Combat Organization, took part in the 1943 Warsaw Ghetto Uprising (becoming its leader after the death of Mordechaj Anielewicz) and also in the city-wide uprising of 1944. After the war, Edelman became a noted cardiologist; from the 1970s onwards, he collaborated with the Workers' Defence Committee; as a member of Solidarity, he took part in the Polish Round Table Talks of 1989. While fighting anti-Semitism in Poland, Edelman was a lifelong anti-Zionist: in a 1985 interview, he said Zionism was a 'lost cause' and questioned Israel's viability. Towards the end of his life, he publicly defended Palestinian resistance, claiming that the Jewish self-defence for which he had fought was in danger of crossing the line into oppression. In August 2002, he wrote an open letter to the Palestinian resistance leaders; though the letter criticized the Palestinian suicide attacks, its tone infuriated the Israeli government and press since it was written in a spirit of solidarity from a fellow resistance fighter, a former leader of a Jewish uprising not dissimilar in desperation to the Palestinian uprising in the occupied territories. Because of this, Edelman never got any official Israeli recognition of his heroism; when Jicak Rabin visited Poland as Prime Minister and Edelman was in the delegation awaiting him at Warsaw airport, he refused to shake Edelman's hand (the reason he gave was that he did not want to shake the hand of a Bundist).[49] To designate Edelman as a 'self-hating Jew' would have been the ultimate obscenity, given that he stands for a certain ethical stance which is rarely encountered today: he knew when to act (against Germans), when to make public statements (for Palestinians), when to get engaged in political activity (for Solidarity), and when just to be there. When his wife and children emigrated in the wake of the growing anti-Semitic campaign in 1968, he decided to stay in Poland, comparing himself to the stones of the ruined buildings at the site of the Auschwitz camp: 'Someone had to stay here with all those who perished here, after all.' This says it all: what mattered was ultimately his bare and muted presence there, not his declarations – it was the awareness of Edelman's presence, the bare fact of his 'being there', which set people free.

APPENDIX *Nota bene!*

The two meanings of '*nota bene*' – 'take special notice, note well' (the correct one) and 'good night' (the false one, based on misreading '*nota*' as 'night') – render all too accurately the fate of the critique of ideology today. In our era of cynical indifference, the message of the critique of ideology is, 'Note well what I'm telling you, awaken to your reality!' while the answer to this call is often: 'You're boring, you make me drowsy, so good night!' How to break this dogmatic slumber, how to pass from 'goodnight' to 'I hear what you're telling me'?

What makes this task so difficult is that ideological dreams are not simply opposed to reality: they structure (what we experience as) reality. If, however, what we experience as reality is structured by fantasy, and if fantasy serves as the screen that protects us from being directly overwhelmed by the raw Real, then *reality itself can function as an escape from encountering the Real*. In the opposition between dream and reality, fantasy is on the side of reality, and it is in dreams that we encounter the traumatic Real. So it is not that dreams are for those who cannot endure reality; rather, reality itself is for those who cannot endure (the Real that announces itself in) their dreams. This is the lesson Lacan draws from the famous dream, reported by Freud in his *Interpretation of Dreams*, of the father who falls asleep while keeping guard over his son's coffin. In this dream, his dead son appears to him, pronouncing the terrible appeal 'Father, can't you see that I am burning?' When the father wakes, he discovers that one of the candles burning on his son's coffin has fallen, igniting the cloth covering it. So why did the father awaken? Was it because the smell of the smoke got so strong that it was no longer possible to prolong sleep by incorporating it in the improvised dream? Lacan proposes a much more interesting reading: it was not the intrusion of the signal from external reality that awakened the unfortunate father, but the unbearably traumatic character of what he encountered in the dream – insofar as 'dreaming' means fantasizing in order to avoid confronting the Real, the father literally woke so that he could go on dreaming. The scenario was the following one: when his sleep was disturbed by the smoke, the father quickly constructed a dream that incorporated the disturbing element (smoke/fire) in order to prolong his sleep; however, what he confronted in the dream was a trauma (of his responsibility for his son's death) much stronger than reality, so he woke into reality in order to avoid the Real.

What this means is that the critique of ideology should not begin with critiquing reality, but with the critique of our dreams. The art of revolutionary dreaming can play a crucial role in pre-revolutionary times. Such dreaming is not limited only to radical forces: one can learn a lot also from the distorted way a conservative or liberal historical agent imagines the threatening shadow of an emancipatory Event. Even a virtual Event can leave traces, can serve as an ambiguous point of reference – therein resides the interest of Christopher Nolan's Batman film *The Dark Knight Rises*, which can only be properly understood against the background of the Event it imagines. Here is the film's (somewhat simplified) storyline.

Eight years after the events of *The Dark Knight*, law and order prevail in Gotham City: under the extraordinary powers granted by the Dent Act, Commissioner Gordon has nearly eradicated violent and organized crime. He nonetheless feels guilty about the cover-up of Harvey Dent's crimes (when Dent tried to kill Gordon's son before Batman saved him, Dent fell to his death, and Batman took the fall for the Dent myth, allowing himself to be demonized as Gotham's villain), and plans to admit to the conspiracy at a public event celebrating Dent, before deciding that the city is not ready to hear the truth. No longer active as Batman, Bruce Wayne lives isolated in his manor while his business crumbles after he invested in a clean-energy project designed to harness fusion power but shut it down after learning that the core could be modified to become a nuclear weapon. Meanwhile, the beautiful Miranda Tate, a member of the Wayne Enterprises executive board, encourages Wayne to rejoin society and continue his philanthropic works.

Here enters the (first) villain of the film. Bane, a terrorist leader who was a member of the League of Shadows, gets hold of a copy of Gordon's speech. After Bane's financial machinations bring Wayne's company close to bankruptcy, Wayne entrusts Miranda with control of his enterprise and also engages in a brief love affair with her. (In this she competes with Selina Kyle, a cat burglar who steals from the rich in order to redistribute wealth, but finally joins Wayne and the forces of law and order.) Learning that Bane has got hold of his fusion core, Wayne returns as Batman and confronts Bane, who says that he has taken over the League of Shadows following the death of its leader, Ra's al Ghul. Crippling Batman in close combat, Bane detains him in a prison from which escape is virtually impossible: inmates tell Wayne the story of the only person to successfully escape, a child driven by necessity and the sheer force of will. While the imprisoned Wayne recovers from his injuries and retrains himself to be Batman, Bane succeeds in turning Gotham City into an isolated city-state. He first lures most of Gotham's police force underground and traps them there; then he sets off explosions which destroy most of the bridges connecting Gotham City to the mainland, announcing that any attempt to leave the city will result in the detonation of Wayne's fusion core, which has been converted into a bomb.

Here we reach the crucial moment of the film: Bane's takeover is accompanied by a vast politico-ideological offensive. Bane publicly reveals the cover-up of Dent's death and releases the prisoners locked up under the Dent Act. Condemning the rich and powerful, he promises to restore the power of the common people, calling on them to 'take your city back'. Bane reveals himself to be 'the ultimate Wall Street Occupier, calling on the 99 per cent to band together and overthrow societal elites'.[1] What follows is the film's idea of people power: summary show trials and executions of the rich, streets littered with crime and villainy, and so on.

After a couple of months, Wayne successfully escapes prison, returns to Gotham as Batman, and enlists his friends to help liberate the city and stop the fusion bomb before it explodes. Batman confronts and subdues Bane, but Miranda intervenes and stabs Batman, revealing herself to be Talia al Ghul, the daughter of Ra's: it was she who escaped the prison as a child, and Bane was the one person who aided her escape. After announcing her plan to complete her father's work in destroying Gotham, Talia escapes. In the ensuing mayhem, Gordon cuts off the bomb's ability to be remotely detonated while Selina kills Bane, allowing Batman to chase Talia. He tries to force her to take the bomb to the fusion chamber where it can be stabilized, but she floods the chamber. Talia dies when her truck crashes off the road, and Batman hauls the bomb beyond the city limits, where it detonates over the ocean and presumably kills him.

Batman is now celebrated as a hero whose sacrifice saved Gotham City, while Wayne is believed to have died in the riots. As Wayne's estate is divided up, his faithful butler Alfred witnesses him and Selina together alive in a café in Florence, while Blake, an honest young policeman who knows about Batman's identity, inherits the Batcave. In short, 'Batman saves the day, emerges unscathed and moves on with a normal life, with someone else to replace his role defending the system.'[2]

BATMAN, JOKER, BANE

The first clue to the ideological underpinnings of this ending is provided by the butler Alfred, who, at Wayne's (would-be) burial, reads the last lines from Dickens's *Tale of Two Cities*: 'It is a far, far better thing that I do, than I have ever done; it is a far, far better rest that I go to than I have ever known.' Some reviewers of the film took this quote as an indication that it

> rises to the noblest level of Western art ... The film appeals to the centre of America's tradition – the ideal of noble sacrifice for the common people. Batman must humble himself to be exalted, and lay down his life to find a new one ... An ultimate Christ-figure, Batman sacrifices himself to save others ... the film does not primarily champion one political philosophy over another, but presents the central premise of Western civilization.'[3]

And, effectively, from this perspective, there is only one step back from Dickens to Christ at Calvary: 'For whosoever will save his life shall lose it: and whosoever will lose his life for my sake shall find it. For what is a man profited, if he shall gain the whole world, and lose his own soul?' (Matthew 16:25–26) Batman's sacrifice as the repetition of Christ's death? Is this idea not compromised by the film's last scene (Wayne with Selina in a Florence café)? Is the religious counterpart of this ending not rather the well-known blasphemous idea that Christ really survived his crucifixion and lived a long peaceful life (in India or even Tibet, according to some sources)? The only way to redeem this final scene would have been to read it as a daydream (hallucination) of Alfred, sitting alone in the Florence café. Another Dickensian feature of the film is a de-politicized complaint about the gap between the rich and the poor. Early in the film, Selina whispers to Wayne while they are dancing at an exclusive upper-class gala: 'A storm is coming, Mr Wayne. You and your friends better batten down the hatches. Because when it hits, you're all going to wonder how you thought you could live so large, and leave so little for the rest of us.' Jonathan Nolan, Christopher's brother who co-wrote the scenario, is (as is every good liberal) 'worried' about the disparity and he admits this worry penetrates the film:

> what I see in the film that relates to the real world is the idea of dishonesty. The film is all about that coming to a head ... The notion of economic fairness creeps into the film, and the reason is twofold. One, Bruce Wayne is a billionaire. It has to be addressed ... But two, there are a lot of things in life, and economics is one of them, where we have to take a lot of what we're told on trust, because most of us feel like we don't have the analytical tools to know what's going on ... I don't feel there's a left or right perspective in the film. What is there is just an honest assessment or honest exploration of the world we live in – things that worry us.[4]

Although viewers know Wayne is mega-rich, they tend to forget where his wealth comes from: arms manufacturing plus stock-market speculations, which is why Bane's stock-exchange games can destroy his empire. Arms dealer and speculator; *this* is the true secret beneath the Batman mask. How does the film deal with it? By resuscitating the archetypal Dickensian trope of a good capitalist who engages in financing orphanage homes (Wayne) versus a bad greedy capitalist (Stryver, as in Dickens). In such Dickensian over-moralization, the economic disparity between rich and poor is translated into 'dishonesty', which should be 'honestly' analysed, although we lack any reliable cognitive mapping. Such an 'honest' approach leads to a further parallel with Dickens – as Jonathan Nolan put it bluntly: '*Tale of Two Cities* to me was the most sort of harrowing portrait of a relatable, recognizable civilization that had completely fallen to pieces. The terrors in Paris, in France in that period, it's not hard to imagine that things could go that bad and wrong.'[5] The scenes of the vengeful populist uprising in the film (a mob that thirsts for the blood of the rich who have neglected and exploited them) evoke Dickens's description of the Terror, so that, although the film has 'nothing to do with politics' (as Christopher Nolan says), it follows Dickens's novel in 'honestly' portraying revolutionaries as possessed fanatics, and thus provides

> the caricature of what in real life would be an ideologically committed revolutionary fighting structural injustice. Hollywood tells what the establishments want you to know – revolutionaries are brutal creatures, with utter disregard for human life. Despite emancipatory rhetoric on liberation, they have sinister designs behind. Thus, whatever might be their reasons, they need to be eliminated.[6]

Tom Charity was right to note 'the movie's defence of the establishment in the form of philanthropic billionaires and an incorruptible police'[7] – in its distrust of the people taking things into their own hands, the film 'demonstrates both a desire for social justice and a fear of what that can actually look like in the hands of a mob'.[8] Ramakrishnan Karthick raises here a perspicacious question with regard to the immense popularity of the Joker figure in the previous film: why such a harsh disposition towards Bane when the Joker was dealt with leniently in the earlier movie? The answer is simple and convincing:

The Joker, calling for anarchy in its purest form ... critically underscores the hypocrisies of bourgeois civilization as it exists, [but] his views are unable to translate into mass action ... Bane on the other hand poses an existential threat to the system of oppression ... His strength is not just his physique but also his ability to command people and mobilize them to achieve a political goal. He represents the vanguard, the organized representative of the oppressed that wages political struggle in their name to bring about structural changes. Such a force, with the greatest subversive potential, the system cannot accommodate. It needs to be eliminated.[9]

However, even if Bane lacks the fascination of Heath Ledger's Joker, there is a feature which distinguishes him from the latter: unconditional love, the very source of his hardness. In a short but touching scene, he tells Wayne how, in an act of love in the midst of terrible suffering, he saved the child Talia, not caring for consequences and paying a terrible price for it (Bane was beaten within an inch of his life while defending her).[10] Karthick is totally justified in locating this event in the long tradition, from Christ to Che Guevara, that extols violence as a 'work of love', as in the famous lines from Che Guevara's diary: 'Let me say, with the risk of appearing ridiculous, that the true revolutionary is guided by strong feelings of love. It is impossible to think of an authentic revolutionary without this quality.'[11] What we encounter here is not so much the 'Christification of Che' but rather a 'Cheization' of Christ himself – the Christ whose 'scandalous' words from Luke ('if anyone comes to me and does not hate his father and his mother, his wife and children, his brothers and sisters – yes even his own life – he cannot be my disciple' (14:26)) point in exactly the same direction as Che's famous quote: 'You may have to be tough, but do not lose your tenderness.' The statement that 'the true revolutionary is guided by strong feelings of love' should be read together with Guevara's much more 'problematic' statement on revolutionaries as 'killing machines':

Hatred is an element of struggle; relentless hatred of the enemy that impels us over and beyond the natural limitations of man and transforms us into effective, violent, selective, and cold killing machines.

Our soldiers must be thus; a people without hatred cannot vanquish a brutal enemy.[12]

Or, to paraphrase Kant and Robespierre yet again: love without cruelty is powerless; cruelty without love is blind, a short-lived passion which loses its persistent edge. Guevara is here paraphrasing Christ's declarations on the unity of love and sword – in both cases, the underlying paradox is that what makes love angelic, what elevates it over mere unstable and pathetic sentimentality, is its cruelty itself, its link with violence. It is this link that raises love over and beyond the natural limitations of man and thus transforms it into an unconditional drive. So while Guevara certainly believed in the transformative power of love, he would never have been heard humming 'all you need is love'. What you need is to *love with hatred*, or, as Kierkegaard put it, the necessary consequence (the 'truth') of the Christian demand to *love one's enemy* is

> the demand to *hate the beloved* out of love and in love . . . So high – humanly speaking to a kind of madness – can Christianity press the demand of love if love is to be the fulfilling of the law. Therefore it teaches that the Christian shall, if it is demanded, be capable of hating his father and mother and sister and beloved.[13]

In contrast to erotic love, this notion of love should be given here all its Paulinian weight: *the domain of pure violence*, the domain outside law (legal power), the domain of the violence that is neither law-founding nor law-sustaining, *is the domain of agape* (unconditional love).[14] Consequently, we are not dealing here with a simple brutal hatred demanded by a cruel and jealous God: the 'hatred' enjoined by Christ is not a kind of pseudo-dialectical opposite to love, but a direct expression of *agape*. It is love itself that enjoins us to 'unplug' from our organic community into which we were born; or, as St Paul put it, for a Christian there are neither men nor women, neither Jews nor Greeks. So, again, if the acts of revolutionary violence are 'works of love' in the strictest Kierkegaardian sense of the term, it is not because the revolutionary violence 'really' aims at establishing a non-violent harmony. On the contrary, the authentic

revolutionary liberation is much more directly identified with violence –
it is violence as such (the violent gesture of discarding, of establishing
a difference, of drawing a line of separation) which liberates. Freedom
is not a blissfully neutral state of harmony and balance, but the very
violent act which disturbs this balance. This is why, back to *The Dark
Knight Rises*, the only authentic love in the film is that expressed by
Bane, the 'terrorist', in clear contrast to Batman.

Along the same lines, the figure of Ra's al Ghul, Talia's father,
deserves a closer look. Ra's is a mixture of Arab and Oriental features,
an agent of virtuous terror fighting to counterbalance the corrupted
Western civilization. He is played by Liam Neeson, an actor whose
screen persona usually radiates dignified goodness and wisdom (he is
Zeus in *The Clash of Titans*), who also plays Qui-Gon Jinn in *The
Phantom Menace*, the first episode of the *Star Wars* series. Qui-Gon is
a Jedi knight, the mentor of Obi-Wan Kenobi as well as the one who
discovers Anakin Skywalker, believing that Anakin is the Chosen One
who will restore the balance of the universe, ignoring Yoda's warnings about Anakin's unstable nature; at the end of *The Phantom
Menace*, Qui-Gon is killed by Darth Maul.[15]

In the *Batman* trilogy, Ra's is also the teacher of the young Wayne.
When, in *Batman Begins*, he finds the young Wayne in a Chinese
prison, he introduces himself as 'Henri Ducard', offering the boy a
'path'. After Wayne is freed, he climbs to the home of the League of
Shadows, where Ducard is waiting, posing as the servant of a man
called Ra's al Ghul. At the end of a long and painful training, Ducard
explains that Bruce must do what is necessary to fight evil, while
revealing that they have trained Bruce with the intention of him leading the League to destroy Gotham City, which they believe has become
hopelessly corrupt. Months later, Ra's unexpectedly reappears, and
reveals that he was not Henri Ducard, but Ra's al Ghul. In the ensuing
confrontation, Ra's elaborates on the League of Shadows' exploits
throughout history (sacking Rome, spreading the Black Death, and
starting the Great Fire of London). He explains that the destruction
of Gotham City is merely another mission by the League to correct
humanity's recurring fits of decadence and, presumably, to protect the
environment. Ra's then has his henchmen burn down Wayne Manor
with the intention of killing Bruce, stating, 'Justice is balance. You

burnt my home and left me for dead; consider us even.' Wayne survives the fire and, as Batman, confronts Ra's. After overpowering him, Batman leaves him for dead on a train that blows up; Ra's uses his last moment to meditate, and is presumed dead, though no body is found in the wreckage. Ra's is thus not a simple embodiment of Evil: he stands for the combination of virtue and terror, for the egalitarian discipline fighting a corrupted empire; he thus belongs to the line that stretches (in recent fiction) from Paul Atreides in *Dune* to Leonidas in *300*. And it is crucial that Wayne is his disciple: Wayne was formed as Batman by him.

TRACES OF UTOPIA

We can see now how Nolan's Batman trilogy clearly follows an immanent logic.[16] In *Batman Begins*, the hero remains within the constraints of a liberal order: the system can be defended with morally acceptable methods. *The Dark Knight* is effectively a new version of the two John Ford western classics (*Fort Apache* and *The Man Who Shot Liberty Valance*) that show how, in order to civilize the Wild West, one has to 'print the legend' and ignore the truth – in short, how our civilization has to be grounded on a Lie: one has to break the rules in order to defend the system.[17] Or, to put it in another way, in *Batman Begins*, the hero is simply a classic urban vigilante, who punishes the criminals when the police cannot do so. The problem is that the police, the official law-enforcement agency, relate ambiguously to Batman's help: while admitting his efficiency, the police force nonetheless perceives Batman as a threat to its monopoly on power and a testimony to its own inefficiency. However, Batman's transgression is here purely formal. It resides in acting on behalf of the law without being legitimized to do so: in his acts, he never violates the law. *The Dark Knight* changes these coordinates: Batman's true rival is not the Joker, his opponent, but Harvey Dent, the 'white knight', the aggressive new district attorney, a kind of official vigilante whose fanatical battle against crime leads him into killing innocent people and destroys him. It is as if Dent is the reply of the legal order to Batman's threat: against Batman's vigilante struggle, the system generates its own illegal excess, its own vigilante, who – much more violent than Batman – directly violates the law. There is thus a poetic justice in the fact that, when Bruce plans to publicly reveal his identity as Batman, Dent jumps in and instead names himself as Batman – he *is* 'more Batman than Batman himself', actualizing the temptation Batman was still able to resist. So when, at the film's end, Batman takes upon himself the crimes committed by Dent to save the reputation of the popular hero who embodies hope for ordinary people, his self-effacing act contains a grain of truth: Batman in a way returns the favour to Dent. His act is a gesture of symbolic exchange: first Dent takes upon himself the identity of Batman, then Wayne – the real Batman – takes upon himself Dent's crimes.

Finally, *The Dark Knight Rises* pushes things even further: is Bane not Dent brought to extremes, to his self-negation? A Dent who draws the conclusion that the system itself is unjust, so that in order to effectively fight injustice one has to turn directly against the system and destroy it? And, as part of the same move, a Dent who loses all inhibitions and is ready to use all murderous brutality to achieve this goal? The rise of such a figure changes the entire constellation: for all participants, Batman included, morality is relativized, it becomes a matter of convenience, something determined by circumstances: it's open class warfare, and everything is permitted in defence of the system when we are dealing not just with mad gangsters but with a popular uprising.

Is this all? Should the film just be flatly rejected by those who are engaged in radical emancipatory struggles? Not really. Things are more ambiguous, and one has to read the film in the way one has done here to reveal a Chinese political poem: absences and surprising presences count. Recall the old French story about a wife who complains to her husband's best friend that he is making illicit sexual advances towards her: it takes some time for the surprised friend to get the point – in this twisted way, she is inviting him to seduce her. It is like the Freudian unconscious which knows no negation: what matters is not a negative judgement on something, but the mere fact that this something is mentioned – in *The Dark Knight Rises*, people's power *is here*, staged as an Event, in a key step forwards from the usual Batman opponents (criminal mega-capitalists, gangsters and terrorists).

Here we get the first clue to the film's deeper ambiguity – the prospect of the OWS movement taking power and establishing people's democracy on Manhattan is so patently absurd, so utterly non-realist, that one cannot but raise the question: why does a major Hollywood blockbuster dream about it. Why does it invoke this spectre? Why even dream about OWS exploding into a violent takeover? The obvious answer (to smear OWS with accusations that it harbours a terrorist-totalitarian potential) is not enough to account for the strange attraction exerted by the prospect of 'people's power'. No wonder the proper functioning of this power remains blank, absent: no details are given about how this people's power functions, what the mobilized people are doing (remember that Bane tells the people they can do what they want – he is not imposing on them his own order). One can even talk of necessary *censorship* here: any depiction of the self-organization of the people during Bane's reign would have ruined the effect of the film, laying bare its inconsistency.

This is why the film deserves a close reading:[18] the Event – the 'people's republic of Gotham City', dictatorship of the proletariat on Manhattan – is *immanent* to the film; it is (to use the worn-out expression from the 1970s) its 'absent centre'. This is why external critique of the film ('its depiction of the OWS reign is a ridiculous caricature') is not enough: the critique has to be immanent, it has to locate within the film itself a multitude of signs which point towards the authentic Event. (Recall, for example, that Bane is not just a brutal terrorist, but a person of deep love and sacrifice.) In short, pure ideology is not possible. Bane's authenticity *has* to leave a trace in the film's texture.[19]

VIOLENCE, WHICH VIOLENCE?

There are nonetheless two commonsense reproaches that impose themselves apropos of our reading of Nolan's film. First, there *were* monstrous mass killings and violence in actual revolutions, from Stalinism to Khmer Rouge, so the film is clearly not just engaging in reactionary imagination. Then there is the second, opposite reproach: the actual OWS movement was not violent and its goal was definitely not a new reign of terror; insofar as Bane's revolt is supposed to extrapolate the immanent tendency of the OWS movement, the film thus ridiculously misrepresents its aims and strategies. The ongoing anti-globalist protests are the very opposite of Bane's brutal terror: Bane stands for the mirror-image of state terror, for a murderous fundamentalist sect taking over and ruling by terror, not for the overcoming of state terror through popular self-organization. What both reproaches share is the rejection of the figure of Bane. The reply to these two reproaches is multiple.

First, one should make clear the actual scope of violence. The best answer to the claim that the violent mob reaction to oppression is worse than the original oppression itself was the one provided by Mark Twain in his *A Connecticut Yankee in King Arthur's Court*:

> There were two 'Reigns of Terror' if we would remember it and consider it; the one wrought in hot passion, the other in heartless cold blood . . . our shudders are all for the 'horrors' of the minor Terror, the momentary Terror, so to speak, whereas, what is the horror of swift death by the axe compared with lifelong death from hunger, cold, insult, cruelty, and heartbreak? A city cemetery could contain the coffins filled by that brief Terror which we have all been so diligently taught to shiver at and mourn over; but all France could hardly contain the coffins filled by that older and real Terror, that unspeakably bitter and awful Terror, which none of us have been taught to see in its vastness or pity as it deserves.

In order to grasp this parallax nature of violence, one should focus on short-circuits between different levels, say between power and social violence: an economic crisis which causes devastation is experienced as uncontrollable quasi-natural power – but it should be experienced as violence.

Secondly, it is not only Nolan's film which is unable to imagine authentic people's power. The 'real' radical emancipatory movements themselves have also been unable to do so: they remained caught in the coordinates of the old society, which is why the actual 'people power' was often such a violent horror.[20] There is a certain revolutionary ruthlessness, the neglect of the human costs of our acts, which can legitimately be questioned. Say, when a country is under occupation and the majority of the population wavers and cannot decide whether or not to join the struggle, the radical resistance is sometimes tempted to provoke heavy retaliations by the occupiers (burning of villages, shooting hostages) to raise the anger of the populace – the terrifying human costs are accepted as the price to pay for the people's mobilization. (To the counter-argument that this is a radical tactic that involves a risk beyond pragmatic considerations, one should reply with another paraphrase of the already-mentioned famous joke from Lubitsch's *To Be Or Not to Be* about 'We do the concentrating, the Poles do the camping': the leaders are not risking their own lives, they are provoking the occupiers, ordinary people are suffering the consequences.)

Furthermore, one should demystify the problem of violence, rejecting simplistic claims that twentieth-century Communism used too much murderous violence, and that we should be careful never to fall into this trap again. As a fact, this is, of course, terrifyingly true – but such a direct focus on violence obfuscates the underlying question: what was inherently wrong with the twentieth-century Communist project, and which immanent weakness of this project forced the Communists (and not only the Communists) in power to resort to unrestrained violence? In other words, it is not enough to say that Communists 'neglected the problem of violence': it was a deeper socio-political failure that pushed them to violence. (The same goes for the notion that Communists 'neglected democracy': their overall project of social transformation enforced on them this 'neglect'.)

In other words, we should absolutely reject the very topic of the 'ethical suspension of the theologico-political' – the idea that we should be ready to constrain our political (or religious-political) engagement when it leads us to violate elementary moral norms, when it makes us commit mass killings and cause other forms of suffering. So what's wrong with the reasoning that follows the lines of 'When you are obsessed with a political (or religious) vision, don't just work to enforce it onto reality, take a step back and try to see how it will affect others, how it will disturb their lives – that there are certain basic moral rules (don't torture, don't use killing as an instrument, etc.) that are above any political engagement'? The point is not that we should turn the suspension around and claim that a radical (theologico-)political engagement justifies violations of basic moral norms. The point is, rather, that our critique of a (theologico-)political vision that justifies mass killings and so on should be *immanent*. It is not enough to reject such a vision on behalf of external moral scruples: there must be something wrong with this vision as such, in its own (theologico-)political terms. In this way, Stalinism is not to be rejected because it was immoral and murderous, but because it failed on its own terms, because it betrayed its own premises.

Last but not least, it is all too simple to claim that there is no violent potential in OWS and similar movements. There *is* violence at work in every authentic emancipatory process: the problem with the film *The Dark Knight Rises* is that it wrongly translated this violence into murderous terror. Let me clarify this point with a detour through my critics who, when they are forced to admit that my statement 'Hitler wasn't violent enough' is not meant as a call for even more terrifying mass killing, tend to turn their reproaches on their head, saying that I just use provocative language in order to make a commonsense non-interesting point. Here is what one of them has written apropos of my claim that Gandhi was more violent than Hitler:

> Žižek is here using language in a way that is designed to be provocative and to confuse people. He doesn't *actually* mean that Gandhi was more violent than Hitler ... What he means to do instead is to alter the typical understanding of the word 'violent' so that Gandhi's non-violent means of protest against the British will be considered more violent than Hitler's incredibly violent attempts at world domination and genocide. Violence, for Žižek in this particular instance, actually means that which causes massive social upheaval. In that way, he considers Gandhi to be more violent than Hitler. But this, like so much of what Žižek writes, is actually nothing new or interesting or surprising. And that's why he writes it in the provocative, confusing, and bizarre manner that he chooses instead of a straightforward manner. If he would have written that Gandhi accomplished more through non-violence that aimed at systemic change than Hitler accomplished through violent means, we would all agree ... but we would also all know that there is nothing profound in such a statement. Instead, Žižek attempts to shock us and, in doing so, he covers up the completely humdrum

conclusion about Gandhi and Hitler that everyone already believed to be true before they read Žižek.

The same is true of Žižek's controversial point about Jews and anti-Semites. There is nothing remarkable about the argument that in the mind of every Nazi who hates Jews there must also be a fictional Jew for that Nazi to hate. And thus any attempt to rid Nazis of the Jews within themselves, as Žižek tells us Hitler once said, would result in the destruction of the Nazis themselves (since the anti-Semites in themselves require the continued existence of the Jews within themselves). In other words, Žižek is once again simply making a muddled word salad in an attempt to dress up commonplaces as profundity. Gandhi's method of changing things worked because he went after the system itself. The anti-Semite can never kill the object of his hatred because his worldview necessitates the fictional Jew.[21]

In both cases, the reproach is the same: that I try to sell the common thesis that Gandhi aimed at changing the system not at destroying people, but since this is a commonplace, I formulate it more provocatively, weirdly expanding the meaning of the word 'violence' to include institutional changes; and the same goes for my statement about 'the Jew is in the anti-Semite, but the anti-Semite is also in the Jew': that it's just a garbled way to deliver the commonplace that, in the mind of every Nazi who hates Jews, there must also be a fictional Jew for that Nazi to hate. But is this the case? What if the key point gets lost in this translation of my 'muddled word salad' into commonsense? In the second case, my point is not just the (effectively obvious) claim that the 'Jew' to whom the Nazi refers is his ideological fiction, but that his own ideological identity is also simultaneously grounded in this fiction (not simply dependent on it): the Nazi is – in his self-perception – *a figure in his own dream about the 'Jews'*. This is far from an obvious commonsense.

So why call Gandhi's attempts to undermine the British state in India 'more violent' than Hitler's mass killings? Precisely to draw attention to the fundamental violence that sustains a 'normal' functioning of the state (Benjamin called it 'mythic violence'), and the no less fundamental violence that sustains every attempt to undermine the functioning of the state (Benjamin's 'divine violence').[22] This is why the reaction of the state power to those who endanger it is so brutal, and why, in its very brutality, this reaction is precisely 'reactive', protective. So, far from eccentricity, the extension of the notion of violence is based on a key theoretical insight – and it is the limitation of violence to its directly visible physical aspect which, far from being 'normal', relies on an ideological distortion. This is also why the reproach that I am fascinated by some ultra-radical violence with comparison to which Hitler and Khmer Rouge 'didn't go far enough' completely misses my point, which is not to go further in *this* type of violence but to change the entire terrain.

It is difficult to be really violent, to perform an act that violently disturbs the basic parameters of social life. When Bertolt Brecht saw a Japanese mask of an evil demon, he wrote how its swollen veins and hideous grimaces 'all betake / what an exhausting effort it takes / To be evil'. The same holds for violence that has any effect on the system. The Chinese Cultural Revolution serves as a lesson here: destroying old monuments proved not to be a true negation of the past. Rather, it was an impotent *passage à l'acte,* an acting out which bore witness to the failure to get rid of the past. There is a kind of poetic justice in the fact that the final result of Mao's Cultural Revolution is the current unmatched explosion of capitalist dynamics in China: a profound structural homology exists between Maoist permanent self-revolutionizing, the permanent struggle against the ossification of state structures, and the inherent dynamics of capitalism. To paraphrase Brecht again: 'What is the robbing of a bank compared to the founding of a bank?' What were the violent and destructive outbursts of a Red Guardist caught in the Cultural Revolution compared to the true Cultural Revolution, the permanent dissolution of all life-forms which capitalist reproduction dictates?

The same, of course, applies to Nazi Germany, where the spectacle of the brutal annihilation of millions should not deceive us. The characterization of Hitler that would have him as a bad guy, responsible for the death of millions, but nonetheless a man with balls who pursued his ends with an iron will, is not only ethically repulsive, it is also simply *wrong*. No, Hitler did not really 'have the balls' to change things. All his actions were fundamentally reactions: he acted so that nothing would really change; he acted to prevent the Communist threat of real change. His targeting of the Jews was ultimately an act of displacement in which he avoided the real enemy – the core of capitalist social relations themselves. Hitler staged a spectacle of Revolution so that the capitalist order could survive. The irony was that his grand gestures of despising bourgeois self-complacency ultimately enabled this complacency to continue: far from disturbing the much despised 'decadent' bourgeois order, far from awakening the Germans, Nazism was a dream which enabled them to postpone awakening. Germany only really woke up with the defeat of 1945.

WEATHERMEN'S FAMILY VALUES

Traumatized by the Stalinist experience, much of today's Left tends to obfuscate the touchy topic of violence, as is clear from Robert Redford's *The Company You Keep* (2012), a film which deals with Leftist ex-radicals confronting their past. To simplify to the utmost, the story centres on recent widower and single father Jim Grant, a former Weather Underground anti-Vietnam War militant wanted for a bank robbery and murder, who has hidden from the FBI for over thirty years posing as an attorney in Albany, New York. He becomes a fugitive when his true identity is exposed, and he must find his ex-lover, Mimi, the one person who can clear his name, before the FBI catches him – otherwise, he will lose everything, including his 11-year-old daughter, Isabel. His search for Mimi takes him across the US, where he contacts many of his Weatherman ex-colleagues; finally, Jim and Mimi meet in a secluded lake cabin close to the Canadian border. She is still passionate about the goals of the Weathermen and unapologetic about her actions thirty years earlier, but Jim tartly responds: 'I didn't get tired. I grew up.' Even if he still believes in the cause, he has now become a responsible family man. Jim asks Mimi to turn herself in and alibi him for the sake of his daughter, Isabel: he doesn't want to leave Isabel behind and repeat the mistake that he and Mimi made 30 years earlier by giving up their own daughter. The next morning, Mimi flees the cabin to sail to Canada, but she turns her boat around and returns to the US to give herself up; the next day, Jim is freed from jail and reunites with Isabel.

It is true that, as a reviewer acerbically put it, *The Company You Keep* exudes nostalgia for the time when terrorists were still people who looked and were dressed like us and bore recognizable Anglo-Saxon names. The film nonetheless has an authentic touch in how it renders in an almost unbearably painful way the disappearance of the radical Left from our political and ideological reality. The survivors of the old radical Left are like sympathetic living dead, remnants of another era, strangers drifting in a strange world – no wonder Redford was attacked by conservatives for sympathy and complicity with terrorists. The film's authentic touch (and also that of the Neil Gordon novel on which the film is based) transpires not only in the generally sympathetic portrayal of ex-Weathermen, but even more in wonderful narrative details like the long detailed descriptions of underground life (how to check if one is being tailed and shake off possible pursuers; how to create a new identity, and so on).

As to the Weather Underground itself, one has to insist that the Weathermen were not on the side of post-68 terror, the regression from politics proper to the Real of raw action: their acts aimed at destroying buildings, not killing people. (The Michigan Bank robbery was done by a splinter group after the Weathermen's formal dissolution.) Weathermen are often accused of destroying the Left in the US, of alienating the support of the broad spectrum of protesters – and were maybe even being manipulated by the FBI – but such a ciriticism gets it wrong. The Weathermen's resort to violence was a desperate attempt to react to the SDS (Students for a Democratic Society) failure to mobilize people and stop the Vietnam war. In other words, the failure of the Left was already evident: the Weathermen's violence was the symptom of this failure, its effect and not its cause. If one looks for the mistakes in the Weathermen's activity, one should look for it elsewhere, in their very organizational structure and practice. For example, 'Weather collectives' practised sexual rotation: all female members were required to have sex with all male members, and women also had sexual relations with other women, as monogamous relationships were considered counterrevolutionary. The point is not that this sexual practice was 'too radical'; on the contrary, such regulated promiscuity fits well today's permissiveness and fear of 'excessive' attachments. While thinking that they were undermining bourgeois ideology, the Weathermen were just laying the ground for its late capitalist stage.

Where *The Company You Keep* fails is in its confronting of that aspect of the Weathermen's activity that is today for us most problematic: their decision to take the path of violent action. While the film obviously sympathizes with the radical Leftist cause, its predominant tone is to reject the path of violence in the terms of maturation, of the passage from youthful enthusiasm (which can easily turn into violent fanaticism) to mature awareness that there are things like family life and responsibility towards one's children that no political cause should make us violate – or, as the hero says to his ex-lover, 'We have a responsibility beyond the Cause. We have a baby.' Read in this way, *The Company You Keep* is, as someone wrote about Neil Gordon's original novel, *le roman des illusions perdues*.[23]

But does such a reference to growing up, family responsibility, and so on, constitute a neutral apolitical wisdom which posits a limit to our political engagement – or is it instead a way for ideology to intervene, preventing us from analysing to the end the political deadlock we find ourselves in? What this second option amounts to is not a covert attempt to justify violent terror, but an obligation to analyse and judge it on its own terms. Let us imagine that Jim were to have no daughter: the problem of the Weathermen's strategy would still exist. Without this type of radical self-examination, we end up endorsing the existing legal and political order as the frame that guarantees the stability of our private family lives. Hardly surprising that, in legal terms, *The Company You Keep* is about the hero's legal rehabilitation, his effort to become a normal citizen with no dark past haunting him.

Even here, however, things are much more subtle. One cannot but admire the mythic atmosphere in which the final reunification of Jim and Mimi is rendered in the film, and even more than in the novel: there is an ethico-metaphysical necessity for them to meet, like in the final meeting of Moose Malloy and Velma in Chandler's masterwork *Farewell, My Lovely*. When Jim and Mimi are on their way to meet each other in a lonely cottage in the midst of a forest close to a lake, the novel resorts to an ingenious narrative procedure: their voyage is rendered as a series of short email reports written alternately by him and her; however, he describes *her* voyage details and she *his*, as if some kind of mystic communion coordinated the voyage. No wonder, when the two ex-lovers finally meet, that their reunion is presented in timeless terms, as a moment of eternity: the gap of over twenty years since their last meeting simply disappears. It is as if the two lovers entered a point in eternity in which past and present directly overlap.

The story ends with a nice ethical twist: a couple does emerge – not the couple of Jim and Mimi, but the couple of Ben Schulberg, the investigative journalist who blew Jim Grant's cover, and Rebeccah Osborne, Jim and Mimi's daughter, who is adopted by an honest FBI agent. Although it may appear that the film follows the standard Hollywood formula of the production of a couple, what resonates here is the topic of an ethical test. Who is tested? Not Jim, and not Mimi (who, on the way to escape to Canada, turns her boat around, back to the US, to surrender herself and save Jim), but Ben himself who, at the film's end, decides not to publish the big story about Rebeccah being Jim and Mimi's daughter, thereby proving that he deserves her.

The mobilization of the family thus serves as a gap-filler that enables the film (and us, its viewers) to avoid the difficult topic of violence, of its justification or unacceptability. It is clear that a ruthless total dedication to violent 'terrorist' struggle could be reasonably legitimized in a country under a brutal occupation or dictatorship – if, say, a French resistance fighter during the Second World War had told his colleagues that he was going to abandon the struggle against the Germans because he grew up and became aware of his responsibility towards his family, his move would be far from ethically self-evident. In a well-known passage from his *Existentialism and Humanism*, Sartre deployed the dilemma of a young man in France in 1942, torn between the duty to help his lone, ill mother and the duty to enter the Resistance and fight the Germans. There is no *a priori* answer to this dilemma: the young man has to assume full responsibility for his decision. It is thus not that the Cause enjoys priority, and that the choice of family obligations equals moral betrayal. The dilemma is real, there is no way of avoiding being hurt.

OUT OF *MALTTUKBAKGI*

So where do we stand today? Maybe, we don't even stand but just lean forward in a very specific way. Near the children's museum in Seoul, there is a weird statue, which, to the non-initiated, cannot but appear as a staged scene of extreme obscenity. It resembles nothing so much as a line of young boys leaning forward behind each other and sticking their heads into the rectum of the one in front; another boy stands at the front of the queue and has the head of the first leaning boy pushed into his crotch. When we inquire what this is about, we are informed that the statue is simply the staging of *malttukbakgi*, a fun game that both Korean girls and boys play up until high school. There are two teams; team A has one person stand up against the wall and the rest of the team have all their heads up in someone else's butt/crotch area to form what looks like a large horse. Team B then jumps up onto the human horse one by one, each jumping with as much force as possible. If anyone from any team falls to the floor, that team loses.

Is this statue not a perfect metaphor for us common people, for our predicament in today's global capitalism? Our view is constrained to what we can see with our head stuck into the arse of a guy just in front of us, and our idea of who is our Master is the guy in front whose penis and/or balls the first guy in the row appears to be licking – but the real Master, invisible to us, is the one freely jumping on our back, the autonomous movement of Capital.

There is a wonderful common Scottish verb, *tartle*, which designates the awkward moment when a speaker temporarily forgets someone's name (usually the name of his or her partner in a conversation), and the verb is used to avoid that occasional embarrassment, as in, 'Sorry, I tartled there for a moment!' Have we all not been tartling in the last decades, forgetting the name 'Communism' to designate the ultimate horizon of our emancipatory struggles? The time has come to fully remember that word.

The present booklet may also appear to tartle, jumping as it does from our debt-driven economy to the struggle for the control of cyberspace, from the impasses of the Arab Spring to the futility of anti-Eurocentrism, from the superego-pressure of ideology to the ambiguous role of violence in our struggles. No single idea underlies this *bric-a-brac*, nothing like Negri's 'multitude' or Piketty's 'soak the rich' to orientate the book's analyses towards a clear political strategy. The author nonetheless hopes that the attentive reader will discern beneath the multiple topics the Communist horizon.

Communism is today not the name of a solution, but the name of a *problem*, the problema of *commons* in all its dimensions – the commons of nature as the substance of our life, the problema of our biogenetic commons, the problema of our cultural commons ('intellectual property'), and, last but not least, commons as the universal space of humanity from which no one should be excluded. Whatever the solution, it will have to deal with *these* problems. This is why, as Alvaro Garcia Linera once put it, our horizon has to remain Communist – a horizon not as an inaccessible ideal, but as a space of ideas within which we move.

Notes

INTRODUCTION

1. Aaron Schuster, 'Comedy in Times of Austerity' (manuscript).
2. James Harvey, *Romantic Comedy in Hollywood: From Lubitsch to Sturges*, New York: Da Capo, 1987, p. 56.
3. Chesterton, G. K., 'A Defense of Detective Stories', in H. Haycraft (ed.), *The Art of the Mystery Story*, New York: The Universal Library, 1946, p. 6.
4. Quoted from http://th-rough.eu/writers/bifo-eng/journey-seoul-1.
5. We should nonetheless also bear in mind that *there is no 'normal' time for modernization*: modernization never comes at its proper time, it always occurs 'too fast', as a traumatic rupture.
6. See Stacey Abbott, *Celluloid Vampires: Life After Death in the Modern World*, Austin: University of Texas Press, 2007.
7. Richard Taruskin, 'Prokofiev, Hail . . . and Farewell?', *New York Times*, 21 April 1991.
8. B. R. Myers, *The Cleanest Race*, New York: Melville House, 2011, p. 6. It is difficult to restrain oneself from adding a comment here: but what if the father is not the husband?
9. Jacques-Alain Miller, 'Phallus and Perversion', *lacanian ink* 33, p. 23.
10. Jacques-Alain Miller, 'The Logic of the Cure', *lacanian ink* 33, p. 19.
11. Miller, 'Phallus and Perversion', p. 28.
12. Quoted from http://www.theatlantic.com/magazine/archive/2004/09/mother-of-all-mothers/3403/.
13. Myers, op. cit., p. 9.
14. Are then – to put it bluntly – North Koreans incestuous psychotics who reject entering the symbolic order? The answer is no – why? Because of the distance towards the symbolic order proper which persists even in official ideological texts. That is to say, even North Korea's

official ideological discourse ('Text', as Myers calls it) does not engage in direct divinization of the Leader; instead, the divinization is elegantly attributed to 'naive' Western visitors fascinated by the Leader's wisdom: 'while the Text likes to draw bemused attention to outsiders, including Americans and South Koreans, who allegedly regard Kim Il Sung as a divine being, it never makes such claims for him itself' (Myers, op. cit., p. 111). Is this not a clear case of 'subject supposed to believe', of the naïve other onto which our own belief is transposed? Similarly, the fact that, in North Korean textbooks the leader (Kim Il Sung, Kim Jong Il . . .) is presented as a person whose body is so pure that it doesn't need to shit, should not be dismissed as ideological madness, since it just brings to extreme the logic of the 'king's two bodies': North Korean subjects are not psychotics who 'literally believe their leader doesn't shit', they just consider shitting is not part of the leader's sublime body.

I DIAGNOSIS *HORS D'OEUVRE?*

1. Quoted from http://www.spectator.co.uk/the-week/leading-article/8789981/glad-tidings/.

2. Quoted from http://www.rationaloptimist.com/. See Matt Ridley, *The Rational Optimist: How Prosperity Evolves*, New York: Harper, 2011.

3. Steven Pinker, *The Better Angels of Our Nature: Why Violence Has Declined*, London: Penguin Books, 2012.

4. Fredric Jameson, *Representing Capital*, London: Verso Books, 2011, p. 149.

5. Fredric Jameson, *Valences of the Dialectic*, London: Verso Books, 2009, pp. 580–81.

6. Jameson, *Representing Capital*, p. 149.

7. Jameson, *Valences of the Dialectic*, p. 580.

8. The *de facto* dismemberment – or, rather, 'congoization' – of Libya after the French-British intervention (the country is now composed of territories ruled by local armed gangs who sell the oil directly to their customers) indicates that Congo is no longer an exception: one of the strategies of today's capitalism that needs to secure a steady supply of cheap raw materials unencumbered by a strong state power is to maintain the dismemberment of a state damned with the curse of rich minerals or oil.

9. Carlo Vercellone, 'The Crisis of the Law of Value and the Becoming-Rent

of Profit', in Fumagalli and Mezzadra (eds.), *Crisis in the Global Economy*, Los Angeles: Semiotext(e), 2010, p. 88.

10. Andre Gorz, *L'immatériel*, Paris: Galilee ,2005, p. 55.

11. Vercellone, op. cit., p. 117.

12. Ibid., p. 86.

13. Wang Hui, 'Debating for Our Future: Intellectual Politics in Contemporary China' (manuscript obtained from the author).

14. Ibid.

15. Karl Marx, *Capital*, Vol. 1, New York: International Publishers, 1967, pp. 254–5.

16. Ibid., pp. 236–7.

17. The *comme d'habitude* in the French original of course doesn't refer to 'as usual' as a simple empty ritual, but to a personal daily ritual which expresses the very core of my personality and, in this sense, stands precisely for 'my way'. But this in no way undermines the point of the reference to the two versions of the song – if anything, it makes it clear that the French *comme d'habitude* is much more authentically personal than the American 'my way', which as a rule evokes empty conformist individualism. Furthermore, does the same not hold also for a society: universal healthcare is 'our way' of practising solidarity, not just grey impersonal legal regulation.

18. The title of an editorial in the *New York Times*, 11 December 2012.

19. Quoted from *Der Spiegel*, 5 August 2012.

20. Quoted from Luciano Canfora, *Critica della retorica democratica*, Roma-Bari: Laterza, 2011, p. 33.

21. See Paul Goble, 'Window on Eurasia: Andropov Wanted to Do Away with National Republics', available online at wttp://windowoneurasia2.blogspot.com/2012/11/window-on-eurasia-andropov-wanted-to-do.html.

22. When Warren Buffett found it scandalous that he – the third richest man in the world – pays less taxes than his secretary, one of his free-market critics tried to justify this fact in the following way: the secretary pays her taxes on her stable guaranteed income, while Buffett earns his money with risky investments and so he deserves a lower tax degree as a compensation for his risks. The problem with this reasoning is that it forgets the obvious: yes, Buffett is taking risks with his investments, but he is already more than compensated for them with the profits he makes.

23. See Mauricio Lazzarato's *The Making of the Indebted Man*, Cambridge: MIT Press, 2012.

24. Ibid., p. 139.
25. I rely in this description of Lazzarato's theory on Martin O'Shaughnessy – see http://lafranceetlacrise.org/2012/08/23/lazzarato-and-the-governmental-power-of-debt-la-fabrique-de-lhomme-endette-or-the-making-of-indebted-man.
26. Karl Marx, *Capital*, Vol. 1, London: Penguin Books, 1990, p. 280.
27. Such use of the term 'entrepreneur' is thus an exemplary case of what Hegel calls 'abstract universality'. What is abstract universality? It is the abstraction from some specific content that obliterates a key distinction constitutive of this abstraction itself. Say one can, of course, conceive dieting and starvation as the species of the same genus, eating-less-than-needed; however, to compare the two is in itself an obscenity committed, among others, by a recent report in the *New York Times*, 'The Mental Strain of Making Do With Less': 'Diets don't just reduce weight, they can reduce mental capacity. In other words, dieting can make you dumber. Understanding why this is the case can illuminate a range of experiences, including something as far removed from voluntary calorie restriction as the ordeal of outright poverty ... Perhaps the problem is not poor people but the mental strain that poverty imposes on anyone who must endure it' (Sendhill Mullainathan, *New York Times*, 21 September 2013).
28. One witnessed the same situation in state-socialist regimes: when, in a mythical scene from Soviet hagiography, Stalin takes a walk in the fields, meets there a driver whose tractor has broken down, and helps him to repair it with wise advice, what this effectively means is that not even a tractor can function normally in state-socialist economic chaos.
29. Peter Buffett, 'The Charitable-Industrial Complex', *New York Times*, 26 July 2013.
30. Peter Sloterdijk, *Zorn und Zeit*, Frankfurt: Suhrkamp, 2006, p. 55.

2 CARDIOGNOSIS *DU JAMBON CRU?*

1. Alenka Zupančič, 'When I Count to Ten, You Will be Dead ...', *Mladina-Alternative*, Ljubljana, 2013, p. 31.
2. See Jaron Lanier, *Who Owns the Future?*, London: Allen Lane, 2013.
3. See Alain Badiou and Jean-Claude Milner, *Controverse*, Paris: Editions du Seuil, 2012.
4. Quoted from http://krugman.blogs.nytimes.com/2013/06/17/1984-hungarian-edition/?_r=0.

5. Ibid.

6. Quoted from http://www.marxists.org/archive/marx/works/1843/critique-hpr/intro.htm.

7. Ibid.

8. Personal message from Engin Kurtay, Istanbul.

9. Quoted in Ben Stein, 'In Class Warfare, Guess Which Class is Winning', *New York Times*, 26 November 2006.

10. The attitude towards reality that underlies this topic is brought to extreme in the so-called 'concave hollow Earth hypothesis' (to which, according to some sources, even Hitler subscribed): the idea that we humans live on the *inside* surface of a hollow spherical world, a gigantic spherical hole in the endless mass of eternal rock and ice, with the Sun as the immobile star shining in the centre of the hole. (How can we then account for sunrise and sundown? The advocates of this hypothesis deployed incredibly complex theories of twisted rays of light.)

11. Two years later, a similar story was told in Michael Anderson's *Logan's Run*, in which a hedonistic society lives in a huge bubble and takes for granted that there is no life outside of it.

12. See Peter Sloterdijk, *In the World Interior of Capital: Towards a Philosophical Theory of Globalization*, Cambridge: Polity, 2013.

13. Sloterdijk, op. cit., p. 12.

14. Ibid., p. 46.

15. Ibid., p. 171.

16. Ibid.

17. See http://www.reuters.com/article/2013/12/01/us-italy-fire-idUSBRE9B00ED20131201.

18. Quoted from http://www.nbcnews.com/news/other/deadly-factory-fire-highlights-near-slavery-conditions-italy-f2D11681836.

19. Louis Nayman, 'Lincoln: Better Off Undead', *In These Times*, 15 November 2012.

20. Ibid.

21. Ibid.

22. In his intervention during the conference 'Global Capitalism and the New Left', Istanbul, 11–12 October 2013.

23. Peter Sloterdijk, *Critique of Cynical Reason*, Minneapolis: University of Minnesota Press, 1988, p. 17.

24. See Karl Marx, 'Class Struggles in France', *Collected Works*, Vol. 10, London: Lawrence and Wishart, 1978, p. 95.

25. Ibid.

26. See *Agnotology: The Making and Unmaking of Ignorance*, ed. Robert

Proctor and Londa Schiebinger, Stanford: Stanford University Press, 2008.

27. Quoted from http://www.boston.com/news/nation/articles/2008/01/21/kings_complexity_often_ignored/.

28. Ibid.

29. Ibid.

30. Gerard Wajcman, 'Intimate Extorted, Intimate Exposed', *Umbr(a)*, 2007, p. 47.

31. See http://www.haaretz.com/blogs/routine-emergencies/why-ultra-orthodox-men-wearing-modesty-glasses-is-a-fabulous-idea-1.457453.

32. See Sergio Gonzales Rodriguez, *The Femicide Machine*, Los Angeles: Semiotext(e), 2012.

33. See Wally T. Oppal (Commissioner, British Columbia), *Forsaken: The Report of the Missing Women Commission of Inquiry*, 19 November 2012, available online at www.ag.gov.bc.ca/public-inquiries/docs/Forsaken-ES.pdf.

34. Surprisingly, this obscene underside of the Law emerges also in the domain of self-help guides. The basic stance best encapsulated by the title of a recent Phillip McGraw bestseller, *Self Matters*, teaching us how to 'create your life from the inside out', finds its logical supplement in books with titles like *How to Disappear Completely* – manuals about how to erase all traces of one's previous existence and 'reinvent' oneself. Doug Richmond's *How to Disappear Completely and Never be Found* (Secausus: A Citadel Press Book, 1999) belongs to the series of how-to manuals which form a refreshingly obscene double of the 'official' manuals like those of Dale Carnegie; books which directly address our publicly unacceptable desires – other titles in the series include *Cheaters Always Prosper*, *Advanced Backstabbing and Mudslinging Techniques*, *Revenge Tactics*, *Spying on Your Spouse*, etc. What these examples have in common is the direct marketing of the obscene underside of the Law, of secret transgressive desires.

35. In a strictly homologous way, the Zionist defenders of the Israeli policy want us to know that they control the media (TV and press), preventing too much critique of Israel to appear in them; however, while we are allowed to know this (in order to fear the Zionists' power), we are not allowed to talk about it publicly – the moment we do it, we are accused of anti-Semitism.

36. Another cynical strategy is to blame the enemy: the US Catholic authorities referred to a study whose alleged conclusion was that the

sexual permissiveness from the 1960s on is to be held responsible for widespread paedophilia in the Church . . .

37. Quoted from www.siol.net/slovenija/novice/2010/04/rode_za_vecernji_list.aspx.

38. Ibid.

39. G. K. Chesterton, *Orthodoxy*, San Francisco: Ignatius Press, 1995, p. 164.

40. What one usually gets from theorists is a private admission that, of course, this is contradictory, but that, nonetheless, such a contradictory ideological edifice *works*, and works spectacularly: it is the only way to ensure fast economic growth and stability in China. Need we add that this is the 'private use of reason' at its purest?

41. See 'Even What's Secret is a Secret in China,' *Japan Times*, 16 June 2007, p. 17.

42. *The Merchant of Venice*, Act 4, scene i.

43. I owe this point to Udi Aloni.

44. http://news.yahoo.com/australian-court-oks-logo-ban-cigarette-packs-004107919--finance.html.

45. Charles Rosen, *Schoenberg*, London: Fontana/Collins, 1975, p. 77.

46. Jean Laplanche, *Problématiques I: L'angoisse*, Paris: PUF, 1980, p. 353.

47. Sigmund Freud, 'Dostoyevsky and Parricide', in *Penguin Freud Library*, Vol. 14: *Art and Literature*, London: Penguin 1985, p. 455.

48. Jacques Derrida, *Acts of Literature*, New York: Routledge ,1992, p. 201.

49. Ecologists like to point out how the introduction of a foreign species into a specific ecosystem can fatally destabilize it: a new predator eating local animal species disturbs the entire cycle of life, a new plant suffocates other plants and destroys the entire food chain, etc. But the main intruders are we humans, whose explosive growth devastates ecosystems, so that nature has to establish new fragile ecological balances.

50. Quoted from www.siol.net/slovenija/novice/2010/04/rode_za_vecernji_list.aspx.

3 PROGNOSIS *UN FAUX-FILET, PEUT-ÊTRE?*

1. Friedrich Nietzsche, *Ecce Homo*, Mineola: Dover, 2004, p. 40.

2. Available in, among others, the recording of his notorious Moscow concert in 1949 (Russian Revelation, RV 70004), with a brief spoken introduction by Robeson himself in perfect Russian.

3. See Paul Fussell, *The Great War and Modern Memory*, Oxford: Oxford University Press, 2000.

4. I rely here on Fussell, op. cit.

5. Incidentally, this idea was used in a famous scene from Hitchcock's Second World War thriller *Foreign Correspondent*. The good guys, who are following a Nazi agent, find themselves in an idyllic Dutch landscape with windmills. Everything seems peaceful, and there is no trace of the agent, when one of the good guys detects something strange, which denaturalizes the picture-perfect scene. He exclaims: 'Look at that windmill! Why is it turning opposite to the direction of the wind?' and the idyllic countryside loses its innocence and becomes semiotically charged.

6. Matthew Shadle, 'Theology and the Origin of Conflict: The Shining Path Insurgency in Peru', *Political Theology*, Vol. 14, No. 2 (2013), p. 293.

7. Ibid.

8. Ibid., p. 295.

9. Far from being simply located on the margins of Europe, the Jews emerged in the twentieth century as a kind of all-European *Ur-Vater*, the chief of the pre-Oedipal gang. Exactly as in Freud's myth about the murder of the primordial father, they were collectively killed by Europeans (the Holocaust as the ultimate crime) in order to re-emerge as the superego agency making all Europeans guilty.

10. In his intervention at the fourth 'The Idea of Communism' meeting in Seoul, 27–29 September 2013.

11. Contrary to what one would expect, the accent on class politics does not necessarily entail 'totalitarianism'. The Popular Front Communist policy (Stalin in the 1930s, Mao in the 1940s), which was apparently more 'open', advocated a united front made up of all progressive forces, including the 'patriotic bourgeoisie', with the exclusion of traitors to the country. The paradox is that such an 'open' policy was effectively much more 'totalitarian': in a proto-Fascist way, it established the all-national unity, the overcoming of 'sectarian' class distinctions, but at the price of demonizing and excluding the Enemy from the national body. This Enemy is not just a class enemy but a traitor whose elimination can only guarantee national harmony (like Jews for Fascists).

12. Those who claim that the working class is disappearing are right to some extent – it is disappearing from our sight. There is a new working class emerging all around us, from the United Arab Emirates to South Korea, a nomadic class of invisible migrant workers separated from

their homes and families, living in isolated dormitories in the suburbs of prosperous cities, with almost no political or legal rights, no health-care or retirement arrangements. To mobilize them and to enable them to organize themselves for an emancipatory cause would be a true political event.

13. In a debate at the fourth 'The Idea of Communism' meeting in Seoul, 27–29 September 2013.

14. Quoted from http://www.zionism-israel.com/ezine/New_Antizionism. htm.

15. Walter Benjamin, 'Theories of German Fascism', *Selected Writings*, Vol. II, Cambridge (Ma): Harvard University Press, 1999, p. 321.

16. Jane Perlez and Pir Zubair Shah, 'Taliban Exploit Class Rifts to Gain Ground in Pakistan', *New York Times*, 16 April 2009.

17. John Caputo and Gianni Vattimo, *After the Death of God*, New York: Columbia University Press, 2007, p. 113.

18. Stalinism was far from an unambiguous example of a strong state – in a weird dialectical turn towards 'organs without body', Stalin once remarked that, while constructing socialism, the state was withering away through the very process of the strengthening of its organs (meaning, of course, principally the secret police apparatus).

19. In his famous Preface to the *Contribution to the Critique of Political Economy*, Marx wrote (in his worst evolutionary mode) that humanity only poses to itself tasks which it is able to solve. One is tempted to turn this statement around and claim that humanity as a rule poses to itself tasks which it cannot solve, and thereby triggers an unpredictable process in the course of which the task (goal) itself gets redefined.

20. John Caputo and Gianni Vattimo, op. cit., pp. 124–5.

21. See his 'A Loving Attack on Caputo's "Caputolism" and his Refusal of Communism', in *Political Theology*, Vol. 14, No. 3 (2013).

22. Ayn Rand, *Atlas Shrugged*, London: Penguin Books. 2007, p. 871.

23. See Karl Marx, *Capital*, Vol. 1, London: Penguin Classics, 1990. p. 165.

24. Incidentally, it is not known to whom 'it has been said' refers – is it a determinate individual or just a reference to common wisdom?

25. In logic and theory of judgement, we sometimes encounter a similar paradox of intransitivity: if A is better than B and B is better than C, it does not always follow that A is better than C – when one compares A and C directly, C can appear as the better. It would be all too easy to explain away this paradox as relying on a change in criteria (when one looks at all systems, one applies a set of criteria, but when one compares them individually, the criteria will imperceptibly shift): in

some way this has to be true, but the point is that the shift is immanent, not arbitrary. That is to say, the shift can occur because of the differentiality of features: let us say that we compare the beauty of three people – A appears more beautiful than B and B more beautiful than C. However, when we compare A and C, it may happen that a strong contrast in some minor feature will ruin the beauty of A, so that A will appear inferior to C.

26. www.reuters.com/article/2012/06/24/us-usa-campaign-healthcare-idUSBRE85N01M20120624.

27. http://www.dailypaul.com/170397/whos-afraid-of-ron-paul.

28. Rony Brauman, 'From Philanthropy to Humanitarianism', *South Atlantic Quarterly* 103:2/3 (spring/summer 2004), pp. 398–9 and 416.

29. G. K. Chesterton, 'The Man Who Thinks Backwards', http://www.online-literature.com/chesterton/2573, last paragraph.

30. Franco Bifo Berardi, *After the Future*, Oakland: AK Press, 2011, p. 175. But is this inconsequentiality really a new phenomenon? Aren't 'bland revolutions' part of our tradition, from medieval peasant revolts to Chartists? In November 1914, Emiliano Zapata and Pancho Villa entered Mexico City with their troops ... and, after a couple of weeks of debate, went back home, basically not knowing what to do with their power.

31. Berardi, op. cit., p. 177.

32. Ibid., p. 176.

33. Michael Hardt and Antonio Negri, *Multitude*, New York: The Penguin Press, 2004, p. 339.

34. Ibid., p. 336.

35. Louis Althusser, *Philosophy of the Encounter*, London: Verso Books, 2006, p. 37.

36. See #*Accelerate*#. *The Accelerationist Reader*, edited by Robin McKay and Atrmen Avanessian, Falmouth: Urbanomic, 2014.

37. With all the growing importance of intellectual work, we should never lose sight of the massive displacement of physical work to China, Indonesia, etc. – but does this global outsourcing of material work really allow us to maintain the so-called 'labour theory of value'? Is knowledge as a factor of value not a fact today, a fact foretold long ago by Marx?

38. Berardi, op. cit., pp. 177–8.

39. I rely here on Rowan Williams's 'On Representation', presented at the colloquium *The Actuality of the Theologico-Political*, Birkbeck School of Law, London, 24 May 2014.

40. Jacques-Alain Miller, 'Un réel pour le XXIᵉ siècle', in *Un réel pour le XXIᵉ siècle*, Paris: Scilicet, 2013, p. 18.

41. See T. J. Clark, 'For a Left with No Future', *New Left Review* 74 (March/April 2012).

42. Franco Bifo Berardi, 'Humankind is Reaching its End' (in Slovene) *Ljubljanski dnevnik*, 24 May 2014, p. 11.

43. Quoted from http://substitute.livejournal.com/986052.html.

44. Personal communication from Xenia Cherkaev.

45. V. I. Lenin, 'The Socialist Revolution and the Right of Nations to Self-Determination' (January–February 1916), www.marxists.org/archive/lenin/works/1916/jan/x01.htm.

46. Quoted from Moshe Lewin, *Lenin's Last Struggle*, Ann Arbor: University of Michigan Press, 2005, p. 61.

47. Quoted from edition.cnn.com/2014/03/19/opinion/motyl-putin-speech.

48. Christopher Hitchens, *Arguably*, New York: Twelve, 2011, p. 634.

49. Ibid., p. 635.

50. Another sign of this immanent tension is the fact that, in the last days of Communism, the protesting crowds often sang the official songs, including national anthems, reminding the powers of their unfulfilled promises. What better thing for an East German crowd to do in 1989 than to sing the GDR national anthem? From the late 1950s to 1989, because its words (*'Deutschland einig Vaterland'* ('Germany, the united Fatherland')) no longer fitted the emphasis on East Germans as a new socialist nation, it was illegal to sing it in public; at official ceremonies, only the orchestral version was performed. The GDR was thus a unique country in which singing the national anthem was a criminal act! Can one imagine the same thing under Nazism?

51. Hitchens, op. cit., p. 635.

52. V. I. Lenin, *Collected Works*, Vol. 33, Moscow: Progress Publishers, 1966, p. 463.

53. Quoted from http://www.voxeurop.eu/en/content/news-brief/2437991-orban-considers-alternative-democracy.

54. G. K. Chesterton, *Orthodoxy*, San Francisco: Ignatius Press, 1995, pp. 146–7.

55. Along the same lines, some liberal critics of anti-Semitism claim not only that anti-Semitism is predominantly Leftist nowadays, but also that anti-Semitism was from the very beginning part of the Communist project. (Suffice it to note that the majority of the members of Lenin's Politburo in the first years of the Soviet power were of Jewish origins – a unique case in the Western world. Whatever Lenin was, he wasn't anti-Semitic.)

56. Ilya Ponomarev, the only member of the Russian Duma who voted against the move to incorporate Ukraine's autonomous republic of

Crimea into his country, made a valid point in explaining his vote: he emphasized that Russia has good arguments for its claim to Crimea, but he disagreed with the procedures used to take it back from Ukraine. This is the core of the problem: it is not about arguments and justification of claims (at this level, all sides are two-faced: the West, which supported Kosovo's secession from Serbia, opposed the secession of Crimea; Russia, which advocates referendum in Crimea, rejects referendum in Chechenia, and so on). What makes the annexation of Crimea problematic is the way it was organized (under Russian military pressure), plus the larger geopolitical struggle behind it.

4 EPIGNOSIS *J'AI HÂTE DE VOUS SERVIR!*

1. Julien Gracq, *The Opposing Shore*, New York: Columbia University Press, 1986, p. 284.
2. Just prior to *The Opposing Shore*, Gracq wrote a play, *The Fisher King* (*Le roi pêcheur*), his retelling of the Parsifal myth with an original twist: in his version, Amfortas tries to convince Parsifal *not* to approach the Grail, warning him that, when one comes too close to it, the destructive side of the Grail is revealed – and, at the play's end, he convinces Parsifal, who leaves the castle (Kundry is here the one who pushes Parsifal towards the Grail). The event – Parsifal's contact with the Grail and his assuming of the royal power – thus never happens. (Furthermore, Gracq focuses on Amfortas's wound, which is repeatedly described in the terms of menstrual blood, as something filthy, while simultaneously associated with the Grail, as if there is a deeper link – even an identity – between the two.) Gracq himself generalizes this final twist: 'In the books I've written, there is an element they all share: *the event never takes place*' (Julien Gracq, radio debate with Gilbert Ernst on 12 July 1971, published in *Cahier de l'Herne*, No. 20 (1972), p. 214). So what happens at the end of *The Opposing Shore*? Is it an event or, rather, a pseudo-event?
3. It is worth noting that, back in the early 1990s, in a Gracq-like mode, Badiou wrote that a victory of Milosevic in the post-Yugoslav war would be more interesting politically than the victory of the forces opposed to him – a clear preference for the nationalist pseudo-event over the non-eventual life. At a deeper level, the problem is Badiou's dismissal of the mere order of being, of economy, as non-eventual.
4. Quoted from http://www.marxists.org/archive/marx/works/1844/manuscripts/preface.htm.

5. See Kojin Karatani, *The Structure of World History*, Durham: Duke University Press, 2014.
6. Friedrich Nietzsche, *Sämtliche Werke: Kritische Studienausgabe*, Vol. 2, Berlin: Walter de Gruyter, 1980, p. 679.
7. Friedrich Nietzsche, *Sämtliche Werke: Kritische Studienausgabe*, Vol. 10, Berlin: Walter de Gruyter, 1980, p. 529.
8. Karatani, op.cit., p. 303.
9. I resume here in a condensed way the line of argument from the penultimate chapter of *The Year of Dreaming Dangerously* (London: Verso Books, 2013).
10. See Peter Sloterdijk, *Repenser l'impôt*, Paris: Libella, 2012.
11. See Thomas Piketty, *Capital in the Twenty-First Century*, New York: Bellknap Press, 2014.
12. See Daniel H. Pink, *Drive: The Surprising Truth about What Motivates Us*, New York: Riverhead Books, 2009.
13. Quoted from http://dotsub.com/view/e1fddf77-5d1d-45b7-81be-5841 ee5c386e/viewTranscript/eng.
14. Karatani, op. cit., p. 304.
15. I resume here the line of argument from Interlude 2 of *Living In the End Times*, London: Verso Books, 2012.
16. Quoted from http://www.mtholyoke.edu/acad/intrel/kant/kant1.htm.
17. Quoted from http://www.aljazeera.com/indepth/opinion/2013/02/201 32672747320891.html.
18. Frantz Fanon, *Black Skin, White Masks*, New York: Grove Press, 2008, pp. 201–6.
19. Quoted from http://www.marxists.org/archive/marx/works/1853/07/22.htm.
20. Quoted from http://www.marxists.org/archive/marx/works/1853/06/25.htm.
21. Quoted from https://www.marxists.anu.edu.au/archive/marx/works/1849/01/13.htm. On account of the (obviously) problematic nature of this passage, one should quote it also in the original:

Die ganze frühere Geschichte Östreichs beweist es bis auf diesen Tag, und das Jahr 1848 hat es bestätigt. Unter allen den Nationen und Natiönchen Östreichs sind nur drei, die die Träger des Fortschritts waren, die aktiv in die Geschichte eingegriffen haben, die noch jetzt lebensfähig sind – die *Deutschen*, die *Polen*, die *Magyaren*. Daher sind sie jetzt revolutionär.

Alle andern großen und kleinen Stämme und Völker haben zunächst die Mission, im revolutionären Weltsturm unterzugehen. Daher sind sie jetzt kontrerevolutionär ... Es ist kein Land in Europa, das nicht in irgendeinem Winkel eine oder mehrere Völkerruinen besitzt, Überbleibsel einer früheren Bewohnerschaft, zurückgedrängt und unterjocht von der Nation, welche später Trägerin der geschichtlichen Entwicklung wurde. Diese Reste einer von dem Gang der Geschichte, wie Hegel sagt, unbarmherzig zertretenen Nation, diese *Völkerabfälle* werden jedesmal und bleiben bis zu ihrer gänzlichen Vertilgung oder Entnationalisierung die fanatischen Träger der Kontrerevolution, wie ihre ganze Existenz überhaupt schon ein Protest gegen eine große geschichtliche Revolution ist ... Aber bei dem ersten siegreichen Aufstand des französischen Proletariats, den Louis-Napoleon mit aller Gewalt heraufzubeschwören bemüht ist, werden die österreichischen Deutschen und Magyaren frei werden und an den slawischen Barbaren blutige Rache nehmen. Der allgemeine Krieg, der dann ausbricht, wird diesen slawischen Sonderbund zersprengen und alle diese kleinen stierköpfigen Nationen bis auf ihren Namen vernichten.

Der nächste Weltkrieg wird nicht nur reaktionäre Klassen und Dynastien, er wird auch ganze reaktionäre Völker vom Erdboden verschwinden machen. Und das ist auch ein Fortschritt.

The key sentence is sometimes translated 'The chief mission of all other races and peoples, large and small, is to perish in the revolutionary holocaust.' and, as such, used against Marx as the forefather of holocaust – however, the word 'holocaust' is not used in this sentence, where it is said that the mission of counterrevolutionary nations is *'im revolutionären Weltsturm unterzugehen'* ('to perish/founder in the revolutionary worldstorm').

22. Quoted from https://www.marxists.org/archive/marx/works/1882/letters/82_09_12.htm.
23. Quoted from https://www.marxists.org/archive/marx/works/1882/letters/82_06_26.htm.
24. Quoted from http://www.aljazeera.com/indepth/opinion/2013/02/2013 2672747320891.html.
25. Chandra Bhan Prasad, a leading Dalit intellectual, celebrated English by anointing the 'Dalit Goddess, English'. See http://www. openthemagazine.com/article/nation/jai-angrezi-devi-maiyya-ki. I owe this data to my good friend S. Anand (New Delhi).

26. I owe this line of thought to Saroi Giri, New Delhi. We can say something similar about today's China: it is wrong to claim that China faces the choice of becoming a truly capitalist country or of maintaining the Communist rule which thwarts full capitalist development. This choice is a false one: in China, capitalist growth is exploding not in spite of the Communist rule but because of it, i.e., far from being an obstacle to capitalist development, Communist rule guarantees the best conditions for unbridled capitalism.

27. Let us risk another extreme example of such a liberating wound. On 7 October 2013 the media reported that a 'Baby factory' had just opened in India, where surrogate mothers will carry Western couples' babies for about $8,000. The factory, built by doctor Nayna Patel, will house hundreds of surrogate mothers in the multi-million-pound complex, which will have a gift shop and hotel rooms for people coming to collect newborns. Women will make babies for a fee as a way of escaping extreme poverty, impregnated using sperm and embryos sent by courier, with childless couples visiting India only to pick up their new son or daughter. Dr Patel views her work as a 'feminist mission' to bring needy women together with would-be mothers who are unable to conceive – no doubt a statement of brutal cynicism. However, cannot we imagine a situation in which lending a womb to another woman would definitely amount to a feminist act of solidarity that challenged traditional notions of substantial femininity?

28. But what about the opposite experience of our own language as provincial, primitive, marked by pathologies of private passions and obscenities which obscure clear reasoning and expression, the experience of which pushes us towards using the universal secondary language in order to think clearly and freely? Is this not the logic of the constitution of a national language to replace the multiplicity of dialects?

29. Jacques Lacan, *The Psychoses: The Seminar of Jacques Lacan, Book III, 1955–56*, London and New York: Routledge, p. 243.

30. Ibid.

31. George Orwell, *The Road to Wigan Pier* (1937), quoted from http://www.orwell.ru/library/novels/The_Road_to_Wigan_Pier/english/e_rtwp.

32. A bizarre episode from Chapman's life demonstrates that he was well aware of what a true engagement means: in 1887, when he was a law student, he assaulted and beat a man for insulting his girlfriend, Minna Timmins. Tormented by remorse, he punished himself for this act by putting his left hand into fire – it was so badly burnt that it had to be amputated.

33. John Jay Chapman, *Practical Agitation*, New York: Charles Scribner & Sons, 1900, pp. 63–4.

34. Bülent Somay, *'L'Orient n'existe pas'* (doctoral thesis, Birkbeck School of Law, London, 2013).

35. See Walter Lippman, *Public Opinion*, Charleston: BiblioLife, 2008.

36. When, in the Summer of 2013, Western European states grounded Evo Morales' presidential plane in which he was returning from Moscow to Bolivia, suspecting that Edward Snowden was hidden in it on his way to Bolivian exile, the most humiliating aspect was the Europeans' attempt to retain their dignity: instead of openly admitting that they were acting under US pressure, or pretending that they simply followed the law, they justified the grounding on pure technicalities, claiming that the flight was not properly registered with their air traffic control. The effect was miserable – Europeans not only appeared as US servants, but they even wanted to cover up their servitude by invoking ridiculous technicalities.

37. As Wendy Brown noted at a public debate at Birkbeck College.

38. As for 'direct democracy', the case of Switzerland is instructive. Switzerland is often celebrated as 'the closest state in the world to direct democracy', yet it is precisely because of its forms of 'direct democracy' (referenda, local people's initiatives, etc.) that Switzerland gave the vote to women only in 1971, that it was able to prohibit construction of minarets a couple of years ago, that it resists the naturalization of immigrant workers, and so on. Plus, the way referenda are organized has a peculiarity: together with the paper on which to write one's decision, each voter gets a leaflet containing the government's 'suggestion' on how to vote. Not to mention the fact that Switzerland, this model of direct democracy, has one of the most non-transparent mechanisms of decision-making: big strategic decisions are made by councils out of public debate and control.

39. Alain Badiou/Elisabeth Roudinesco, 'Appel aux psychanalystes. Entretien avec Eric Aeschimann', *Le Nouvel Observateur*, 19 April 2012.

40. Personal communication (April 2013).

41. Quoted from Nicolas Fleury, *Le réel insensé: Introduction à la pensée de Jacques-Alain Miller*, Paris: Germina, 2010, pp. 93–4.

42. Translated by John Ashbery, quoted from http://www.poetryfoundation.org/poetrymagazine/poem/241582.

43. Saroj Giri, 'Communism, Occupy and the Question of Form', *Ephemera*, Vol. 13(3), p. 594.

44. Ibid., p. 595.
45. Ibid., p. 590.
46. I owe this reference to Hegel's *Notrecht* to Costas Douzinas, who developed it in his intervention 'The Right to Revolution?' at the Hegel-colloquium *The Actuality of the Absolute* organized by the Birkbeck School of Law in London, 10–12 May 2013. Passages from Hegel's *Philosophy of Right* are quoted from www.marxists.org/reference/archive/hegel/works/pr/prconten.htm?.
47. Marx, Letter of 5 March 1852 to Joseph Weydemeyer, *MECW* 39, p. 65.
48. In India, thousands of impoverished intellectual workers are employed in what is ironically called 'like-farms': they are (miserably) paid to sit the whole day in front of a computer and endlessly press the button 'like' on pages which ask the visitors or customers to click on 'like' or 'dislike' for a product in question. In this way, a product can artificially appear as very popular and thereby seduce ignorant prospective customers into buying it (or at least checking up on it), following the logic of 'there must be something in it if so many customers are satisfied by it'. So much for the reliability of customer reactions. (I owe this information to Saroj Giri, New Delhi.)
49. Information given to me by Shulamith Aloni, who, as the minister of education in Rabin's government, was also part of the Israeli delegation.

APPENDIX *NOTA BENE!*

1. Tyler O'Neil, 'Dark Knight and Occupy Wall Street: The Humble Rise', *Hillsdale Natural Law Review*, 21 July 2012, available online at http://hillsdalenaturallawreview.com/2012/07/21/dark-knight-and-occupy-wall-street-the-humble-rise/.
2. R. M. Karthick, 'The Dark Knight Rises a "Fascist"?', *Society and Culture*, 21 July 2012, available online at http://wavesunceasing.wordpress.com/2012/07/21/the-dark-knight-rises-a-fascist/.
3. Tyler O'Neil, op. cit.
4. Christopher Nolan, interview in *Entertainment* 1216 (July 2012), p. 34.
5. http://www.buzzinefilm.com/interviews/film-interview-dark-knight-rises-christopher-nolan-jonathan-nolan-07192012.
6. Karthick, op. cit.
7. http://edition.cnn.com/2012/07/19/showbiz/movies/dark-knight-rises-review-charity/index.html?iref=obinsite.

8. Forrest Whitman, 'The Dickensian Aspects of *The Dark Knight Rises*,' 21 July 2012, available online at http://www.slate.com/blogs/browbeat/2012/07/23/the_dark_knight_rises_inspired_by_a_tale_of_two_cities_the_parts_that_draw_from_dickens_.html.

9. Karthick, op. cit.

10. Tom Hardy, the actor who plays Bane, also played Charles Bronson/Michael Peterson, the legendary British prisoner known for the mixture of violence, quest for justice and artistic sense which makes him similar to Bane, in *Bronson* (2010).

11. Quoted from Jon Lee Anderson, *Che Guevara: A Revolutionary Life*, New York: Grove, 1997, pp. 636–7.

12. Ibid.

13. Søren Kierkegaard, *Works of Love*, New York: Harper & Row, 1962, p. 114.

14. A supreme literary example of such 'killing out of love' occurs in Toni Morrison's *Beloved*, where the heroine kills her daughter to prevent her falling into slavery.

15. One should note the irony of the fact that Neeson's son is a devoted Shia Muslim, and that Neeson himself often talks about his forthcoming conversion to Islam.

16. I rely here on an idea developed by Srecko Horvat (Zagreb).

17. For a more detailed analysis of *The Dark Knight*, see Chapter 1 of Slavoj Žižek, *Living in the End Times*, London: Verso Books, 2010.

18. I leave out of consideration the Aurora cinema killings, which in no way reflect specifically on the film.

19. And one should also not shirk from imagining an alternative version of the film, similar to what Ralph Fiennes did with *Coriolanus*: in his film, it is as if Coriolanus, obviously out of place in the delicate hierarchy of Rome, only becomes what he is, gains his freedom, when he joins the Volscians (with their leader Aufidius playing the role of Bane). He does not join them simply in order to take revenge on Rome; he joins them because he belongs there. In joining the Volscians, Coriolanus does not betray Rome out of a sense of petty revenge but regains his integrity. His only act of betrayal occurs at the end when, instead of leading the Volscian army onto Rome, he organizes a peace treaty between the Volscians and Rome, breaking down under the pressure of his mother, the true figure of superego Evil. This is why he returns to the Volscians, fully aware what awaits him there: the well-deserved punishment for his betrayal. So what about imagining a Batman who rejoins Bane's forces in Gotham City; after helping them to almost defeat the state

power, he breaks down, mediates an armistice, and then goes back to the rebels, knowing he will be killed for his betrayal?

Such experiments with alternative versions often contain a critico-ideological potential. The premise of Mark Millar's *Superman: Red Son* (DC Comics, 2003) is that Superman had been raised in the Soviet Union; the story (which mixes alternative versions of DC superheroes with alternative-reality versions of real political figures such as Stalin and Kennedy) begins with Superman's rocket ship landing on a Ukrainian collective farm rather than in Kansas, so that, instead of fighting for 'truth, justice, and the American Way', Superman is described in Soviet radio broadcasts as 'the Champion of the common worker who fights a never-ending battle for Stalin, socialism, and the international expansion of the Warsaw Pact'. Does *Red Son* not provide a nice case of Brechtian 'alienation' (*Verfremdung*)? The disturbing effect of Superman's rocket ship landing in the Soviet Union, the spontaneous feeling that 'something is wrong', that Superman landed in a wrong place, makes us aware of how the figure of Superman is firmly rooted in the American ideological universe.

20. Incidentally, the debate about waterboarding being torture or not should be dropped as an obvious nonsense: why, if not by causing pain and fear of death, does boarding make hardened terrorist-suspects talk? This is why one should reject the 'realist' argument according to which waterboarding is a mere 'mental trickery torture', in which the prisoner thinks he is going to drown but actually isn't in much danger: we should weigh the benefit and potential life-saving effect of the information that can be obtained through such trickery versus the wrong of the trickery itself. However, waterboarding is experienced by its victim as a real threat of drowning, in the same way that a mock shooting of a prisoner (described long ago by Dostoyevsky) is a terrifying experience even if the prisoner actually isn't in much danger. So we are back at the utilitarian calculus – the brief suffering of one against the death of many.

21. http://lazersilberstein.tumblr.com/post/26499132966/according-to-slavoj-zizek-no-one-understands-slavoj-zizek.

22. There is a homologous procedure in our language. In the domain of politics, one often uses (ironically) the passive form of an active verb – say, when a politician who is forced to 'voluntarily' step down, one comments on it that he was 'stepped down'. In China, during the Cultural Revolution, one even used the neutral form – like 'struggle' – in an artificial passive or active version. When a cadre accused of

revisionism was submitted to a session of 'ideological struggle', it was said that he was 'struggled', or that the revolutionary group was 'struggling' him. (Here, the intransitive verb was changed into a transitive one: we not only struggle, we struggle *someone*.) Such distortions of 'normal' grammar adequately express the underlying logic; consequently, instead of rejecting them as violent distortions of the normal use of language, we should praise them as disclosures of the violence that underlies this normal use.

23. It is impossible to miss a nice detail in the film's plot: it is the two ex-Weather *women* (played by Susan Sarandon and Julie Christie) who remain faithful to their old commitment, while all ex-Weather *men* made a compromise on behalf of family responsibilities – contrary to the standard myth that women are more attached to families while men are ready to risk all for a Cause.